Cheap
Threats

Cheap
Threats

Why the United States Struggles to Coerce Weak States

Dianne Pfundstein Chamberlain

Georgetown University Press
Washington, DC

Library of Congress Cataloging-in-Publication Data

Pfundstein Chamberlain, Dianne, author
Cheap threats : why the United States struggles to coerce weak states /
Dianne Pfundstein Chamberlain.
     pages   cm
     Includes bibliographical references and index.

   Summary: The United States has a huge advantage in military power over other states, yet it is frequently unable to coerce weak adversary states with threats alone. Instead, over the past two decades, the leaders of Iraq, Haiti, Serbia, Afghanistan, and Libya have dismissed US threats and invited military clashes. Why have weak states risked and ultimately suffered catastrophic defeat when giving in to US demands earlier might have allowed their survival? Why was it necessary to use force at all? Pfundstein Chamberlain finds that the United States' compellent threats often fail because the use of force has become relatively cheap for the United States in terms of political costs, material costs, and casualties. This comparatively low-cost model of war that relies on deficit spending, air power, high technology, and a light footprint by an all-volunteer force has allowed the United States to casually threaten force and frequently carry out short-term military campaigns. Paradoxically, this frequent use of "cheap" force has made adversary states doubt that the United States is highly motivated to bear high costs over a sustained period if the intervention is not immediately successful.

ISBN 978-1-62616-282-2 (hardcover : alk. paper) — ISBN 978-1-62616-281-5 (pbk. : alk. paper) — ISBN 978-1-62616-283-9 (ebook) 1. United States—Military policy. 2. United States—Military relations—Developing countries. 3. Developing countries—Military relations—United States. 4. Military art and science—Decision making. 5. Strategy. I. Title.
UA23.P495 2016
327.1'170973—dc23
2015025240

17 16   9 8 7 6 5 4 3 2 First printing
Printed in the United States of America

Cover design by Jim Keller. Cover image by iStock by Getty Images.

For Ken, who is dearly missed

Contents

Illustrations

Acknowledgments

The idea for this book first took root during the summer of 2009 when I was a graduate student attending the Summer Workshop on the Analysis of Military Operations and Strategy (SWAMOS) at Cornell University. It soon blossomed into my dissertation at Columbia University, where I was skillfully and compassionately advised by Robert Jervis and Richard Betts. I am very grateful for the serious and constructive feedback they have given me throughout the life of this project. I also thank members of the Saltzman Institute for War and Peace Studies, especially Johannes Urpelainen, for their feedback. At Columbia, I also had the opportunity to work closely with the late Kenneth Waltz. He became both an additional adviser on this project and one of my dearest friends.

I was fortunate enough to spend the 2012–13 academic year as a postdoctoral research fellow in the International Security Program at the Belfer Center for Science and International Affairs, Harvard Kennedy School, where I devoted my time to revising this project. I thank Steve Miller, Steve Walt, and other members of the Belfer Center for their feedback and Sean Lynn-Jones for his assistance in preparing proposals for this book. I also thank the Department of Political Science at the University of Massachusetts, Amherst, for taking me on as an assistant professor in fall 2013 and for supporting the final phases of this research. My editor at Georgetown University Press, Don Jacobs, has been a tireless advocate for this project, and the manuscript benefited greatly from his suggestions and from those made by Robert Art and an anonymous reviewer.

Through the long slog of graduate school and early years in the academy, I have enjoyed friendships with many extraordinarily talented and kind individuals. During my years at Columbia, Michael Beckley, Erica Borghard, Simon Collard-Wexler, Jennifer Hudson, Jeffrey Lenowitz, Brad Jennison, Costantino Pischedda, Kelly Rader, Mira Rapp-Hooper, Andrew Watkins, and Peter van der Windt challenged me intellectually and eased the growing pains of graduate school. My friends at the Belfer Center, including Paul Avey, Evelyn

Krache Morris, Jon Markowitz, and Marisa Porges, pushed me to refine my thinking about cheap threats and about American security policy.

I do not exaggerate when I assert that I could not have written this book without my family's assistance. My parents, Don and Roberta, unfailingly supported my education, from the days when I was a six-year-old drawing picture books about ancient Egyptian mummification to my years in New York pondering the finer points of coercion. My wonderful sister Lauren provided much-needed emotional reinforcement. They believed in me more than I believed in myself in the early days of this project.

Finally, I must thank my darling husband, Robert, both for his keen critiques of the work and for his unflinching belief in its merit. He supports my ambitions without hesitation, and I do not think I will ever get over the surprise of having found such a compassionate, challenging, and dedicated partner. Let us go forward together!

Introduction
Too Cheap to Compel

On March 18, 2011, President Obama demanded that Libyan leader Muammar Qaddafi implement a cease-fire and halt his advance on the rebel-held city of Benghazi, and he promised to implement military action against Qaddafi if the United States' terms were not met.[1] Despite the fact that Obama threatened Qaddafi with the world's most powerful military, the Libyan leader chose to resist the United States' demands, and as a result the United States and its North Atlantic Treaty Organization (NATO) allies launched Operation Odyssey Dawn shortly afterward. Why would Qaddafi choose to resist in the face of such a threat?

Since the end of the Cold War, the United States has carried out military action against several weak states after a compellent threat failed to convince these states to change their behavior. A compellent threat comprises a demand that a target modify its present behavior and a promise to inflict military force on the target if it chooses not to comply.[2] Over the past two decades, the leaders of Iraq, Haiti, Serbia, Afghanistan, and other states have dismissed US compellent threats and invited military clashes with the world's sole superpower. This inability to coerce target states with military threats is even more surprising given that the United States does not bluff. As this study demonstrates, in all post–World War II crises in which the United States issued an explicit compellent threat and the target resisted US demands, the United States executed its threat. The United States has consistently demonstrated that it is willing and able to execute military threats against its opponents. How, then, can we explain this inability of the world's most powerful state to coerce many of the world's weakest targets?

This book develops a new theory, the *costly compellence* theory, which asserts that the United States' compellent threats are likely to fail when they are cheap to issue and to execute because such threats do not signal that the United States is highly motivated to prevail against a stubbornly resistant opponent. Target states resist

1

not because they doubt the credibility of the United States' threats, but because they doubt the United States' underlying motivation to secure its preferred outcome in a prolonged conflict. Compellent threats are cheap in the post–Cold War period because the United States has developed a model of war-fighting that minimizes the human, political, and financial costs it incurs when it employs military force. That is, the decision to launch military action no longer generates significant casualties, political blowback, or long-term fiscal sacrifice for the United States, and thus the threat of force is not a convincing signal that the world's sole superpower is willing to persevere to extract compliance from a stubbornly resistant target state.

This theory draws on game-theoretic insights about costly signaling to present a new approach to interstate coercion. It suggests that the United States' decision to pursue a model of war-fighting that limits its own costs for employing force, combined with the absence of a peer competitor to rein in its behavior, renders the United States' compellent threats ineffective against weak states. It also suggests that it may be uniquely challenging for a unipole to accurately signal its interests in a crisis with a weak state because it will be difficult for an overwhelmingly powerful state to incur excessively high costs in a contest with a relatively weak opponent.[3]

The willingness of weak states to resist in the face of threats issued by the world's most powerful state challenges many theories about the way power operates in international politics. Hegemonic stability theory, theories of interstate coercion, and bargaining theories of war's outbreak do not provide satisfactory explanations for this phenomenon. Moreover, our understanding of state resolve—a factor often cited as a key determinant of effective coercion—is flawed. The costly compellence theory draws on a new definition of state resolve and insights about costly signaling to develop a framework for understanding unipolar compellence in the post–Cold War world. Given that the United States seems to find no shortage of weak and misbehaving states to coerce, we must understand why its threats fail if we hope to coerce target states more successfully in the future.

Before surveying the status of current theories on interstate coercion, it is important to note that the costly compellence theory is intended to explain only cases in which the United States is attempting to compel a weak state to change its current behavior—that is, it is intended to apply only to cases in which the United States seeks a change in the status quo. Deterrent threats, which are intended to prevent the target from taking some future action, are excluded from this study. So, for example, the logic of the costly compellence theory would not apply to the United States' 2012 effort to deter the Bashar al-Assad regime in Syria from using chemical weapons because the threat was intended to prevent future action by the regime. The 2011 threat against Qaddafi, however, demanded a change in his regime's ongoing behavior, and thus it falls within the scope of costly compellence.

Failed Threats: A Puzzle for Security Theory

The phenomenon of weak states resisting threats issued by the unipole challenges many existing theories about the way power operates in international politics. Why would a weak state resist a military threat and submit to a war with the most powerful state in the system? For Geoffrey Blainey, the answer is simple: It would not. When one state enjoys overwhelming superiority in military power, the outcome of a war should be so obvious that no other state would willingly challenge the powerful state.[4] A. F. K. Organski and Jacek Kugler, on the other hand, argue that unipolarity is stable only until a challenger threatens to overtake the sitting hegemon.[5] Similarly, Robert Gilpin argues that a hegemon becomes vulnerable to a rising challenger as the costs of maintaining the international system begin to exceed its resources and as the rising challenger's costs for changing the system begin to decline.[6] These theorists argue that a dramatic imbalance in relative power is peaceful as long as there is no obvious rising challenger in the system. Weak states will recognize their own weakness and avoid a confrontation with the sitting hegemon.

None of the adversaries that have failed to submit to US coercion in the last two decades, however, could be considered rising challengers. Neither Blainey, nor Organski and Kugler, nor Gilpin can account for the fact that states as weak and marginalized as Serbia and Iraq have resisted the United States' compellent threats and submitted to a military conflict with the most powerful state in the system.[7] The United States may not face the possibility of hegemonic war with a rising challenger in the near future, but the inability of hegemonic stability theory to explain the wars we observe suggests that we need a new understanding of preponderant power.

Standard theories of coercion also struggle to explain this phenomenon. Coercion works by convincing the target that it will suffer pain if it chooses not to comply with the coercer's demands. As Thomas Schelling asserts, "it is the *threat* of damage, or of more damage to come, that can make someone yield or comply."[8] Unlike brute force, which succeeds by forcing the target to change its behavior, interstate coercion succeeds by *persuading* the target to change its behavior. That is, the object of coercion is to convince the target to undertake a specified action while the target retains the ability to resist the coercer's demands. An enemy that has been overrun and forced to comply with one's demands has not been coerced. Coercion succeeds only when the target retains the capability to resist and chooses to make concessions.

Within the broader category of coercion, we can distinguish between deterrent threats, which prevent future action through the promise of pain, and compellent threats, which are intended to induce the adversary to take some action or change his current behavior.[9] Successful deterrent threats maintain the status quo, while successful compellent threats alter the status quo or return the world to some preexisting status quo. Alexander L. George and William E. Simons's concept of "coercive diplomacy" is narrower than Schelling's concept of compellence, which includes both coercive diplomacy and blackmail as defined by George,[10] but all three concepts—compellence, coercive diplomacy, and blackmail—involve the threat or limited use of force to persuade an adversary to undertake, halt, or reverse an action. As noted above, this study focuses solely on the United States' use of compellent threats—that is, threats intended to induce a change in the target state's behavior.

Robert A. Pape argues that a target state will resist attempts at coercion when the expected benefits of resistance exceed the expected costs of resistance.[11] According to this model, the ability to threaten more pain should increase the likelihood of target compliance, *ceteris paribus*. If this basic model of coercion is accurate, then it would suggest that the United States should be uniquely capable of coercing target states. Yet the record of post–Cold War compellence shows that, in a period in which the United States has had both the capability and the willingness to target states all over the world, the ability to inflict devastating costs does not guarantee coercive success.

This suggests that successful coercion rests on more than the capability to inflict pain on a target state. The concept of "credibility"—the target's belief that the coercer will execute the threatened action—dominates much of the relatively limited literature on compellence. The inherent logic is that a threat that is more credible will be more effective in convincing the target state to yield to the threatener's demands. In fact, Schelling argues that "face," or the "interdependence of a country's commitments," is "one of the few things worth fighting for."[12] That is, we must maintain today's commitments so that tomorrow's threats will be credible.[13] In the logic of compellent threats, this means that the effective use of threats today depends on our willingness to follow through on threats yesterday. If this is true, then the United States' threats should be highly effective if it consistently demonstrates a willingness to follow through on its threats. As we will discover in the second chapter, however, the United States never bluffs with compellent threats—and yet, target states still choose to resist.[14]

Daryl G. Press also identifies credibility as a major determinant of coercive success. He argues that if the coercer can accomplish what it threatens at low cost, then the threat will be more likely to be perceived as credible and thus more likely to be effective against the target state.[15] It may be true that threats that can be executed with relative ease are viewed as credible by target states. If a threat's effectiveness is a function of its credibility and credibility is a function of the ease of execution, then a state that can employ force with relative ease should be able to wield compellent threats very effectively. The record of US compellence reveals, however, that this is not the case: The second chapter will demonstrate that the United States' compellent threats have been more likely to fail in the post–Cold War period, precisely when it has been relatively cheap and easy for the United States to execute military action around the world.

Studies that focus on threat *credibility* frequently conflate the concept with threat *effectiveness*. In reality, a threat may fail to change a target's behavior even when the target believes that the coercer will execute the threatened punishment. In other words, the target may believe that the coercer's threat is credible and still choose to resist.

The first chapter will demonstrate that credibility is a necessary but not sufficient cause of threat effectiveness and that we must distinguish between a threat's *immediate* and *ultimate credibility* to understand why the United States' compellent threats fail against weak states.

Coercion in US Practice

Standard theories present a straightforward logic for how coercion succeeds: A credible threat to inflict pain (or, in the case of a limited use of force, to inflict more pain in the future) should convince a target state to accede to the coercer's demands. Existing studies yield a variety of observations on the record of coercion in US foreign policy and a variety of suggestions about the conditions associated with success. Most of these studies examine a broader category of US action than compellent threats, but they still provide a useful baseline for evaluating the effectiveness of US coercion.

Barry M. Blechman and Stephen S. Kaplan find that US coercion was successful over the short term (six months after the incident) in 75 percent of cases from 1946 to 1975, although the success rate falls below 50 percent after three years.[16] In their 1994 study, which updates and includes the results of their earlier (1971) edition, George and Simons identify two cases in which coercive diplomacy was successful, three cases in which coercive diplomacy was unsuccessful, and two cases in which the results were ambiguous.[17] Although it is not an exhaustive study of the United States' use of coercion during the period under investigation, this study yields a success rate of two out of seven cases, or roughly 29 percent. In addition to several contextual factors,[18] George and Simons find that one of the key variables affecting the outcome of a coercive attempt is the scope of the demands made of the target. The more expansive the demands, the less likely the target is to comply.[19]

Robert J. Art and Patrick M. Cronin pick up where George and Simons leave off and add several cases to the data set on US coercive diplomacy, up to and including the attempt to coerce Afghanistan in 2001. By including George and Simons's data, Art and Cronin count seven successful cases of coercive diplomacy and ten failed cases out of twenty-two, for a success rate of 32 percent and a failure rate of

45 percent.[20] In contrast to George and Simons, they do not find that the type of demand is associated with the likelihood of target compliance.[21] Blechman and Tamara Cofman Wittes examine eight cases of military coercion from the George H. W. Bush and Bill Clinton administrations and find a success rate of roughly 38 percent.[22] They find that effective coercion is associated with making limited demands of the target state.[23]

Although these studies employ different methods, some common conclusions do emerge. Blechman and Kaplan's study is the most optimistic, claiming a 75 percent success rate for US objectives over the short term but less than 50 percent over the long term. Their study is restricted to the use of military force during the Cold War, a non-random subset of the universe of US coercion. The other post–Cold War studies by George and Simons, Art and Cronin, and Blechman and Wittes (who also limit their study to strictly military coercion) all yield success rates of roughly one-third. This suggests that the effectiveness of US coercion may have changed over time.

When we examine these results more closely, an additional observation emerges. With the exception of Art and Cronin's work, all these studies of US coercion identify the type of objective as a major factor associated with coercive outcomes: Targets are more likely to concede to limited demands.[24] If it is true that limited demands are associated with coercive success, then we should observe that the United States' threats are more effective when its demands are most limited. We will investigate the veracity of this claim with the new data set on US compellent threats presented in the second chapter and in the case studies that follow.

Resolve: The Need for a New Definition

In addition to credibility, the concept of "resolve" or "motivation" also plays a prominent role in existing theories of coercion. This concept has escaped close scrutiny thus far, but we must examine theories of motivation and resolve to build an argument about why the United States' compellent threats fail against weak states. Our understanding of interstate coercion suffers from a failure to employ the concept of resolve consistently. In the rest of this chapter, I present a new definition that is necessary to understand why the United

States struggles to coerce weak target states with compellent military threats.

Resolve figures prominently in Cold War arguments about deterrence, and it is helpful to examine the specific language used to describe the concept to demonstrate the inconsistency in the term's use. For example, Glenn H. Snyder notes:

> Often the reasons why the balance of power has been successful or unsuccessful in preventing war have turned on perceptions of intention and resolve rather than on perceptions of capability. Britain and France failed to deter Hitler in 1939 not so much because they were weak in material strength, but largely because Hitler discounted their will to fight after they had demonstrated weakness in crisis after crisis.[25]

Although he does not define "resolve" precisely, Snyder seems to equate the term with determination. It is not clear, however, what a highly resolved state is determined to *do*. Snyder's discussion of the "Chicken" model of crisis dynamics suggests that "resolve" is the willingness to stand firm in a dispute. On the other hand, his discussion of nuclear deterrence suggests that resolve refers to "intentions to invoke various possible levels of violence"[26]—that is, the willingness to escalate a crisis and the willingness to inflict violence on the opponent. Snyder suggests that a highly resolved state is one that is highly motivated, but it is unclear how a high level of determination translates into behavior.

Robert Jervis also argues that resolve "reflects the strength of the state's motivation to prevail on a given issue."[27] In a limited war, the state with higher resolve is more willing to run the risk of dangerous escalation and therefore more likely to prevail, presumably because it is more highly motivated to achieve its interests.[28] Military capability matters less in such a situation than the willingness to use this capability, or, rather, it matters less than the opponent's belief in one's willingness to use this capability.

Both Snyder and Jervis argue that the state that is perceived as more highly resolved than its opponent is most likely to prevail in a crisis. In other words, the state that cares more and can communicate to the opponent that it cares more about what is at stake will win. It is not clear from these studies, however, what the term "re-solve" means. Both Snyder and Jervis seem to equate resolve with "determination" or "motivation." A closer analysis of these and other arguments about resolve reveals that a more precise definition of the term is necessary to better understand crisis dynamics in general and unipolar threat failures in particular.

Resolve in Models of War's Outbreak: The Will to Initiate Military Action

Many formal models of war's outbreak treat crises as contests of re-solve. Because each state faces strong incentives to overstate its own resolve in the hope that it can obtain its desired outcome without fighting, it can be very difficult for states to communicate accurately in a crisis.[29] James D. Morrow defines resolve as the "relative attrac-tiveness of conceding now to war."[30] In his model of war's outbreak, a state's willingness to escalate at each stage of the crisis is determined by its expectations about relative power.[31] In other words, a state's resolve is a function of its material capabilities.

James D. Fearon employs a similar notion of resolve. In his model of the role of audience costs, "resolve" is a state's willingness to esca-late a crisis to war, based on its prewar estimates about the value of the object in dispute and the likely costs of an ensuing war.[32] A state with high resolve is one willing to run a high risk of war to achieve its objectives. Thus, for two states with the same initial valuation of the object in dispute, the state with the lower costs for fighting will be considered to have higher resolve than the state with high costs for fighting.

Todd S. Sechser argues that a compellent threat fails when an overwhelmingly powerful coercer does not compensate its target suf-ficiently for the reputational loss that it suffers for complying with the coercer's demands.[33] He defines resolve as "the target's value for the cost of fighting . . . relative to the stakes of the crisis."[34] A closer examination of the model reveals, however, that state behavior is actually driven by prewar estimates of the costs of fighting, with low-cost states escalating and high-cost states acquiescing to the coercer's demands.[35]

In this sample of formal models of war's outbreak, outcomes are driven by uncertainty about prewar estimates of the costs of fighting. States infer their adversaries' resolve by evaluating their capabilities. Resolve in these models is purely a function of material power and not of a state's commitment to its objectives. These models of war's outbreak capture a specific component of resolve: the willingness to initiate a war with the opponent. States with higher anticipated costs of fighting are considered "low-resolve" and less willing to escalate, while those with low costs of fighting are considered "high-resolve." No state, however, can estimate perfectly the costs of war in advance. These bargaining models of war's outbreak do not capture a state's willingness to persist in war if actual costs exceed its prewar estimates.

Resolve in War: The Will to Suffer

Studies of war's outcome define the concept of resolve very differently than do studies of war's outbreak. In general, studies of war's outcome define "resolve" as the willingness to persist in war despite mounting costs. Thus, a highly resolved state is one that is willing to suffer high costs. In many of these studies, a highly resolved state is also more likely to prevail over a less cost-tolerant opponent.[36] A war is won by the state that has the higher level of motivation to prevail in the dispute—that is, by the state that has the higher level of resolve. The way to win, therefore, is to exploit the adversary's willingness to suffer costs in war.

A focus on the adversary's cost tolerance plagued US strategic thinking during the Vietnam War. John E. Mueller argues that American strategists assumed they could "break" the will of the North Vietnamese but finally discovered that they were willing to withstand more punishment than the United States was willing to inflict.[37] Although some studies find that there is no correlation between casualties suffered and war's outcome,[38] the willingness to suffer did seem to play a role in the Vietnam War. As long as the North Vietnamese did not lose, they could hope to hold out long enough that the Americans would give up and go home.

In a response to Mueller, Richard K. Betts notes that an exclusive focus on the resolve of the Vietnamese communists is misleading. We must also consider the United States' breaking point to understand the balance of resolve during the Vietnam War.[39] The United

States' reluctance to tolerate the costs of the protracted conflict was a function of its more limited objectives. In other words, a state's willingness to suffer costs in war is a function of its motivation to prevail over its opponent.

The willingness to endure suffering should be a particularly powerful indicator of motivation for a democracy. Immanuel Kant argues that republics are less likely than other states to engage in wars because the public both controls the levers of government and bears the costs of war.[40] There is evidence that high human costs can undermine support for an ongoing war. For example, Mueller finds a significant relationship between US casualties and public support for the wars in Korea and Vietnam. As casualties increased, support among the American public for each of the wars dropped.[41] More recently, David Karol and Edward Miguel find that the ten thousand casualties of the Iraq War cost President George W. Bush 2 percent of the popular vote in the 2004 election.[42] The willingness to absorb human costs is a powerful indicator of a state's motivation to achieve its objectives.

These arguments about cost tolerance and war's outcome claim to focus on the same concept as that examined in bargaining theories by Morrow, Fearon, and Sechser—state resolve. However, these two groups of theories examine two very different symptoms of state motivation. In a typical bargaining model, a highly resolved state is one that is willing to initiate a war because it expects the costs of fighting will be low. In a study of war's outcome, however, a highly resolved state is one that is willing to persist in war despite suffering high costs. We must separate these concepts to develop a more precise understanding of the sources of compellent threat failure. It is not necessarily true that a state that is willing to initiate military action that it believes will be cheap is also willing to persist in a protracted and costly military conflict.

Resolve in War: The Will to Kill

A third indicator of state resolve has received less attention in scholarship on both crisis bargaining and war's outcome. If it is true that a state's cost tolerance affects war's outcome, then it must also be true that the opponent's willingness to *inflict* those costs affects war's outcome. Recall that Snyder refers to a highly resolved state as one that is willing to "invoke various possible levels of violence."[43] Gil Merom argues that the willingness to inflict violence is an important determinant of the outcomes of asymmetric wars. In particular, democracies struggle to inflict the level of violence necessary to defeat small states.[44]

If inflicting more violence makes a target more likely to concede, then the willingness to be brutal indicates that a state is highly motivated to defeat its opponent.[45] Although understudied, the willingness to inflict violence constitutes a distinct and critical component of state resolve. Carl von Clausewitz reminds us that "the degree of force that must be used against the enemy depends on the scale of political demands."[46] A state's willingness to inflict high levels of violence on its opponent indicates that it is highly motivated to achieve its objectives.[47]

The Three Faces of State Resolve: A New Definition and Sources of Compellent Threat Failure

Bargaining models of war's outbreak define resolve as a state's willingness to go to war with its opponent, based on its prewar estimate of the costs of fighting. Studies of war's outcome define resolve as a state's willingness to continue to kill and be killed in pursuit of its objectives. Standard bargaining models of war's outbreak capture resolve *for* war, while studies of war's outcome capture resolve *in* war. The two concepts are related, but there is no reason to assume, as current theories implicitly do, that high resolve to go to war is necessarily accompanied by high resolve to fight a war with persistent intensity.

Properly defined, state resolve consists of three related but distinct components: the willingness to initiate military action, the willingness to persevere in war despite mounting costs,[48] and the willingness to inflict violence on the opponent. In the same way that a fever is a symptom of an underlying disease, so too are these three components the physical expression of a state's underlying resolve. A state may be characterized by the extent to which it is initiation-willing (as in bargaining theories of war), cost-tolerant (as in studies of war's outcome), and violence-inflicting. In the universe of compellent threats, the willingness to initiate military action corresponds to the willingness to execute a threat. The willingness to execute a threat is not necessarily accompanied, however, by the willingness to prosecute an ensuing war with the commitment and intensity necessary to exact target compliance. In other words, a state may be willing to execute a compellent military threat against a target because it expects that the ensuing fight will be low-cost. If casualties and financial costs exceed its prewar estimates, however, this state may withdraw from the fight precisely because it has a low level of resolve, measured in terms of cost tolerance.

This tripartite definition of state resolve suggests that the United States' threats may fail to compel compliance for two reasons. A target may resist because it does not believe that the United States will execute its threat. Or a target may resist a credible threat—that is, one that it believes will be executed—because it believes that the United States lacks the underlying motivation to persist in a protracted and costly conflict to defeat the target after the threat fails to induce compliance. These two types of compellent threat failures should yield very different patterns of target-state behavior if and when the unipole executes its threat. If the target resists because it doubts the threat's credibility, then we would expect the target's military resistance to crumble very soon after the initiation of hostilities because it resisted in the belief that the unipole would not attack. If, on the other hand, the target believes that the unipole will execute the threat but not fight hard enough to secure what it wants from the target, then the target will pursue a military strategy designed to inflict costs on its opponent and to force the opponent to kill target-state civilians.[49]

In other words, this tripartite specification of state resolve suggests that the willingness to execute compellent threats may not necessarily correspond to a willingness to persist in a long and costly conflict with a target state. Thus, a target state cannot infer from the willingness to issue and to execute compellent military threats that the unipole is highly motivated to defeat it in a protracted conflict. Instead of assuming, as many standard theories of coercion do, that credibility is a sufficient cause of threat effectiveness, we must build on these insights about resolve to develop a new framework for understanding why the United States' compellent threats succeed or fail.

Cheap Threats: Overview

The first chapter develops the costly compellence theory in detail and explains the underlying logic of costly signaling. It derives hypotheses on the United States' use of compellent threats during the Cold War and post–Cold War periods and presents evidence that the United States has developed a model of war-fighting that renders the use of force relatively cheap. The second chapter presents an original data set on the United States' use of compellent threats in crises from 1945 to 2007. The data show that the United States has employed compellent threats more frequently since the end of the Cold War and that these threats have been less effective than their Cold War counterparts in altering target-state behavior. Both of these findings are consistent with the predictions of the costly compellence theory. An extensive discussion of the method employed to construct the data set is located in the appendix.

Chapters 3 through 6 evaluate four cases in which the United States issued a compellent threat against another state: the Cuban Missile Crisis, the 2011 intervention in Libya, the 1991 war with Iraq, and the 2003 invasion of Iraq. The first two crises constitute a pair of "most-likely" cases for which costly compellence makes opposite predictions, while the two Iraq cases present a unique opportunity to isolate the United States' efforts to coerce the same target in successive crises. For each case, I evaluate the logic of the costly compellence theory and three competing theories of threat effectiveness, including the argument that compellent threats that make limited demands are more effective than those demanding expansive concessions. The cases span both the Cold War and post–Cold War periods, and the Iraq chapters draw on exciting new primary evidence on the Iraqi regime uncovered after the 2003 invasion. Taken as a whole, the case chapters supplement and reinforce the findings of the data set: Costly compellence outperforms competing theories in explaining both the successes and failures of US compellent threats. The final chapter expands on the implications of costly compellence for our understanding of unipolarity and for US policymakers. Cheap threats may be ineffective, but the evidence suggests that they are here to stay.

Notes

1. Obama, "Situation in Libya."

2. Unless otherwise indicated, the term "threat" always refers to a compellent threat.

3. This study refers to the United States as a "unipole," a label that the first chapter will explore in greater detail.

4. Blainey, *Causes of War*, 122.

5. Organski and Kugler, *War Ledger*, 206.

6. Gilpin, *War and Change*, 186–87.

7. The inability of hegemonic stability theory to predict these conflicts may stem from the fact that it was only intended to explain conflict between great powers, and it has accurately predicted the absence of such a conflict in the post–Cold War period. The logic of these theories still suggests, however, that a weak state should be unwilling to challenge the unipole because it is unlikely to win—and this is not what we observe in cases where weak states resist the United States' compellent threats.

8. Schelling, *Arms and Influence*, 3.

9. Ibid., 69–71.

10. George, "Coercive Diplomacy: Definition and Characteristics," in George and Simons, *Limits of Coercive Diplomacy*, 2nd ed., 7.

11. Pape, *Bombing to Win*, 16. Note that Pape's concept of coercion differs from Schelling's definition, which encompasses both deterrence and compellence. Pape defines coercion as "persuading an opponent to stop an ongoing action or to start a new course of action by changing its calculations of costs and benefits" (p. 12), a concept that is very similar to Schelling's definition of "compellence."

12. Schelling, *Arms and Influence*, 124.

13. Jonathan Mercer asserts that the extent to which an actor develops a reputation depends on how the observer attributes the actor's behavior in a given situation. In other words, following through on a threat does not automatically generate a reputation for resolve that will be projected into future crises. See chapter 1, "Reputation and Deterrence Theory," in *Reputation and International Politics*.

14. Threats may also fail due to a breakdown in communication between the coercer and the target. See Schelling, *Arms and Influence*, 55. Christopher P. Twomey argues that differences in military doctrine can hinder communication in a crisis and make it more likely that a state will underestimate its opponent. See *Military Lens*, 26, 35. The purpose of this study is not to argue that communication failures are never responsible for compellent-threat failures.

Instead, it presents a theory about why a target state would choose to resist a unipole's demands, even when it has full information about the unipole's capability and willingness to execute the threatened action.

15. Press, *Calculating Credibility*, 21.

16. Blechman and Kaplan, *Force without War*, 87.

17. George and Simons, "Findings and Conclusions," in George and Simons, *Limits of Coercive Diplomacy*, 2nd ed., 269.

18. George and Simons identify many conditions associated with a greater likelihood of target compliance in "Findings and Conclusions," ibid., 270–87.

19. George, "Theory and Practice," ibid., 15. George also notes that this relationship between the scope of the demand and the likelihood of target compliance introduces an important strategic element to the choice of demand and of the coercive strategy to be employed (p. 15).

20. Art, "Coercive Diplomacy: What Do We Know?," in Art and Cronin, *United States and Coercive Diplomacy*, 387.

21. Ibid., 393.

22. Blechman and Wittes, "Defining Moment," 4.

23. Ibid., 26.

24. Since policymakers likely recognize the impact that their demand may have on the target, the choice of demand is likely to be an important strategic consideration. George observes this in "Theory and Practice," 15.

25. Snyder, "'Prisoner's Dilemma,'" 98. A full review of game-theoretic models of international crises is beyond the scope of this study, but Snyder provides a good review of the classic models and their implications for international politics.

26. Ibid., 98. Snyder also notes that "countries probably perceive each other as having a hierarchy of interests, so that giving way on a minor issue would not reliably indicate weakness on a major one" (p. 100). This suggests that perceptions of resolve are a function of the specific circumstances of a crisis, not simply a state's overall reputation for appearing resolved in past crises.

27. Jervis, "Nuclear Superiority," 632.

28. Ibid., 628.

29. Morrow, "Capabilities, Uncertainty, and Resolve," 965.

30. Ibid., 941.

31. Ibid., 942.

32. Fearon, "Domestic Political Audiences," 582. Two recent studies find little evidence that audience costs operate in actual crises. See Snyder and Borghard, "Empty Threats," and Trachtenberg, "Audience Costs."

33. Sechser, "Goliath's Curse," 628–29.

34. Ibid., 634–35.

35. Sechser claims on p. 637 that the "most highly resolved targets will stand

firm [i.e., fight in the first crisis], while all others will capitulate." He then claims that a target that "acquiesces" reveals that its resolve (represented by the variable "c_B") "exceeds a critical threshold," while a target that fights reveals that its resolve (c_B) is *below* the critical threshold. This would seem to suggest that states with high resolve—that is, higher values for c_B—acquiesce to the challenger's threats, while states with low resolve—that is, lower values for c_B—choose to fight, a rather curious result. Closer examination reveals that Sechser is inconsistent in his use of the key variable c_B: He defines it as "the target's value for the cost of fighting . . . relative to the stakes of the crisis" on pp. 634–35, as the "level of resolve" on p. 636, and then as the "costs for fighting" on p. 637. If c_B is understood as the costs of fighting, and not as resolve, then it makes more sense that states with high values for c_B would be unwilling to fight in the first round, while states with low values for c_B would be willing to escalate.

36. Such studies include, for example, Maoz, "Resolve, Capabilities"; Sullivan, "War Aims"; and Mack, "Why Big Nations Lose." The argument that the state with higher resolve will win is a standard explanation for why big states lose limited wars with small states. Mack's study, for example, assumes that the smaller state in a limited war is always more highly motivated than the larger state, and thus it does not seem to be able to account for variation in the outcomes of limited, asymmetric wars. See pp. 184–86.

37. Mueller, "'Breaking Point,'" 498, 509.

38. In "War Power," Rosen finds that there is no clear relationship between battle deaths suffered and a war's outcome. The losing side lost more soldiers than the winning side in just more than half the cases he examined (p. 175).

39. Betts, "Comment on Mueller," 521.

40. Kant, "Perpetual Peace," 100.

41. Mueller, *War, Presidents and Public Opinion*, 60.

42. Karol and Miguel, "Electoral Cost of War," 633.

43. Snyder, "'Prisoner's Dilemma,'" 98.

44. Merom, *How Democracies Lose*, 15.

45. In the post–Cold War era, inflicting violence is costly not only for the victims of the violence but also for the state delivering force. We will return to this point chapter 1.

46. Clausewitz, *On War*, 585.

47. This does not imply that inflicting high levels of violence is an effective strategy in war. The willingness to be brutal is an indication that a state is highly motivated to prevail over its opponent, not that the state is likely to win.

48. In *On War*, Clausewitz suggests that a state should persevere only as long as the effort expended is in proportion to the political objectives sought (p. 81).

49. This tripartite specification of state resolve is also necessary to explain

why the United States would decide to initiate military action when it lacks the motivation to win an ensuing war. In Fearon's model, the leader of a democratic state may escalate a dispute because the audience costs generated by the crisis make escalation less costly than backing down ("lock in"). See "Domestic Political Audiences," 578. The argument presented herein suggests, however, that a unipole may start a war to which it is not very committed because it believes that the ensuing fighting will be relatively cheap and that the target is likely to concede shortly after the initiation of hostilities.

Chapter 1
The Logic of Costly Compellence

Why, when the United States issues a compellent threat, would a weaker state choose to resist? The willingness of weak states to resist the United States' threats challenges many theories of how power operates in international politics. It also frustrates US policymakers, who can deploy the world's most powerful conventional military but struggle to coerce target states before the actual use of force.

The costly compellence theory asserts that it is the very fact that the United States is so powerful that makes its compellent threats less likely to be effective. Because the use of force is relatively cheap for a unipole, the threat to inflict violence is not a convincing signal that the United States is highly committed to achieving its goals vis-à-vis the target. A compellent threat must be both *immediately* and *ultimately credible* to the target state to be effective in changing the target's behavior. The target must believe both that the unipole will execute the threatened action and that the unipole will apply additional, decisive force if the target continues to resist after the threat has been executed.

Game-theoretic logic on signaling suggests that a threat must be costly for the threatener to be an effective signal of high motivation. Thus, only a threat that is costly for the unipole will signal that the unipole is highly motivated to defeat its opponent—that is, only a costly threat will be ultimately credible to a target state. By contrast, a cheap threat may be judged immediately credible by the target because it is so easy for the unipole to execute it, but the unipole's willingness to carry out such a low-cost threat will not convince the target that the unipole is highly motivated, and hence the target is likely to resist. In other words, the costly compellence theory asserts that a state with an overwhelming advantage in power over its opponent will find it very difficult to accurately signal its interests in a crisis. In the rest of this chapter, I develop the logic of costly compellence, derive hypotheses on the United States' use of compellent threats, and demonstrate how the United States has developed a model of war-fighting that renders the use of military force relatively cheap.

Concepts: Unipolar Compellent Threats, Credibility, and Effectiveness

Stephen G. Brooks and William C. Wohlforth assert that a unipolar system is one in which a single state vastly exceeds all other states across the full spectrum of capabilities.[1] Although there is some debate about how to classify the United States' position, I adopt Brooks and Wohlforth's definition and employ the term *unipole* to refer to a state enjoying an overwhelming advantage in relative capabilities over all other states in the system.[2] The *target* state is the recipient of the unipole's threat.[3] For arguments that apply to all types of coercion and not to the special case of a unipole coercing a weaker state, I use the term *coercer* to refer to the state issuing a threat.

A *limited compellent military threat* consists of a demand that a target modify its present behavior and a promise to inflict force on the target if it does not accede to the unipole's demands. Such a threat can either be issued explicitly by a policymaker on behalf of the unipole or delivered by a show of force or the movement of military assets. Whether explicit or implicit, the threat communicates to the target that the unipole will execute limited military action if the target does not alter its behavior according to the unipole's demands.[4] The threat may specify the military action to be taken, such as an aerial bombing campaign. Or the threat may indicate only that the unipole will apply force if the target does not accede to its demands.[5] Regardless of the specific content, a compellent military threat works by persuading the target to change its behavior, not by physically forcing it to do so.

In sum, a unipole's compellent military threat has two necessary components: a demand for a change in the status quo and a promise to use military force against the target if it chooses not to comply. As noted in the introduction, deterrent threats—which are intended to prevent the target from taking some future action—are excluded from this study.

Credibility vs. Effectiveness

To explain why the unipole's compellent threats fail against weak states, we must first distinguish between the concepts of credibility and effectiveness. This distinction is often overlooked,[6] particularly in studies of deterrence, but it must be preserved to understand why a unipole's compellent threats fail against weak states. A *credible* threat is one that the target believes is likely to be executed. Thus, a threat's credibility is a belief that the target may or may not hold about the threat—it is not an inherent quality of the threat itself. An *effective* threat is one that convinces the target state to concede to the unipole's demands before the threat has been executed. That is, a threat is effective when it modifies the target's behavior before the use of force.

To explain why the United States' compellent threats fail against weak states, we must also distinguish between a threat's *immediate* and *ultimate credibility.* Because a coercer as powerful as the United States would remain overwhelmingly powerful after executing a conventional threat against a relatively weak state, the target must evaluate the unipole's threat according to two stages. First, the target considers whether the unipole will execute the threatened action. The target believes that the threat is immediately credible when it believes that the unipole will execute its immediate threat. Second, the target assesses whether it believes the United States is willing to apply additional force after the threatened action fails to modify the target's behavior. A threat is ultimately credible when the target believes that the coercer is willing to escalate its use of violence if the target continues to resist after the immediate threat has been executed. The target's expectations about the unipole's behavior at both stages will determine whether the target will concede to the unipole's initial demands.

In most cases, immediate credibility is a necessary condition for compellent threat effectiveness. If the target is to concede, it must believe that there is at least some chance that the threatened action will be executed. Immediate credibility is not, however, a sufficient cause of threat effectiveness. A threat may be immediately credible but still fail to convince the target to change its behavior before the threat is executed.

To be effective in modifying the target's behavior before the use of force, a compellent threat must convince the target both that the unipole will execute the immediate threat *and* that it will apply more force if the target continues to resist after the threat has been executed. In other words, the threat must be both immediately and ultimately credible in order to convince the target to concede to the unipole's demands. If the target doubts the unipole's willingness to use decisive force after the threatened action fails—that is, if it doubts the threat's ultimate credibility—then it may resist a threat with high immediate credibility. In such a case, the target would choose to resist because it believed that the unipole would execute limited military action against it and would then abandon its objectives rather than escalate its use of force against a stubbornly resistant opponent. The logic of the target's decision is represented in the diagram on the following page.

For example, imagine that the unipole issues a compellent threat demanding that a target state admit inspectors to its nuclear reactors and promising a cruise missile strike in the event of noncompliance. If the target doubts that the cruise missiles will be launched, then it has no reason to concede to the demand to admit inspectors. If, however, the target believes the strike will be executed, then it considers whether it believes the unipole will escalate the use of force if the target continues to refuse admission to the weapons inspectors after the strike. If the target believes that the unipole lacks the motivation to use additional force after the cruise missiles fail, and if it believes that the impact of the strike will be limited relative to the value of its nuclear program, then the target will refuse to admit the weapons inspectors—even though it believes the unipole's threat is immediately credible.

The Logic of Signaling and the Costly Compellence Theory

To be effective, a unipole's compellent threat must be both immediately and ultimately credible to the target. As noted in the introduction, Press argues that ease of execution enhances a threat's credibility and therefore its effectiveness.[7] The logic of costly compellence, however, suggests the opposite: A compellent threat that is easy to execute will not be effective in changing a target's behavior because a

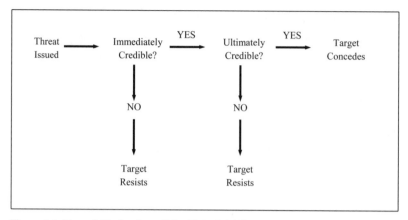

Figure 1.1. Target's Evaluation of the Unipole's Threat

threat that can be executed cheaply does not signal that the unipole is highly motivated to use decisive force at the second stage of the conflict. In other words, cheap threats fail because they lack ultimate credibility.

To be effective, the unipole's compellent threat must convince the target that the unipole is highly motivated to apply additional, decisive force after the immediate threat fails to induce compliance. The target is aware, however, that a unipole that is not highly motivated has strong incentives to behave as if it were. Fearon states the challenge of communicating motivation in similar terms: A target cannot directly observe the coercer's underlying level of motivation, and it also knows that the coercer has an incentive to pretend to be more resolved than it actually is.[8] Thus, the target must infer from the signal—that is, from the threat—how motivated it believes the unipole is to escalate the use of force if the initial threat fails to change the target's behavior.

Given the incentives for the unipole to misrepresent its level of motivation and given that the target is aware of these incentives, how can a compellent threat signal a high level of motivation? Game-theoretic logic suggests that costly signals are more likely to be perceived as believable indicators of high motivation because only a highly motivated actor would be willing to pay the costs associated with such a signal. The formal logic was first developed in research on the role of education in the job market, wherein acquiring education is a signal of a job applicant's quality.[9] If everyone can acquire additional education with relative ease, then education conveys little information about an individual's capability.

Fearon describes the logic for two states engaged in a game of signaling: "A threat may be rendered credible when the act of sending it incurs or creates some cost that the sender would be disinclined to incur or create if he or she were in fact *not* willing to carry out the threat."[10] In this passage, Fearon claims that a costly threat is more "credible" than a low-cost threat. In fact, his argument suggests that a costly threat is more *effective* in coercing a target state because a costly threat signals that the threatener is highly motivated to defeat its opponent. This is an important distinction: The fact that a threat is costly effectively conveys information about the threatener's underlying preferences—its level of motivation—not that the threatener is very likely to carry out the threat.[11] That is, the fact that the threat is costly communicates the threatener's interests and level of motivation, not the likelihood that it will execute the threatened action.

Costly Compellence: Effective Compellent Threats

In fact, there may be an inverse relationship between the extent to which a threat is costly and the extent to which it is perceived as immediately credible, as we will see below. Costly threats are effective not because they are more credible than low-cost threats but because they convince the target that the coercer is highly motivated to defeat it. A compellent threat's immediate credibility is a function of how easy it is for the unipole to execute the threat. All else equal, threats that are less costly for the unipole to execute are more immediately credible to the target. The logic of costly signaling suggests, however, that a threat that is not costly for the unipole will not signal that the unipole is highly motivated to escalate the use of force after the immediate threat fails.

Although a cheap threat may have high immediate credibility because the unipole can execute it with ease, the willingness to execute a low-cost threat does not signal that the unipole is highly motivated. The target resists a cheap threat because it believes both that it can withstand the threatened action and that the unipole lacks the motivation to defeat it in a prolonged and costly military conflict. A costly threat is more effective in changing target-state behavior because the costliness of the threat signals that the unipole is highly motivated to defeat its target, not because it is more immediately credible than a cheap threat.

Thus, the costly compellence theory asserts that threats that are costly for the unipole are more effective than low-cost threats in inducing target-state compliance because they signal that the unipole is highly motivated to defeat its target. Costly threats are ultimately credible. Table 1.1 illustrates how a target is likely to view a costly and a cheap threat, in terms of both their immediate and ultimate credibility.

Consider the same example of the United States threatening the target with a missile strike if it refuses to admit inspectors. If executing the strike will be relatively cheap and easy for the unipole, then the target is likely to judge that the threat has low ultimate credibility. Because the threat can be executed so easily, however, the target will believe that the unipole is likely to execute the strike—that is, the target will believe such a cheap threat has high immediate credibility. The target will resist in the face of such a threat not because it doubts that the United States will execute the missile strike but because it believes that the United States will abandon its objectives after the limited application of force fails to change the target's behavior.

Alternative Explanation: The Cost–Benefit Approach

It is important to note that costly compellence is a theory about coercion *before* war, not coercion *in* war. That is, costly compellence is a theory of how the target assesses the likely course of a coercive engagement with the unipole before the use of force. The straightforward "cost–benefit" approach to threat effectiveness advanced by Pape and others is a theory of coercion *in* war, and it asserts that a target concedes to a threat when the expected costs of resistance

Table 1.1. Costly vs. Cheap Threats

Type of Threat	Immediate Credibility	Ultimate Credibility	Target Response
Costly	Indeterminate	High	Concede
Cheap	High	Low	Resist

outweigh the expected benefits of resistance.[12] Thus, this approach argues that when we observe resistance, the target must have believed that the benefits of resistance outweighed the costs and that when we observe compliance, the expected costs of resistance outweighed the expected benefits. This explanation incorporates the target's estimate about the probability of suffering costs and reaping rewards, but it does not explain why the target would make such assessments. The explanation advanced by the cost–benefit approach for a case in which a target resisted a compellent threat implicitly assumes that the target believed that no additional punishment would be forthcoming after the initial threat was executed—or at least that the probability of additional punishment was sufficiently low that resistance was still the best option. It assumes, in other words, that both the target and coercer can know and perfectly calculate the anticipated costs of war in advance and that the target believes the coercer will limit itself to the realm of coercion and not escalate to brute force after coercion fails.

In reality, however, the United States does not tell a target, "Comply or I will drop exactly 283 bombs on you." The target must always guess how much force it should expect in the event of noncompliance. This is why we need costly compellence: The theory explicitly incorporates the target's assessment about the coercer's level of motivation. Pape argues that strategic bombing generally fails because it cannot inflict enough damage to cripple a modern society or inflict unacceptable pain on the population.[13] The costly compellence theory asserts, however, that threat effectiveness is a function of how costly it is for the unipole to implement its threat, because the costliness of the threat signals how motivated the unipole is to achieve its objectives and hence how much pain it is likely to inflict on the target state with a variety of instruments. A cheap threat will not signal that the unipole is highly motivated to use a large amount of force against the target, making the target more likely to resist.[14]

Hypotheses on Compellent Threat Effectiveness

Given that threats are likely to be more ultimately credible and thus more effective when they are costly, we must now determine the conditions under which it is costly for the unipole to threaten and employ force. A compellent military threat is costly for the unipole for one of two reasons: because issuing the threat exposes the unipole or one of its major allies to the risk of a wider military conflict, or because executing the threat imposes significant human, financial, or political costs on the unipole.

Unipolar Threats Do Not Rock the Boat

The international distribution of power determines whether it is costly to issue a compellent military threat. Schelling argued during the Cold War that a limited war could set off a chain of events that spiraled out of control: "To engage in limited war is to start rocking the boat, to set in motion a process that is not altogether in one's control."[15] When one of the two superpowers in a bipolar system starts a limited war, it risks capsizing the boat of international stability. Disaster can ensue not because the bipole that rocked the boat wished to overturn it, but because the initial act increased the probability that the boat would capsize. In his exposition of the stabilizing effects of bipolarity, Kenneth N. Waltz notes that each bipole must monitor conflicts around the world. Anything that presents either a challenge or opportunity for gain for the opponent also affects one's own relative position.[16] Thus, neither bipole can threaten or execute military action without considering whether doing so will incite a devastating military conflict with its superpower opponent. This condition induces restraint in the bipoles' behavior.

By contrast, a unipole does not "rock the boat" when it issues a compellent military threat against a weaker state. Schelling's argument about the dangers of limited war depends on the mutual vulnerability of bipoles. Without a restraint-inducing global peer competitor, a unipole is free to threaten military action without risking a wider war with a state of comparable strength. Issuing a compellent military threat is a low-risk, low-cost undertaking for a unipole.

Because it is not very risky for a unipole to issue compellent threats, we would expect a unipole to issue compellent threats more frequently than a bipole.[17] Because it is not very risky, and thus not very costly, for a unipole to issue compellent threats, its threats will be less effective in compelling target-state compliance than threats issued by a bipole.

> *Hypothesis 1(a): A unipole issues compellent threats against small states more frequently than a bipole.*
> *Hypothesis 1(b): Compellent threats issued by a bipole are more effective in inducing target-state compliance than threats issued by a unipole.*

Executing Compellent Threats

The manner in which the unipole chooses to employ military force determines whether it is costly to execute compellent threats and thus whether these threats are likely to be effective in inducing target-state compliance before the use of force. Because a threat that can be executed cheaply does not signal to the target that the unipole is highly motivated to prevail in a protracted conflict, strategies that minimize the human, political, and financial costs that the unipole incurs to execute compellent threats undermine the ultimate credibility of those threats.

> *Hypothesis 2: A compellent threat issued by a unipole that actively minimizes the human, political, and financial costs of employing military force is less effective than a threat issued by a unipole that does not employ such cost-minimizing strategies.*

Hypothesis 2 implies that we must consider both the specific characteristics of a unipole's threat and the unipole's overall strategy for employing force to determine the extent to which a threat is costly to execute. That is, both the specific type of force that the unipole threatens to inflict (air strikes, ground troops, etc.) and the general strategies that the unipole employs to generate and inflict violence on target states affect how costly it is to execute compellent threats. There are three different types of costs that we must consider in deciding whether a particular threat will be costly for the unipole: human, political, and financial.

Military Manpower

The most painful losses that a state suffers in war are the deaths of its own people.[18] The willingness to kill its own citizens should be a convincing indication that the unipole is highly motivated to prevail over its opponent. Jervis notes that a state could offer human sacrifices to convincingly signal high motivation to another state.[19] This may seem like a fantastical suggestion, but the decision to send troops into battle is always a decision to sacrifice some citizens to serve the interests of the state. For the purposes of signaling motivation, however, not all militaries are created equal.

Conscription—compulsory military service—dramatically increases the mass of manpower at a state's disposal.[20] Clausewitz noted that the *levée en masse* mobilized the weight of the French nation-state for the first time and unleashed the resources and will of the nation in war.[21] Conscription gives the population a direct stake in the outcome of war by forcing individuals to bear the costs of fighting.[22] For this very reason, conscription is also a politically costly strategy. Conscription exposes a wider range of individuals—including the elite members of society who are directly involved in the processes and decisions of government—to the burdens of military service than does volunteer recruitment. Because conscription forces the general population to pay the human costs of war, it makes the public more likely to punish policymakers for costly military campaigns.

By contrast, volunteer recruitment lowers the political costs of employing force and of executing military threats. Rather than being forced to risk one's life for the state, a volunteer soldier willingly accepts the risks of military service. The public will be less likely to punish policymakers for costly wars when the soldiers fighting and dying do so voluntarily and when they do not have to worry that their own sons and daughters will be forced to serve. The ability to wield a military composed of volunteers frees policymakers to employ force with less risk of reprisal.[23]

Between the extremes of universal conscription and reliance on active volunteers lies the mobilization of reserves. By calling up reserve troops, the unipole can increase the military manpower at its disposal without resorting to a politically costly draft. Unlike conscripts, reservists voluntarily consent to the possibility of active service. The public outcry when such individuals are mobilized will be much less than that which would occur in the wake of a draft. Calling up reserves is more costly, however, than relying solely on active volunteers because reservists are pulled away from their jobs and families to serve.

If the unipole cannot recruit enough volunteers to meet its military manpower needs, and if it is unwilling or unable to call up reserves, then it can avoid the use of conscription by hiring private military contractors to perform functions formerly reserved for the armed services. Private contractors may be expensive in dollar terms,[24] but they lower the political costs of employing force. Even more so than volunteer soldiers, private contractors willingly and temporarily accept the risks of war in exchange for monetary compensation. For this reason, the public will be much less resistant to (and policymakers will be less likely to be punished for) threatening and employing force when the unipole deploys contractors instead of draftees or reservists. Furthermore, because private contractors are not members of the unipole's military, the casualties they suffer may go unreported in official accounts of military engagements. This shields the public even more from the true human costs of its wars.

In sum, strategies that enable the unipole to avoid the use of conscription render the use of military force less costly for policymakers. Such strategies include reliance on an all-volunteer force, the calling up of reserves, and the hiring of private contractors to perform functions formerly reserved for the military. Because these strategies render the use of force cheaper for the unipole, they also undermine the effectiveness of the unipole's compellent threats.[25] Conversely, the decision to adopt conscription by a unipole that had formerly avoided the practice will be a very costly signal of high motivation to prevail over the target.[26]

Military Strategy and Casualty Avoidance

The way that a unipole fights also affects how costly it is to execute compellent threats. Military strategies differ significantly in the extent to which they expose soldiers to the risk of making the ultimate sacrifice. Strategies that minimize the risk of casualties will be less politically costly than those that place the lives of soldiers at great risk, and they will also be less costly for the soldiers themselves. By contrast, strategies that expose troops to great risk—particularly those that involve the use of ground troops—will be much more costly for the unipole to implement, and thus the unipole's compellent threats will be more effective.

For example, a force structure like that proposed by advocates of the Revolution in Military Affairs (RMA) thesis relies on operations that emphasize speed, precision, and firepower over manpower.[27] Operations that employ aerial bombing, sea-based cruise missiles, or unmanned aerial vehicles (UAVs) exploit advanced technology to deliver force from a distance and minimize risks for the unipole's soldiers. By adopting a military model that substitutes technology for manpower, policymakers can minimize the casualties suffered by the unipole's soldiers and thereby minimize the human and political costs of employing force.[28]

The specific action that the unipole promises to inflict on the target also affects how costly it will be to execute the threat.[29] The most costly action that the unipole can threaten and undertake against the target is an attack with a large contingent of ground troops. Placing troops on the ground exposes them to a much higher level of risk than that which they face when the unipole chooses to administer air strikes or launch cruise missiles against the target state. It is much easier for a weak target state to attack soldiers on the ground than to shoot down an advanced air force or to sink the ships from which precision-guided munitions are launched. It is also much more difficult for the unipole to insert ground troops into and remove ground troops from the theater of operations than it is to send a carrier battle group or an air wing.

By contrast, airpower is one of the cornerstones of the RMA model and allows the unipole to deliver force against the target while putting its own forces at very little risk. There is considerable debate about whether airpower can be an effective, independent instrument of coercion. The case that best supports the arguments of airpower proponents is the 1999 NATO campaign over Kosovo, but scholars continue to debate the reason for Slobodan Milošević's so-called capitulation. Critics of airpower argue that strategic bombing can inflict a lot of damage on target states but rarely achieves the coercer's political objectives.[30] Bombing may be effective, however, in support of much more expensive and risky ground operations.[31] Regardless of whether airpower is an effective independent instrument of coercion, it is much less costly for the unipole in both human and political terms to employ airpower and similar operations than to employ ground troops.[32]

Paying the Bills: Allies and Deficit Spending

In addition to the way that the unipole chooses to fight, the way that it chooses to pay for its military operations also affects how costly it is to execute compellent threats. Just as conscription distributes the human costs of war, so does taxation spread the financial costs of war across the population.[33] Michael Howard argues that the tax bureaucracy evolved in early modern Europe because fledgling states needed money to pay for their military campaigns.[34] As Charles Tilly famously noted, "war made the state and the state made war."[35] When citizens bear the financial costs of war directly, they have a much stronger incentive to act as a check on the government's foreign policy. Raising taxes to pay for a military operation is thus a politically costly strategy. Elected officials may be exposed to retaliation if the public does not support a military campaign for which it is asked to sacrifice.[36]

There are some strategies that the unipole can adopt to minimize the financial costs of its military operations and avoid politically costly taxes. The unipole is, by definition, capable of executing military action around the world without assistance. The decision to enlist allies in the campaign against the target state may, however, reduce the financial and political costs of executing the unipole's threat.[37] Such allies may do little to enhance the unipole's battlefield effectiveness, but they can lower the financial costs of executing military threats if they contribute troops, equipment, or money to the unipole's campaign. Acting in conjunction with allies can also lower the political costs for military action if the unipole's population views the approval of such allies as an indication of the action's "correctness." By contrast, acting unilaterally is more expensive in financial terms and may be more likely to anger the public both at home and abroad.

Instead of calling on taxpayers or its allies to foot the bill for military operations today, the unipole can instead pass the costs of its coercive campaigns to future generations. That is, rather than opt for the politically costly strategy of raising taxes, the unipole can pay for its operations with deficit spending. Both allies' contributions and deficit spending shield the unipole's public from the financial costs of using force and make it easier for the unipole to execute military action.[38]

The Will to Kill and Collateral Damage

The willingness to inflict violence on the opponent is one of the three components of state resolve. Inflicting violence is obviously costly to the target of the violence. The extent to which it is costly for the unipole to inflict violence on its target also affects the ultimate credibility of the unipole's threat and thus the likelihood that the target will concede. That is, if the unipole threatens to pursue a campaign of violence against the target for which the unipole will suffer significant costs, then the threat of force is more likely to be viewed as ultimately credible. Let us assume that killing the target's soldiers is an accepted consequence of military operations.[39] The extent to which it is costly for the unipole to kill—either deliberately or accidentally—members of the target's civilian population also affects how costly it is to execute a compellent threat and thus how likely it is to be perceived as ultimately credible.

Some military strategies target and kill civilians by design. Examples of such strategies would include medieval sieges of fortified cities designed to starve the enemy into submission and strategic bombing campaigns intended to induce policy change by inflicting pain on the target state's population. Some strategies can inflict enormous suffering even when civilians are not the direct targets of military operations. The term "collateral damage" refers to the accidental killing of civilians as an unintended by-product of legitimate military operations.

Whether deliberate or not, killing civilians is politically costly for the unipole when two conditions are met. First, prevailing norms in the international system must condemn civilian casualties in war. Second, the unipole's population must be aware that its government is killing target state civilians and must disapprove of this behavior.[40] When these two conditions are met, elected policymakers have strong incentives to eschew strategies that deliberately target civilians and to actively minimize collateral damage caused by the unipole's military.

In the post–Cold War world, both the deliberate and the accidental killing of civilians are condemned by international norms. The norm of the "Responsibility to Protect" has justified interventions that override state sovereignty to save civilians from violence within their own states.[41] Nor is the belief that civilians should be protected in war held exclusively by those fortunate enough to live in states at peace. In a survey of people in twelve war-torn countries, only 3 percent of respondents believed that combatants should attack both combatants and noncombatants.[42] Furthermore, the general public is more aware than ever of the suffering that military operations can inflict on civilian populations. The twenty-four-hour news cycle and social media sites continually report on civilian casualties generated by major operations. Some media outlets even publish graphic images of victims.[43] Just as casualties suffered by a unipole's soldiers raise the political costs of conducting military campaigns, so too does the publication of civilian casualties caused by the unipole's air strikes.[44]

The costly compellence theory suggests that threats that do not explicitly exclude civilians from attack are more effective in inducing target-state compliance because they are more costly for the unipole to execute, and therefore they are more convincing signals that the unipole is highly motivated to prevail.[45] The argument makes no claim about whether targeting civilians is an effective strategy in war. Many studies suggest that strategies that target civilians are both ineffective and counterproductive,[46] but a small number suggest that violence against civilians can be effective under some conditions.[47] Regardless of whether targeting civilians is a war-winning strategy, the willingness to do so is a costly signal that the unipole is highly motivated to prevail over its opponent, and such a threat is more likely to be effective in inducing target compliance before the actual use of force.

The Paradox of Costly Compellence: Summary

To be effective, a unipole's compellent threat must be both immediately and ultimately credible: The target must believe both that the unipole will execute the threatened action and that the unipole will apply additional, decisive force if the target continues to resist after the threat has been executed. That is, the target must believe that the unipole is resolved both to initiate military action against it and to prosecute the ensuing conflict with the sacrifice and intensity necessary to defeat it if the target continues to resist.

The costly compellence theory asserts that threats that are costly for the unipole are more effective in inducing target-state compliance than threats that are relatively cheap because costly threats signal to the target that the unipole is highly motivated to apply decisive force after the threatened action fails to induce compliance. A cheap threat is likely to be immediately credible to the target because it is so easy to execute. A cheap threat does not, however, signal *ultimate* credibility precisely because it is so easy to implement. A target chooses to resist a cheap threat not because it doubts the unipole's willingness to execute it, but because it doubts the unipole's motivation to exact compliance after the limited application of force fails.

The international distribution of power determines whether it is costly to issue a threat, while the unipole's war-fighting model determines whether it is costly to execute a compellent threat. Because a unipole faces no peer competitor capable of restraining its behavior around the world, in most situations it is neither risky nor costly for a unipole to issue a compellent military threat. We expect, therefore, that a unipole will issue compellent threats much more frequently than a bipole. There are a variety of conditions and strategies that determine whether a threat is costly for a unipole to execute and hence whether a target is likely to concede to the unipole's demands before the actual use of force. Maintaining an all-volunteer military, calling up reserves rather than instituting a draft, relying on private military contractors, pursuing military strategies that shield the unipole's troops from casualties, funding military operations with deficit spending, executing its threats in conjunction with allies, and limiting collateral damage suffered by target civilians limit the unipole's costs for military action.[48] The costly compellence theory tells us that we should expect compellent threats issued by a unipole that pursues these strategies to be more immediately credible but less ultimately credible, and hence less effective, than those issued by a unipole more willing to incur the costs of its military operations, because these cost-minimizing strategies render the threat of force an uninformative signal of how motivated the unipole is to exact compliance from a stubbornly resistant target state. The costly compellence theory thus reveals a paradox: Strategies to make the use of force less costly and more efficient enhance the immediate credibility of a unipole's compellent threats, but they also undermine the ultimate effectiveness of these threats.

If the unipole chooses to employ strategies to make the use of force less costly, does that not mean that it can inflict a lot of damage on the target at low cost to itself, making the target *more* likely to concede?[49] To believe this argument, we (and target states) must believe that applying cheap and limited instruments of force—strategic bombing, cruise missile strikes, surgical attacks by units of special operations forces, drone strikes, etc.—in large doses is an effective way of forcing compliance from a stubbornly resistant target state. Otherwise, there would be no reason for a target to comply when threatened with such a campaign. There is in fact limited evidence to support the claim that large doses of cheap instruments are effective at inducing compliance from a resistant target. As noted above, much of the work on airpower (including Pape's) refutes the argument that strategic bombing, even in large doses, is an effective independent instrument of coercion in war. It may be relatively easy for the unipole to employ cheap instruments, but that is precisely why cheap instruments do not signal that the unipole is highly motivated to defeat the target state and why the threat to employ them does not induce compliance.

Costly Compellence and the United States: Observable Implications

The costly compellence theory suggests that a unipole will issue compellent threats more frequently than will a superpower in a bipolar system and that its compellent threats will be ineffective in obtaining target-state compliance if and when it pursues the cost-minimizing strategies for employing force described above. To test these hypotheses about the frequency and effectiveness of the United States' compellent threats, we must first assess both the country's position in the international system and the manner in which it employs force. This will allow us to determine the conditions under which it is costly for the United States to issue and execute compellent threats and thus the conditions under which such threats are likely to be effective.

Issuing Threats: The United States as Unipole

Brooks and Wohlforth argue that the United States "has a greater share of power than any single state has ever had in 300 years."[50] A brief examination of US economic and military resources demonstrates that the United States is indeed in a class by itself. The World

Bank estimates 2013 US gross domestic product (GDP) at roughly $16.8 trillion ($53,000 per capita), nearly twice that of the United States' nearest competitor. China surpassed Japan in 2010 to become the world's second largest economy and recorded a GDP of $9.2 trillion ($6,800 per capita) in 2013. Japan followed China with a 2013 GDP of $4.9 trillion ($39,000 per capita), which was a contraction from the previous year.[51]

In addition to commanding the world's largest economy, the United States also commands the world's largest defense establishment. US defense spending was $581 billion in 2014 (roughly 3.3 percent of GDP), down from a recent high of roughly $700 billion in 2011. This contraction in the defense budget reflects sequestration mechanisms that were part of the Budget Control Act of 2011.[52] Although in recent years the United States had accounted for roughly half of total global defense spending, US spending on defense in 2014 was roughly 36 percent of the global total for that year. By contrast, China's official defense budget was roughly $129 billion in 2014, or 1.3 percent of its GDP.[53] China's record of impressive economic growth and increasing defense budgets has led some to conclude that the United States is in relative decline and that the world will soon be multipolar.[54] Michael Beckley argues, however, that the United States' advantage over China in economic, technological, and military power is both real and likely to persist.[55] Arguments heralding the United States' decline cannot dispute the fact that the United States commands vastly more economic and military resources than any other state and is uniquely capable of employing force around the world.[56] In other words, the United States is a unipole.[57]

Executing Threats: The Low Cost of Employing American Force

Since the end of the Second World War, the United States has gradually adopted several strategies to insulate the bulk of its population from the burdens of war. These trends accelerated dramatically with the end of the Cold War in 1990. The United States eliminated conscription and relies instead on a volunteer military supplemented with private contractors. The US military has also embraced many aspects of the RMA to protect the All-Volunteer Force (AVF) from the worst realities of combat. The United States has relied on contributions from its allies and deficit spending to fund its post–Cold War campaigns. Furthermore, norms about the use of violence have evolved such that the US military takes great pains to limit the harm that it inflicts on target states. In combination, these trends dramatically limit the United States' costs for employing military force.

The United States and Military Manpower

Samuel P. Huntington argued that the American liberal ethos clashes directly with the notion of compulsory military service. In his view, the volunteer militias of the Revolutionary War perfectly embodied America's ideal relationship between the civilian and the state.[58] Despite its valorization of the citizen-soldier from Lexington and Concord, the United States has not always relied solely on volunteer soldiers to prosecute its wars. A system of conscription was employed during the American Civil War and during both world wars. Although President Harry S. Truman briefly ended the practice in 1947, conscription was reinstated in 1948, and a selective service system remained in place until 1973.[59] Conscription in the United States was never truly universal, however, even during the two world wars.[60] The practice has been controversial in the United States not only because it clashes with the American "liberal ethos," but also because of inequities in its implementation,[61] as wealthier and more privileged men were often able to avoid service through a variety of deferment programs.[62]

The end of conscription in 1973 and the adoption of the AVF mean that the general public in the United States is no longer exposed to the burden of military service. Volunteers are not drawn equally from across society: Southern states continue to be overrepresented among new accessions, while the Northeastern and Mid-Atlantic regions have accession rates much lower than the national average.[63] Surveys of new recruits suggest that they are drawn from the lower middle or middle class and not from the high end of the income distribution.[64] One study links the elimination of conscription to the current underrepresentation of veterans in Congress.[65] The AVF has increased personnel retention and allowed the United States to develop the most highly skilled military in the world,[66] but it also shields the general public—and particularly the elite segments of society from which policymakers are likely to be drawn—from the burdens of military service, thereby lowering the costs to the United States of employing force.

When the United States shifted to the AFV, it also changed the way reserves are integrated into the military. The total-force policy crafted by Gen. Creighton Abrams at the end of the Vietnam War expanded the role of the reserves so that any significant military operation would require the use of reserve components. This would mean, in theory, that policymakers would only be able to execute operations for which they had the support of the American public.[67] Since the end of the Cold War, however, the need to call up the reserves has not served as a check on the United States' ability to launch military operations. Reservists were called up for the 1991 Gulf War and for peacekeeping in the Balkans, but many of these individuals volunteered to go, and they were not kept on active duty for more than six months. By contrast, for the wars in Iraq and Afghanistan, reservists and units from the National Guard have been called up at very short notice, without adequate training, and have remained on active duty much longer than anticipated.[68] Furthermore, both military personnel on active duty and reservists have been deployed for multiple tours in these wars,[69] which has allowed the United States to avoid costly conscription at the expense of the well-being of its soldiers and their families. The need to call up these reservists did not, however, provoke outcry in the United States or make it politically infeasible to conduct two failing wars in the Middle East.

Reservists are not the only option available for a unipole that wishes to avoid conscription. The United States' growing use of military contractors is part of a larger post–Cold War trend to privatize elements of American foreign policy. Both political parties have promoted this "outsourcing" of foreign policy as a way to save money and improve efficiency.[70] Although it is not a new phenomenon, the United States' use of contractors has received a lot of attention in recent years because private military firms have been very active in Iraq and Afghanistan. A conservative 2007 estimate by the Department of Defense counted 180,000 private contractors in Iraq, compared to 160,000 US troops there at that time.[71] In other words, the United States needed more than twice the manpower to prosecute the war in Iraq than it could provide from its own military, and the ability to hire contractors both allowed the United States to prolong its presence in Iraq and avoid the politically costly decision to send conscripts to the Middle East.

Casualties

The perception that the American public is relatively squeamish about casualties creates strong incentives for policymakers to continue with these strategies to avoid conscription and to rely on missions that limit the risks of casualties for US troops. The belief that Americans cannot stomach casualties does influence planning for US operations. For example, President Bill Clinton's promise not to send ground troops as part of the 1999 NATO mission to coerce Serbia reflected a desire to minimize NATO casualties. The decision to bomb targets in Yugoslavia from high altitudes lowered the risk to NATO personnel, but it may have also hindered accurate targeting and made collateral damage more likely.[72] Fears about US casualties also influenced planning for the 2001 invasion of Afghanistan.[73]

In fact, several studies of US public opinion on more recent conflicts suggest that Americans will tolerate casualties only under specific conditions. Eric V. Larson and Bogdan Savych find that the public will tolerate casualties if it believes that the stakes are high, but it is much less willing to tolerate heavy losses for limited goals.[74] They also find that, in the post–Cold War era, public support is higher for air campaigns than for missions involving ground troops.[75] Christopher Gelpi, Peter D. Feaver, and Jason Reifler find that the American public's willingness to support a military operation as casualties mount depends on "the interactive effect of two underlying attitudes: expectations about the likelihood that the military operation will be a success and belief in the initial rightness of the decision to launch the military operation."[76] Richard C. Eichenberg examines polls of American public opinion from 1981 through 2005, including polls on the 2003 US invasion of Iraq. He finds that "support . . . increases when the intervention is successful, regardless of the level of casualties."[77]

In other words, the evidence suggests that the American public is willing to tolerate high casualties and risky operations involving ground troops only when the stakes are high and the operation is going well. This means that policymakers face strong incentives to avoid risky strategies such as the use of ground troops, particularly when the goal is not a core US interest and the outcome is uncertain.[78] Military leaders also face strong incentives to limit casualties when it costs \$35,000 to \$50,000 to train a new army volunteer to report to his or her first duty station and tens of thousands of dollars to educate and train a long-serving officer in the AVF.[79] In other words, both policymakers and military leaders face strong incentives to limit casualties.

The RMA, Airpower, and Drones: Substituting Technology for Manpower

One of the most important manifestations of this desire to minimize US casualties has been the adoption of many elements of the RMA thesis.[80] Proponents argue that the superiority of US technology—and airpower in particular—has transformed the character of warfare such that the United States can impose its will on any opponent while suffering few casualties. The rapid expulsion of Iraqi forces from Kuwait in 1991 seemed to usher in this new era of US military dominance. The report on Operation Desert Storm by the House Armed Services Committee asserts that airpower was the decisive instrument in the war with Iraq. In fact, it cites the reliance on technology as a key factor accounting for the high performance of US forces and the low level of casualties incurred.[81] In other words, at the dawn of the post–Cold War period, the link between technology and low casualties had already emerged.

As noted above, airpower is perhaps the most attractive weapon in the RMA arsenal because it offers the ability to deliver force from a relatively safe distance.[82] It should be no surprise, therefore, that airpower has played a large role in US operations since the end of the Cold War. The Gulf War began with an extensive bombing campaign. The 1999 campaign over Kosovo was conducted exclusively from the air. The 2003 invasion of Iraq began with a decapitation strike aimed at Iraqi leadership, after which US forces launched simultaneous air and ground attacks. In fact, we will see in the sixth chapter that the George W. Bush administration based its planning for the 2003 invasion of Iraq on many of the central tenets of the RMA.

The United States has also grown increasingly reliant on the use of UAVs to deliver force from a distance and to shield its own forces from casualties.[83] The rise of the UAV is itself a part of the growing use of robots in combat, particularly during the wars in Iraq and Afghanistan.[84] P. W. Singer argues that the low-cost 1991 victory in Iraq, combined with the specter of Vietnam and the humiliating pullout from Somalia in 1993, spurred investment in unmanned systems precisely because they minimize US casualties.[85] According to a 2012 report by the Congressional Research Service, unmanned aerial systems (UAS) constituted 41 percent of the United States' inventory of aircraft, up from only 5 percent in 2005. This inventory includes more than seven thousand unmanned systems.[86]

The United States' use of drones to target and kill suspected terrorists, insurgents, and their associates first received attention during the George W. Bush administration, but the use of drone strikes increased dramatically during Barack Obama's presidency.[87] The use of unmanned aircraft for targeted killings raises thorny ethical issues about assassination and oversight, particularly as the Central Intelligence Agency (CIA) has begun to build and operate its own fleet of armed drones.[88] Unmanned aircraft are particularly attractive, however, because substituting drones and robots for soldiers minimizes US casualties. Many drones are cheap compared to manned aircraft, and without a pilot on board they can be sent on risky missions without risking American lives.[89] Reliance on high-tech instruments that separate US soldiers from their foes may be interpreted by some as an indication that the United States is unwilling to pay high costs to defeat its opponents.

Some might argue that the shift to counterinsurgency (COIN) in the wars in Iraq and Afghanistan invalidates the assertion that the United States relies on technology and airpower to minimize its costs for employing force. Indeed, the new *US Army / Marine Corps Counterinsurgency Field Manual* emphasizes that the military's main role in COIN is to protect the population and that the use of excessive force can undermine the ability to achieve political objectives.[90] The counterinsurgency manual thus places a much larger emphasis on the use of ground troops than does the RMA model of warfare. Instead of reinstating the draft to meet this need for ground forces, however, the United States relied on the cost-saving strategies described above, including the repeated deployment of reservists and members of the National Guard and the hiring of private contractors, and by shifting troops between theaters when necessary. As we will see in the concluding chapter, the increasing use of unmanned systems to prosecute the so-called war on terror, the 2011 standoff strike on Libya, and the new strategic guidance released by the Department of Defense in 2012 all point to reinvigoration of the technology-intensive American war-fighting model described in this chapter.[91]

Deficit Spending and Allies: Strategies to Avoid Taxation

Substituting technology for manpower is an attractive strategy for a unipole trying to minimize the political costs of employing force,[92] but it can also be very expensive in dollar terms. This would seem to undermine the argument that pursuing an RMA-based military model lowers the costs of executing military action. The US defense establishment is not cheap. Total US defense spending was roughly $580 billion in 2014 (roughly 3.3 percent of GDP), which amounted to slightly more than one-third of total global defense spending that year.[93] US defense spending was nearly half of total global spending as recently as 2012.[94] US defense spending amounted to $1,822 per capita in 2014, more than eight times the global average of $225 per capita.[95]

The United States spends a lot of money on defense. In fact, annual US defense spending exceeds the GDPs of many countries.[96] When the $580 billion figure for annual defense spending is compared to the size of the US economy and to historical trends in defense spending, however, the number is not as outrageous as it initially appears. During the height of World War II, the United States spent more than 37 percent of its GDP on defense, while the figure was 14 percent at the end of the Korean War in 1953. During the first half of the Cold War, annual spending on national defense hovered around 8 to 9 percent of GDP, and then it finally settled to around 5 to 6 percent of GDP after the Vietnam War ended and before the drawdown in spending that followed the end of the Cold War. US national defense spending as a percentage of GDP bottomed out at just under 3 percent in 2000 before climbing to a high of 4.7 percent in 2010. Even at the height of the Vietnam War—a grinding counterinsurgency more comparable to the wars in Iraq and Afghanistan than the Second World War—the United States was willing to spend 8 to 9 percent of its GDP on defense. Current US defense spending is not insignificant. As a percentage of GDP, however, US defense spending is moderate in comparison to twentieth-century trends.[97]

Although the US defense establishment is expensive, its baseline cost remains relatively stable over time, and taxpayers are accustomed to paying for it. Thus, it is the way that the United States chooses to pay for its military operations that determines whether it is costly for it to execute compellent threats. Although the United States did not face the same pressures as did states in early modern Europe competing for survival, it has sometimes raised taxes to pay for its wars. A federal excise tax on long-distance telephone calls was enacted to pay for the Spanish–American War. Federal income tax withholding was established during the Second World War and remains in place to this day.[98] If we examine the United States' major military operations in the post–Cold War period, however, we find that it does not want to pay for the wars that it fights—at least, not immediately.

The United States' total incremental costs for the Gulf War were estimated at $61 billion.[99] Allies pledged roughly $54 billion to offset these costs. The Defense Department's report notes that without these financial contributions from its allies, "the US would have had to pay these costs either through a tax increase or through deficit spending, adding to the nations' [sic] fiscal difficulties."[100] In other words, the mission was important to the United States and to the preservation of international peace but not so important that US policymakers would call on the public to pay for it with higher taxes.

The recent wars in Iraq and Afghanistan have been significantly more expensive than the Gulf War. The International Institute for Strategic Studies estimates the total cost of the war on terror from 2001 through 2012, including the wars in Afghanistan and Iraq and homeland security costs, at $1.4 trillion.[101] Joseph E. Stiglitz and Linda J. Bilmes, on the other hand, estimate that total costs for the Iraq War alone will exceed $3 trillion.[102] Although the wars in Iraq and Afghanistan have been enormously expensive, Americans have not been asked to pay for them with higher taxes. Instead, President Bush and congressional Republicans actually passed a series of tax cuts from 2001 through 2004, with the 2003 tax breaks for the affluent alone carrying an estimated price tag of $1 trillion over ten years.[103] In fact, the United States borrowed most of the money to pay for the war in Iraq.[104] The Bush administration also circumvented normal budgeting procedures by funding the wars with "emergency 'supplemental' war requests [that] were often kept secret until the last possible moment."[105]

In other words, in the post–Cold War period, the United States has relied on its allies to help offset the costs of its military operations and on deficit spending to pay for the rest. Even as battles over government debt and possible default raged in 2013, there were no calls to raise taxes to pay off the country's wars. Strategies that permit the United States to avoid raising taxes to pay for military operations lower the unipole's costs for executing compellent threats.

Minimizing Collateral Damage

Norms about the killing of noncombatants have evolved such that it is now politically costly to kill the target state's civilians. The United States' behavior toward noncombatants has also evolved over the last century. The campaign to pacify the Philippines after the United States acquired the islands from Spain in 1898 was brutal. American soldiers burned villages, shot prisoners, and committed many atrocities against the local inhabitants.[106] During the strategic bombing campaigns of World War II, the enlightened democracies of Great Britain and the United States deliberately rained ferocious destruction onto the people of Germany and Japan.[107]

Since the dropping of the atomic bombs on Japan—of which a majority of Americans approved at the time[108]—the trend in post–World War II America has been a retreat from strategies that target civilians and a movement toward both acknowledging when mistakes have been made and proactively protecting civilians from harm. For example, civilian casualties became a focal point for critics of US participation in the Vietnam War. The United States' reliance on massive firepower in densely populated areas in Vietnam did cause civilian casualties, and the use of napalm and defoliants also exposed the Vietnamese population to both immediate and long-term suffering. The most famous American atrocity was the My Lai Massacre in March 1968, in which an army company on a search-and-destroy mission killed as many as 567 unarmed men, women, and children.[109] In public statements, however, both Gen. William

Westmoreland and President Lyndon Johnson stressed that civilian casualties were the unintended and tragic consequences of legitimate military operations.[110] This suggests that policymakers were aware of the political fallout generated by collateral damage, a change from the World War II era when civilian targeting was part of the Allies' strategy.

Plans for the United States' post–Cold War air campaigns have reflected a new attitude about civilian casualties. Advances in precision targeting both complement this desire to minimize collateral damage and allow the United States to use its firepower more discriminately. For example, the decapitation campaign at the beginning of the Gulf War was a precision strike designed to target Iraqi leaders and spare civilians. Gen. Colin Powell, the chairman of the Joint Chiefs of Staff, further restricted the bombing of targets in Baghdad after a February 13 strike on the Al-Firdos bunker accidentally killed hundreds of civilians.[111] In some cases the United States also avoided killing Iraqi soldiers. Concerns about press reports of the "turkey shoot" along the "Highway of Death" restricted bombing of retreating Iraqi soldiers at the end of the war, allowing many to escape back into Iraq.[112]

Concerns about civilian casualties also drove debates about targeting during the 1999 Kosovo campaign. The NATO allies' wish to oversee target lists and the desire to minimize collateral damage gave rise to a complicated approval system for individual targets. Some targets, such as bridges and petroleum storage locations, were ruled off-limits due to fears about civilian casualties despite their strategic importance.[113] As we will see in chapter 6, planning for the 2003 invasion of Iraq also reflected a desire to minimize collateral damage. Although the US military was criticized for its treatment of Iraqi civilians, the evidence suggests that civilian casualties in Iraq were low by historical standards.[114] The United States also took pains to minimize collateral damage in the war in Afghanistan. In June 2009, Gen. Stanley McChrystal issued new restrictions on the use of air strikes in Afghanistan because of collateral damage resulting from strikes aimed at insurgents. He noted that "air power contains the seeds of our own destruction if we do not use it responsibly."[115]

The evidence from US and NATO campaigns in the post–Cold War period suggests that attitudes about inflicting violence on target states have evolved over the last century. The United States now goes to great lengths to limit collateral damage, and in some cases it even refrains from killing its opponent's soldiers. This is a stunning reversal from the Second World War, when the deliberate targeting of civilians was a major component of the Allies' strategy to defeat Germany and Japan. Efforts to limit the violence inflicted on target states may be desirable from a normative standpoint.[116] These efforts also minimize the United States' political costs for employing military force and thereby erode the signaling properties of its compellent threats.

Testing Costly Compellence: The Plan of Attack

The United States is the most powerful country in the world across the major indices of state power. No other state comes close to matching its combination of economic and military dominance. In other words, the United States is a unipole, and thus it is not very costly for it to issue compellent threats under most circumstances. The United States has also developed a model that limits its own costs for the use of military force: It abandoned conscription in 1973 and has since relied on an all-volunteer force supplemented by reservists and private military contractors, it has embraced many elements of the RMA thesis—particularly airpower—to substitute technology for manpower in its military operations, it has opted to enlist allies to offset the costs of its military operations and to use deficit spending to pay for its campaigns, and it now takes great pains to minimize the pain inflicted on target-state civilians. In combination, all of these strategies render the use of force relatively cheap for the United States, and thus it is not very costly for it to execute compellent threats in the post–Cold War period.

With these observations about the independent variables in mind, the costly compellence theory generates some specific observable implications for the United States' use of compellent threats. Hypothesis 1(a) asserts that a unipole issues compellent threats more frequently than a bipole. It suggests that we should observe that the United States has issued compellent threats more frequently in the post–Cold War period than it did during the period of bipolarity (1945–1989).

According to hypothesis 2, the United States' compellent threats should be less effective in the post–Cold War period because it has chosen to employ cost-minimizing strategies that render the use of force relatively cheap. In addition, certain types of threats—such as those that exclude the use of ground troops or are implemented with the assistance of allies—that are less costly for the United States to implement are also less likely to be effective in inducing target-state compliance.

To determine whether the empirical record is consistent with these predictions, the following chapter presents a new data set on the United States' use (and nonuse) of compellent threats in international crises from 1945 to 2007. Although it is impossible to test the independent impact of each of the cost-minimizing strategies discussed in this chapter, this data set allows us to evaluate the relative frequency with which the United States has issued compellent threats in the Cold War and post–Cold War eras and to evaluate the relative success rates of US compellence across the two periods. The data set also allows us to evaluate the explanatory power of competing explanations for compellent threat failure, particularly the theory that the scope of the coercer's demands determines a threat's likelihood of success.

Notes

1. Brooks and Wohlforth, *World out of Balance*, 13. They also specify that unipolarity is a definition based on relative capabilities and not political influence, and thus it is distinct from a system of empire (p. 12).

2. For debates on unipolarity and its consequences for international politics, see, for example, *World Politics* 61, no. 1 (January 2009, special issue), and Monteiro, *Theory of Unipolar Politics*.

3. Some of the arguments in this chapter could be applied to any state with an overwhelming advantage in military power that threatens a weaker state. For example, a regional hegemon may enjoy an advantage over a local target similar to that which the unipole enjoys over all other states in the system. The dynamics that we would observe for such a regional hegemon threatening a local target should be similar to those that we observe for the unipole. This would be a promising avenue for future study of the costly compellence theory.

4. It is obviously more difficult to communicate the unipole's demands through the use of tacit threats than through explicit statements. In the case of a tacit threat issued by a limited show of force, the timing of the unipole's

action in response to offensive behavior by the target state may communicate the unipole's demands quite clearly. In other cases, the unipole's demands may be less obvious to the target. The purpose of this study is not to argue that miscommunication is never a source of threat failure. Rather, I start from the assumption that the actors involved in a crisis are aware of the unipole's demands and intent to use force if those demands are not met to demonstrate that miscommunication is not a necessary condition for compellent threat failure.

5. Even if the unipole's threat does not specify the action to be taken, we will assume that the target does not believe that the unipole threatens it with total war or nuclear annihilation.

6. This distinction has not received the attention that it deserves because many of our theories of coercion are derived from Cold War studies of nuclear deterrence that implicitly equate credibility with effectiveness. If the target of a deterrent threat takes no action, then this inaction is usually taken as evidence that the threat was credible. In fact, the target's inaction may be evidence that the threat is effective in influencing the target's behavior, even though the target may doubt its credibility. The costs associated with a nuclear deterrent threat are so astronomically high that the deterrent may be effective even if the target questions the threat's credibility. See Freedman, "Strategic Coercion," 25. Credibility may be a sufficient cause of threat effectiveness in the case of nuclear deterrent threats, but this is not the case for conventional compellent threats.

7. Press, *Calculating Credibility*, 21. Jakobsen makes a similar argument in *Western Use of Coercive Diplomacy*, 30. A recent large-N study argues that a threat's credibility is an important predictor of resistance by weak states, but the model measures "credibility" simply by coding whether the state issuing the threat is contiguous to the target. See Allen and Fordham, "From Melos to Baghdad," 1042–43.

8. Fearon, "Signaling Foreign Policy Interests," 69. "Resolve" in this context refers to the willingness to initiate military action.

9. Spence, "Job Market Signaling," 358.

10. Fearon, "Signaling Foreign Policy Interests," 69.

11. Fearon specifies this more carefully in the abstract of his study: "The author distinguishes between two types of costly signals that state leaders might employ in trying to credibly communicate *their foreign policy interests* to other states." In ibid., 68, emphasis added.

12. Pape, *Bombing to Win*, 16.

13. Ibid., 316–18.

14. The argument advanced in this book is not entirely incompatible with the straightforward cost–benefit approach. Costly threats are effective because they signal to the target that the unipole is highly motivated and hence more likely to apply the amount of force necessary to defeat the target on the

battlefield—that is, to exact a brute-force victory after coercion fails. One could understand costly compellence as a theory of when the target is likely to assess that the costs of resistance will be high. The main variable driving this assessment, however, is the costliness of the threat to the coercer, not the costliness of the immediate threat to the target, as the cost–benefit approach would suggest.

15. Schelling, *Arms and Influence*, 105–6.

16. Waltz, *Theory of International Politics*, 170–71.

17. The unipole's freedom to issue military threats is not without limits. In some regions around the world, the unipole's interests or allies would be put at risk in the event of an escalating military crisis. In such situations—for example, in a region with a hostile, nuclear-armed adversary—the local risk environment more closely approaches that which exists under bipolarity. The unipole will be more restrained in issuing threats in such regions.

18. I do not use the term "manpower" in this section to imply that men are the only individuals who serve in the military. The English language lacks a gender-neutral word with the same meaning, so rather than draw attention to an invented term of my own, I reluctantly opt for this one.

19. Jervis, *Logic of Images*, 251.

20. For an excellent review of different types of conscription and its history in the United States, see Cohen, *Citizens and Soldiers*.

21. Clausewitz, *On War*, 592.

22. As Howard notes, the rise of conscription and other changes in European states transformed the face of warfare by the end of the nineteenth century: War was no longer the realm of ruling aristocrats but the expression of the state as a whole. In *War in European History*, 110.

23. For example, British leaders believed that reliance on an all-volunteer force lowered public resistance to the 1982 Falklands War. See Cohen, *Citizens and Soldiers*, 112.

24. We will review the United States' use of private contractors and the associated costs later in this chapter.

25. The unipole's decision to avoid conscription may also lessen the impact of military action on the target state. A volunteer force may be less fearsome to a target state simply because it is smaller than it would be if the unipole employed conscription. On the other hand, a force composed entirely of long-serving volunteers will probably be considerably more proficient than a conscript force.

26. By extension, if the unipole were willing to conscript individuals who are generally shielded from military service, such as women and even children, then deploying the military would be even more costly.

27. For a review of different schools of thought on the RMA, see O'Hanlon, *Technological Change*, chapter 2. For a more critical perspective, see Biddle, *Military Power*.

28. An RMA-based force may limit casualties, but it also has some major drawbacks. A high-tech, casualty-minimizing force structure limits in the short term the unipole's ability to conduct protracted ground campaigns. A force structure based on the RMA thesis is both poorly suited to counterinsurgency and ill equipped for a war of attrition with a conscript army numbering in the millions.

29. The unipole does not necessarily specify the action to be taken against the target. In cases where it does, the specific action with which it threatens the target affects how costly it would be to execute the threat. In cases where the unipole does not specify the action it will take, the target may guess what to expect based on the unipole's recent pattern of threat execution.

30. Works skeptical of the effectiveness of airpower as an independent instrument of coercion include, for example, Pape, *Bombing to Win*; Pape, "Limits of Precision-Guided Air Power"; Byman and Waxman, "Great Air Power Debate"; Press, "Myth of Air Power"; and Crane, "Sky High." Others argue that airpower can play a powerful independent role in coercing target states. See, for example, Cohen, "Mystique of U.S. Air Power"; Warden, "Success in Modern War"; and Stigler, "Clear Victory."

31. Pape, *Bombing to Win*, 316–18.

32. The United States' increasing use of UAVs continues this trend of using airpower to deliver force without risk to its soldiers, as we will see later in this chapter.

33. This argument focuses on the costs of military operations, not the baseline costs of the unipole's defense establishment. These baseline costs are unlikely to change much in the short term, and taxpayers are accustomed to paying them.

34. Howard, *War in European History*, 49.

35. Tilly, "History of European State-Making," 42.

36. Compulsion is not the only means of extracting financial resources from the population. For example, citizens may be encouraged to contribute to a war effort through the purchase of government bonds. Just as conscription is a more politically costly means of raising an army, so too is taxation a more politically costly way of extracting resources from the population.

37. The question of why a unipole would choose to recruit allies is a complicated one. The unipole may seek allies for reasons unrelated to the costliness of the proposed operation, but given that the unipole is capable of carrying out the threatened action on its own, the net effect of enlisting allies will often be a reduction in the costs borne by the unipole to execute the compellent threat.

38. All else equal, the decision not to employ taxation should limit the resources available to the unipole to prosecute military campaigns. As we will see later in this chapter, however, US policymakers have been able to substitute

deficit spending and ally contributions for taxes. Whether such a strategy is viable over the long term is unclear.

39. Recent US military operations suggest that this may not be true. For example, the United States refrained from liquidating retreating Iraqi soldiers at the end of the Gulf War because it did not want to appear too brutal. See chapter 19, "The Gate Is Closed," in Gordon and Trainor, *Generals' War*.

40. Note that neither condition is sufficient on its own to make collateral damage costly: International norms must condemn the killing, *and* the general public must be made aware of this killing.

41. For an overview of this norm and its role in international politics, see the *International Coalition for the Responsibility to Protect* at http://www.responsi bilitytoprotect.org/.

42. Greenberg Research, "People on War Report," 13–14.

43. For example, Al Jazeera's website, particularly the Arabic-language version (http:www.aljazeera.net/portal), often publishes gruesome photos of civilian and military casualties; during the 2009 protests in Iran, videos of wounded and dying protestors appeared on YouTube (https://www.youtube.com).

44. In some cases, the unipole's efforts to minimize collateral damage may coincide with those that it undertakes to minimize casualties for its own soldiers. For example, a precision-guided missile strike on the target's leader both protects the unipole's troops from the risks of a ground invasion and minimizes civilian casualties relative to a less discriminate bombing campaign. On the other hand, a strategy that employs overwhelming firepower to protect the unipole's troops may actually increase the suffering of target-state civilians.

45. If the target values the lives of its civilians, then threats issued by a unipole with a reputation for minimizing collateral damage may also be less effective because the target will have less to fear from the unipole's strike.

46. For example, in *Bombing to Win*, Pape argues that punishment strategies do not work (p. 316). Kalyvas reviews dozens of studies of indiscriminate violence against civilians and finds that such strategies tend to backfire. See *Logic of Violence*, 171.

47. Downes argues that the British blockade of Germany in World War I convinced the German government to negotiate for an armistice (*Targeting Civilians in War*, 253). Kalyvas suggests that indiscriminate violence can be effective when there is a "high imbalance of power" between two actors (*Logic of Violence*, 171). In a study of Russian shelling of Chechen villages, Lyall finds that indiscriminate violence suppresses insurgent attacks, at least in the short term ("Does Indiscriminate Violence Incite," 357).

48. Strategies that limit the unipole's costs may also hinder its ability to conduct intense military campaigns. For example, if calling up reserves is necessary

for an intense military operation, then the unipole will be more likely to opt for a limited use of force. The need to call up reserves may then limit the unipole's ability to commit to a decisive campaign at the second stage.

49. This is consistent with the logic advanced by Press in *Calculating Credibility*.

50. Brooks and Wohlforth, *World out of Balance*, 12–13.

51. GDP is listed in current US dollars, and figures are from World Bank, "GDP (current US$)." Per capita figures are from World Bank, "GDP per capita (current US$)." In 2014, the International Monetary Fund reported that China's economy had surpassed the United States' when measured in terms of purchasing power parity (PPP), which takes into account differences in national price levels. Many argue that this is not an accurate picture of China's economy either, especially for things that cannot be easily adjusted for the cost of living. See, for example, Schiavenza, "China Economy Surpasses US."

52. See the Executive Summary in United States Department of Defense, *Quadrennial Defense Review 2014*, iv. The impact of these cuts will be discussed in greater detail in the concluding chapter.

53. Figures are from International Institute for Strategic Studies (IISS), *Military Balance 2015*, 34, 484, 486, 490. Numbers for China are official central-government spending at market exchange rates and exclude extrabudgetary funds. There are many challenges in interpreting China's figures for both economic performance and military spending. For a review of Chinese defense budgets and efforts to compare them with American figures, see Blasko et al., *Defense-Related Spending*.

54. Layne, "Waning of U.S. Hegemony"; Rachman, "Think Again."

55. Beckley, "China's Century?"

56. The United States is not the world's most powerful and important actor on any and every issue in international politics, nor does it have the ability to translate its immense power resources into its preferred outcome on every issue. There is, however, no state capable of acting as a check on the United States' behavior.

57. The logic of costly compellence and the findings of this study do not depend on the label we assign to the United States. Regardless of whether one believes we should call the United States a unipole, what matters is the fact that the United States is vastly more powerful than the states it attempts to coerce with compellent threats in the post–Cold War period.

58. Huntington, *Soldier and the State*, 149, 167.

59. Rostker, *I Want You!*, 2. For more on conscription in the American Civil War and proposals for the Spanish–American War, see Parker, "Should Our Volunteers?"

60. For a more complete description of the different types of military service, see Cohen, *Citizens and Soldiers*, 23. Cohen also provides a thorough review of military service in the United States through the establishment of the AVF.

61. On the inequity of Civil War conscription, see Flynn, "Conscription and Equity," 12, and Parker, "Should Our Volunteers?," 577.

62. See Flynn, "Conscription and Equity," 7–8.

63. Office of the Under Secretary of Defense for Personnel and Readiness, *Population Representation*, 12.

64. Rostker, *I Want You!*, 8.

65. Bianco and Markham, "Vanishing Veterans," 283. They also find that veteran status has a small impact on voting, which suggests that a decline in veteran representation in Congress may have an impact on US policy (p. 285).

66. Rostker, *I Want You!*, 8.

67. Marsh, "Active and Reserve Forces," 96.

68. Korb, "Fixing the Mix," 4–5.

69. Kagan, "Manpower Crisis," 100.

70. Stanger, *One Nation under Contract*, vii. For a thorough history of private military contractors, see Singer, *Corporate Warriors*.

71. Singer, *Corporate Warriors*, 245.

72. Lacquemont, "Casualty-Aversion Myth," 44.

73. Bowman, "War Casualties."

74. Larson and Savych, *American Public Support*, 214.

75. Ibid., xxi.

76. Gelpi, Feaver, and Reifler, *Paying the Human Costs*, 20.

77. Eichenberg, "Victory Has Many Friends," 141.

78. The perception of what constitutes a "high" number of casualties seems to have shifted with the end of the Cold War. As Larson notes, "the concern about casualties among political leaders and the public, although humane, is not entirely rational—U.S. battle deaths are actually somewhat rare, typically very few, and are dwarfed by the number of deaths to U.S. service personnel from other causes" (*Casualties and Consensus*, p. 6). The fact that the Gulf War was judged successful and with fewer casualties than had been expected may have reset the public's expectations about acceptable casualty rates.

79. Thomas, "U.S. Army." The quoted figure of $35,000 to $50,000 is a 2004 estimate of the cost to train a new soldier from the time of walking into a recruiting office until reaching his or her first duty station, and the cost varies depending on the specific training received.

80. For a review of the different schools of thought, see O'Hanlon, *Technological Change*, chapter 2.

81. Aspin and Dickinson, *Defense for a New Era*, xix–xx.

82. The claim that airpower could be a revolutionary, independent, war-

winning instrument is not new. In a series of articles in the *Saturday Evening Post* from 1923 to 1925, Brig. Gen. Billy Mitchell, a major advocate for an independent air service, argued "that a powerful air force could make war a briefer, more humane, and cheaper affair by obliterating an enemy's industrial centers." In Biddle, *Rhetoric and Reality*, 137.

83. UAVs, or drones, are defined by the Department of Defense as "powered, aerial vehicles that do not carry a human operator, use aerodynamic forces to provide vehicle lift, can fly autonomously or be piloted remotely, can be expendable or recoverable, and can carry a lethal or nonlethal payload." The term "unmanned aerial system" (UAS) refers to the combination of the unmanned vehicle itself and the ground-control systems and data links necessary to operate the vehicle. See Gertler, *U.S. Unmanned Aerial Systems*, 1. UAS seems to be replacing UAV as the preferred name for these systems, particularly in US government reports, but the popular media still refers to them as drones or UAVs.

84. On the history of UAVs and robotics in modern warfare, see Singer, *Wired for War*.

85. Ibid., 59.

86. Gertler, *U.S. Unmanned Aerial Systems*, 9. This figure excludes small "micro systems" and includes only the Department of Defense inventory and not that of the Central Intelligence Agency (CIA).

87. On the use of drones in Obama's first term, see Mayer, "Predator War." The US government does not publish official figures on drone strikes, but some organizations are tracking reported strikes and casualties. For example, see the "Covert Drone War" project of the Bureau of Investigative Journalism at https://www.thebureauinvestigates.com/category/projects/drones/.

88. Most notably, in October 2012, in the wake of the fatal attack on the US embassy in Benghazi, Libya, the CIA asked for up to ten additional armed drones to add to its inventory of thirty to thirty-five vehicles. See Miller, "CIA Seeks to Expand."

89. Singer, *Wired for War*, 33.

90. United States Department of the Army, *Counterinsurgency Field Manual*, 54.

91. For the new strategic guidance, see United States Department of Defense, *Sustaining U.S. Global Leadership*.

92. In "Democracy and the Preparation for War," Gartzke finds that, contrary to popular wisdom, democracy is not the key factor that determines whether a state employs a capital-intensive form of warfare. He argues instead that "capital-abundant states buy more weapons while labor-abundant states hire more personnel" (p. 468). To the extent that capital-abundant states are more likely to be democratic, this explains the apparent tendency for democracies to protect their forces.

93. IISS, *Military Balance 2015*, 484.

94. IISS, *Military Balance 2013*, 548, 554.

95. IISS, *Military Balance 2015*, 484, 490. I employ figures from IISS here because they are calculated consistently across countries, which makes for more accurate comparisons.

96. For a list of 2014 GDP figures, see World Bank, "GDP (current US$)."

97. Figures from Office of Management and Budget, "Table 3.1."

98. Preble, *Power Problem*, 80.

99. United States Department of Defense, *Conduct of the Persian Gulf War*, 634. Figures are those reported in 1992 and not adjusted for inflation. "Incremental costs" include the costs of "deploying, operating, and supporting forces used in Operations Desert Shield and Desert Storm," and they exclude the investment and baseline costs associated with the force structure (p. 633).

100. Ibid., 634.

101. IISS, *Military Balance 2012*, 45.

102. Stiglitz and Bilmes, *Three Trillion Dollar War*, 24.

103. Hacker and Pierson, "Abandoning the Middle," 33.

104. Stiglitz and Bilmes, *Three Trillion Dollar War*, 29.

105. Ibid., 22.

106. Clodfelter, *Warfare and Armed Conflicts*, 271–72.

107. See Pape, *Bombing to Win*, 104, 254–55.

108. Conway-Lanz, *Collateral Damage*, 13–14.

109. Clodfelter, *Warfare and Armed Conflicts*, 784–85. In pointing out American atrocities in the Philippines and Vietnam, I do not suggest that it was the policy of the US government or of the US military to inflict violence on local populations. Rather, I point them out to suggest that the United States' willingness to tolerate acts of violence against civilians, including both collateral damage and atrocities committed in the heat of battle, has declined over time.

110. Conway-Lanz, *Collateral Damage*, 217.

111. Gordon and Trainor, *Generals' War*, 324–27.

112. See chapter 19, "The Gate Is Closed," in ibid.

113. Clark, *Waging Modern War*, 225.

114. Kahl, "In the Crossfire," 15.

115. Quoted in Filkins, "U.S. Tightens Airstrike Policy."

116. Recall that the costly compellence theory does not assert that targeting civilians is an effective strategy *in* war. Rather, it simply suggests that the unwillingness to do so minimizes the United States' costs for employing force.

Chapter 2
US Compellent Threats, 1945–2007

This chapter presents a new data set on the United States' use of compellent threats in international crises. The data reveal that the United States has employed compellent threats more frequently in the post-1989 period than it did during the Cold War and that targets resisted US compellent threats more frequently in the post–Cold War period than they did from 1945 to 1989, consistent with the predictions of costly compellence. These trends remain consistent even if we set aside cases in which the United States requested regime change—that is, cases in which the United States made extreme demands of the target state.

The data also demonstrate that the United States does not bluff. In all cases in which the United States issued an explicit compellent threat and the target resisted, the United States followed through on the threatened action. At first glance, this makes the willingness of weak target states to resist the United States' compellent threats even more puzzling. This observation is consistent, however, with the costly compellence theory: Targets resist cheap threats because they do not signal that the United States is highly motivated to prevail in a long and costly conflict. The chapter concludes with an overview of the methods employed in the case chapters.

The Data Set on US Compellent Threats in Crises from 1945 to 2007

The Need for a New Data Set

The costly compellence theory asserts that costly threats are more effective than cheap threats in generating target-state compliance because cheap threats lack *ultimate credibility*. The international distribution of power determines whether it is costly to issue a threat, and the unipole's war-fighting model determines whether it is costly to execute a threat. A cheap threat fails not because the target doubts the threat's *immediate credibility*, but because a cheap threat does not convince the target that the unipole is highly motivated to prevail over it in a long and costly conflict after coercion fails. The theory yields the following hypotheses:

> *Hypothesis 1(a): A unipole issues compellent threats against small states more frequently than a bipole.*
> *Hypothesis 2: A compellent threat issued by a unipole that actively minimizes the human, political, and financial costs of employing military force is less effective than a threat issued by a state that does not employ such cost-minimizing strategies.*

The United States became a unipole with the demise of the Soviet Union in 1989, and it has developed a model for the application of military violence that dramatically limits its costs for employing force and for executing compellent threats. Thus, according to the logic of costly compellence, we should observe that the United States has issued compellent threats more frequently in the post–Cold War period than it did under bipolarity. If we date the rise of the United States' cost-minimizing model to 1990, then we would expect to observe a decline in average threat effectiveness in the post–Cold War period.[1] If, however, we observe that threats are more effective in this period or that the rate remained unchanged after the rise of the cheap war-fighting model, then the logic of costly compellence would be called into question.

None of the existing studies of coercion in US foreign policy contain the data necessary to evaluate these hypotheses, nor are the standard data sets on war and conflict appropriate for testing them. As discussed in the introduction, several of these studies employ a case study approach to identify conditions that are associated with successful coercive diplomacy.[2] Such studies examine cases in which the United States did or did not threaten the use of force, and they also include cases of nonmilitary coercion. These small-N studies are not comprehensive enough, however, to permit us to draw general conclusions about the United States' use of compellent threats.

There are also several large data sets on the United States' use of military force.[3] The universe of cases they examine is not limited to compellent threats or to coercion. One recent example, the Military

Intervention by Powerful States (MIPS) data set by Patricia L. Sullivan and Michael T. Koch, lists all cases in which the United States used armed force to achieve political objectives from 1946 to 2003.[4] From this list, it could be possible to isolate and evaluate cases in which compellent military threats were issued and force was employed. The major disadvantage of a "use of force" data set, however, is that it does not include cases in which force was *not* employed. The most effective compellent threats are those that are not executed— those that convince the target to yield before the application of violence. Consequently, a data set that examines cases in which the United States used force excludes the cases in which compellent threats have been employed most effectively.

On the other hand, a data set that includes only cases in which a compellent threat was actually issued will not allow us to evaluate the conditions under which the United States is likely to issue a threat. Sechser's data set examines compellent threats issued from 1918 to 2001 and is an important contribution to the study of international coercion.[5] It includes cases involving the United States, but it does not include cases in which threats were *not* issued.

To evaluate claims about the conditions under which threats are more or less likely to be issued, we must start from a universe of cases in which coercion was possible but not inevitable. For this reason, the data set on US compellent threats presented in this chapter is derived from a collection of international crises. This data structure allows us to evaluate both hypotheses of interest to the costly compellence theory: that the United States issues threats more frequently as a unipole and that its efforts to make the use of force cheap undermine the effectiveness of its compellent threats.

Starting Point for the Data Set: International Crises

I employed data and case histories from the International Crisis Behavior (ICB) Project as the starting point for the data set on US compellent military threats in crises from 1945 to 2007.[6] The ICB Project began in 1975 as a response to the lack of systematic research on international crises, and data collection has proceeded over five different phases since then.[7] The ICB data set contains a list of all international crises from 1918 to 2007. For each crisis in the data set, the project records data on the crisis actors, the international system, the crisis trigger, the actors' behavior, and the crisis resolution. The data set is now available online, and the raw data can be downloaded directly from the project's website.[8] The most recent release of ICB data (Version 10) includes 455 international crises from the end of World War I through 2007.[9]

Crises are relatively rare events in international politics. On average, there were slightly more than five international crises per year from 1918 to 2007. The United States employs military force much more frequently than it is involved in an international crisis. According to Blechman and Kaplan, from 1946 to 1976 the United States used its military for political purposes 215 times.[10] According to the ICB Project, the United States was involved in thirty-nine crises during the same period, including intrawar crises.[11] International crises are less rare, however, than interstate wars. The Correlates of War (COW) Project identifies fifty-six interstate wars during the period 1918 to 2007,[12] when the ICB Project records 455 international crises. Thus, international crises are less rare than interstate wars but more rare than cases in which the United States has employed military force for political aims.

The ICB list of international crises does not constitute a random sample of international events. By definition, a crisis is a disruption in the normal pattern of state interactions. A crisis is characterized by heightened tension and an increased risk of military action. The list of international crises is, however, a systematic collection of state interactions in which compellent threats may be employed. This does not mean that threats will never be issued outside the scope of an international crisis. It is possible but unlikely that a state would issue a compellent threat outside a crisis. It is more likely that a state would issue a deterrent threat in a noncrisis setting, but such threats are beyond the scope of this analysis.

The major advantage of employing the ICB Project crisis list as a starting point for the data set on US compellent threats is that the universe of cases includes both situations in which threats were issued and situations in which they were not issued. It also includes cases in which threats were successful and those in which they failed. Starting from a list of crises allows us to examine both the frequency with which the United States employs compellent threats and the frequency with which target states change their behavior in response to these threats.

Constructing the Data Set: Baseline Data from the ICB Project

To construct the data set, I first isolated crises in which the United States was identified as a crisis actor.[13] To compare the United States' behavior under bipolarity with its behavior as a unipole, I restricted the universe of crises to the post–World War II period (1945–2007). Excluding crises that occurred before the end of World War II, there were 349 international crises from 1945 to 2007. This is an average of roughly 5.5 international crises per year. The United States was involved in sixty-three of these post–World War II crises, or roughly one crisis per year.

There were 285 international crises during the Cold War (1945–1989), or roughly 6.3 international crises per year. In the post–Cold War period (1990–2007), there were 64 international crises, or roughly 3.6 international crises per year. The United States was involved in 49 Cold War crises, roughly 1.1 per year. In the post-1989 period, the United States was involved in 14 crises, an average of 0.8 per year. The data show that there were nearly twice as many international crises per year during the Cold War as there were in the eighteen years following the dissolution of the Soviet Union. The data also show that the United States was involved in fewer crises per year in the post–Cold War period.

If we examine US involvement relative to the universe of crises, however, the picture is somewhat different. For the total period 1945–2007, the United States was involved in roughly 18 percent of all international crises. The United States was identified as a crisis actor in 49 of 285 Cold War crises (1945–1989), roughly 17.2 percent. In the post–Cold War period, however, the United States was involved in 14 of 64 international crises, roughly 21.9 percent. International crises are less frequent on average in the post-1989 period than they were during the Cold War, but the United States was involved in a greater percentage of all crises in the post–Cold War period than it was during bipolarity.

Coding Compellent Threats

I consulted the case summary available through the ICB data viewer as the starting point for coding several variables for each crisis. I examined additional primary and secondary sources for most crises because the case summary and the ICB coding of relevant variables did not provide enough information to determine whether a threat was issued and/or the target's response to a threat. For each crisis, I identified the United States' opponent, determined whether the United States issued a compellent threat, recorded the target's response to a threat when issued, and evaluated whether the United States executed its threat. When a threat was explicitly articulated and not implied through the movement of forces, I coded the type of threat by consulting the statement made by or imputed to the individual responsible for issuing the threat. In cases where the United States issued a threat, I also recorded the specific demand that the United States made of the target.

A compellent military threat has two necessary components: a demand that the target change its behavior and a promise to inflict military force if it does not comply. Threats that are intended to prevent the target from taking future action are therefore excluded from the data set.[14] In addition, the United States' threat must have been intended to achieve a change in the target state's behavior by promising to use force in a manner consistent with coercion, not brute force.

Threats were classified according to five types: ultimatum, open-ended, vague, active implicit, and passive implicit. The first three of these—ultimatum, open-ended, and vague threats ("explicit threats," types 5, 4, and 3, respectively)—are communicated explicitly by the United States to the target. The other two types of threat—active implicit and passive implicit ("implicit threats," types 2 and 1, respectively)—are communicated solely by the movement or application of limited force.[15] A more detailed description of how these and other variables were coded is located in the appendix.

Results: Frequency of US Compellent Threats

The United States was involved in sixty-three crises from 1945 to 2007. Fourteen of these crises occurred in the post–Cold War period (1990–2007).[16] The United States issued a compellent threat in nineteen of the sixty-three crises in which it was involved from 1945 to 2007 (30.2 percent). During the Cold War (1945–1989), the United States issued a compellent threat in eleven of forty-nine crises in which it was involved (22.4 percent). In the post–Cold War period, however, the United States issued a compellent threat in eight of fourteen crises in which it was involved (57.1 percent). In other words, the United States issued a compellent threat in one in five crises during the Cold War and in nearly three in five crises in the post–Cold War period.[17] On average, the United States issued 0.24 compellent threats per year during the Cold War and 0.44 compellent threats—nearly twice as many per year—in crises during the post–Cold War period. Measured in terms of either the universe of crises or the rate per year, the United States issued compellent threats more frequently as a unipole than it did during the Cold War.[18] These findings are consistent with the predictions of costly compellence.

No clear correlation between the crisis stakes and the United States' willingness to issue a compellent threat emerges from these data. A "threat to influence" was the issue at stake for the United States in most crises during the Cold War (forty-five of forty-nine crises, or 92 percent) and in a smaller majority of crises in the post–Cold War period (nine of fourteen crises, or 64 percent). These crises concerned the United States' ability to exert its influence on other states.[19] There were four crises during the Cold War in which the United States faced the risk of "grave damage," but the United States issued a compellent threat in only one of these serious crises (the Cuban Missile Crisis). There is considerable variation in the issues over which the United States was willing to issue a compellent threat in the post–Cold War period. In addition to the crises involving the threat of grave damage, the United States also issued compellent threats in two post–Cold War crises where it faced a political threat and three in which it faced a "threat to influence." In other words, the United States' willingness to issue a compellent threat does not seem to be correlated with the seriousness of the crisis stakes.

It is also important to consider the cases in which the United States chose *not* to issue a compellent threat. The United States was involved in fourteen crises in the post–Cold War period, including several with Iraq, the Haiti regime crisis, and several crises over North Korea's nuclear ambitions. The United States chose not to issue a compellent threat in the nuclear crises with North Korea and Iran, which arguably posed the greatest risk to US interests of all the crises in this period.[20] In fact, there is evidence from the 1993–94 crisis with North Korea that the fear of damaging escalation convinced US policymakers to pursue nonviolent coercion rather than employ a compellent threat.[21] Although the number of high-stakes, no-threat cases is too small to allow us to draw firm conclusions, it is interesting to note that the United States chose not to pursue military coercion in some of the most dangerous crises of the post– Cold War period. This suggests that there may be circumstances in which the risks of escalation do constrain the unipole's willingness to issue a compellent threat. The logic of costly compellence suggests, however, that a threat issued in a high-stakes crisis should have more ultimate credibility than one issued without risk.

In sum, the data demonstrate that the United States has been much more willing to employ compellent threats since the end of the Cold War than it was during the period of bipolarity, consistent with the logic of costly compellence. There is no clear correlation between the crisis stakes and the United States' willingness to issue compellent threats. Table 2.1 presents all international crises from 1945 to 2007 in which the United States was a crisis actor. The highlighted column in the center of the table indicates whether the United States issued a compellent threat against the opponent(s) during the crisis. The compellent-threat variable was coded in the affirmative if the United States issued a threat of any type.

Results: Compellent Threat Effectiveness

After determining whether the United States issued a threat in each crisis, I then evaluated how both the target and the United States responded to the threat. I evaluated how the target responded to the United States' demands (*resist* or *concede*), whether the United States subsequently executed the threat, and whether there were any allies involved in the US effort to coerce the target (the "threat by coalition" variable). Finally, I considered how the target responded to the threat's execution—whether the target backed down after the launch

Table 2.1. US Crises, 1945–2007

Crisis #	Crisis Name	Dates	Opponent	Other Actors	Did US Issue Compellent Threat?	Gravity of Crisis (US)	Gravity of Crisis (Opponent)
108	Azerbaijan	23 Aug 1945–9 May 1946	USSR	Iran, UK	No	Threat to influence	Territorial threat
111	Turkish Straits	7 Aug–26 Oct 1946	USSR	Turkey	Yes	Threat to influence	n/a
114	Truman Doctrine	21 Feb–22 May 1947	USSR	Greece, Turkey	No	Threat to influence	n/a
123	Berlin Blockade	24 Jun 1948–12 May 1949	USSR	UK, France	No	Threat of grave damage	Threat of grave damage
125	China Civil War	23 Sep 1948–3 Dec 1949	China	None	No	Threat to influence	Political threat
132	Korean War I	25 Jun–30 Sep 1950	China	North Korea, South Korea	No	Threat to influence	Territorial threat
133	Korean War II	30 Sep 1950–1 Jul 1951	China	North Korea, South Korea	No	Threat to influence	Threat of grave damage
140	Korean War III	16 Apr–27 Jul 1953	China, North Korea	South Korea	Yes	Threat to influence	Threat of grave damage, threat of grave damage
144	Guatemala	12 Dec 1953–29 Jun 1954	Guatemala, USSR	Honduras	No	Threat to influence	Political threat
145	Dien Bien Phu	13 Mar–21 Jul 1954	Vietminh	France, UK	No	Threat to influence	n/a
146	Taiwan Strait I	Early Aug 1954–23 Apr 1955	China	Taiwan	No	Threat to influence	Territorial threat
152	Suez Nationalization War	26 Jul 1956–12 Mar 1957	USSR	France, UK, Israel, Egypt	No	Threat to influence	Threat to influence
159	Syria–Turkey Confrontation	18 Aug–29 Oct 1957	Syria, USSR	Turkey	No	Threat to influence	Political threat, n/a

Table 2.1. *continued*

Crisis #	Crisis Name	Dates	Opponent	Other Actors	Did US Issue Compellent Threat?	Gravity of Crisis (US)	Gravity of Crisis (Opponent)
165	Iraq–Lebanon Upheaval	8 May–end Oct 1958	USSR, pro-Soviet states in region	Lebanon, Jordan, UK	No	Threat to influence	n/a
166	Taiwan Strait II	17 Jul–23 Oct 1958	China	Taiwan	No	Threat to influence	Threat of grave damage
168	Berlin Deadline	27 Nov 1958–15 Sep 1959	USSR	France, UK	No	Threat to influence	Threat of grave damage
180	Pathet Lao Offensive	9 Mar–16 May 1961	Pathet Lao, USSR	Thailand	Yes	Threat to influence	Political threat, n/a
181	Bay of Pigs	15 Apr–24 Apr 1961	Cuba	USSR	No	Threat to influence	Political threat
185	Berlin Wall	Early Aug–28 Oct 1961	USSR	DDR, GDR, France, UK	No	Threat to influence	Threat to influence
186	Vietcong Attack	18 Sep–15 Nov 1961	North Vietnam (Vietcong forces)	South Vietnam	No	Threat to influence	n/a
193	Nam Tha	6 May–12 Jun 1962	Pathet Lao, USSR	Thailand, North Vietnam	No	Threat to influence	Political threat, n/a
196	Cuban Missile	16 Oct–20 Nov 1962	USSR	Cuba	Yes	Threat of grave damage	Threat of grave damage
206	Panama Flag	9 Jan–12 Jan 1964	Panama	None	No	Threat to influence	Limited military threat
210	Gulf of Tonkin	30 Jul–mid-Aug 1964	North Vietnam	None	No	Threat to influence	Limited military threat
211	Congo II	4 Aug–30 Dec 1964	Rebel forces in Congo	Belgium, USSR	No	Threat to influence	Territorial threat

#	Name	Date						
213	Pleiku	7 Feb–late Mar 1965	North Vietnam	South Vietnam	Yes	Threat to influence	Threat to influence	Threat of grave damage
215	Dominican Intervention	24 Apr–31 Aug 1965	(Civil war in Dominican Republic)	None	No	Threat to influence	Threat to influence	n/a
222	Six-Day War	17 May–11 Jun 1967	USSR	Israel, Egypt, Syria, Jordan	No	Threat to influence	Threat to influence	Threat to influence
224	Pueblo	21 Jan–23 Dec 1968	North Korea	None	Yes	Threat to influence	Threat to influence	Threat of grave damage
225	Tet Offensive	30 Jan–31 Mar 1968	North Vietnam	South Vietnam	No	Threat to influence	Threat to influence	n/a
230	Vietnam Spring Offensive	22 Feb–8 Jun 1969	North Vietnam	South Vietnam	No	Threat of grave damage	Threat to influence	n/a
233	EC-121 Spy Plane	15 Apr–26 Apr 1969	North Korea	None	No	Threat to influence	Threat to influence	n/a
237	Invasion of Cambodia	13 Mar–22 Jul 1970	North Vietnam, Vietcong forces	South Vietnam, Cambodia	No	Threat to influence	Threat to influence	Threat to influence
238	Black September	15 Sep–29 Sep 1970	Syria, USSR	Jordan, Israel	Yes	Threat to influence	Threat to influence	Threat to influence, n/a
239	Cienfuegos Submarine Base	16 Sep–23 Oct 1970	USSR	Cuba	No	Threat of grave damage	Threat of grave damage	n/a
246	Vietnam—Ports Mining	30 Mar–19 Jul 1972	North Vietnam	South Vietnam	No	Threat to influence	Threat to influence	Threat of grave damage
249	Christmas Bombing	23 Oct 1972–27 Jan 1973	North Vietnam	South Vietnam	Yes	Threat to influence	Threat to influence	Threat of grave damage
255	October / Yom Kippur War	5 Oct 1973–31 May 1974	USSR	Israel, Egypt, Syria, Jordan	No	Threat to influence	Threat to influence	Threat to influence
259	Mayaguez	12 May–15 May 1975	Cambodia	China	Yes	Threat to influence	Threat to influence	Threat of grave damage
260	War in Angola	12 Jul 1975–27 Mar 1976	Angola, USSR	Cuba, South Africa, DRC, Zambia	No	Threat to influence	Threat to influence	Political threat, threat to influence

Table 2.1. *continued*

Crisis #	Crisis Name	Dates	Opponent	Other Actors	Did US Issue Compellent Threat?	Gravity of Crisis (US)	Gravity of Crisis (Opponent)
274	Poplar Tree Incident	17 Aug–16 Sep 1976	North Korea	None	No	Threat to influence	Threat to influence
292	Shaba II	11 May–30 Jul 1978	Zaire	Belgium, France	No	Threat to influence	n/a
303	Afghanistan Invasion	Mid-Mar 1979–28 Feb 1980	USSR	Afghanistan, Pakistan	No	Threat to influence	Threat to influence
309	US Hostages in Iran	4 Nov 1979–20 Jan 1981	Iran	None	Yes	Threat to influence	Political threat
343	Invasion of Grenada	19 Oct 1983–28 Oct 1983	Grenada	None	No	Threat to influence	Political threat
354	Nicaragua MiG-21s	6 Nov 1984–12 Nov 1984	USSR, Nicaragua	None	No	Threat to influence	n/a, political threat
363	Gulf of Syrte II	24 Mar–21 Apr 1986	Libya	None	No	Threat to influence	Territorial threat
386	Libyan Jets	21 Dec 1988–12 Jan 1989	Libya	None	No	Threat to influence	Threat to influence
391	Invasion of Panama	15 Dec 1989–3 Jan 1990	Panama	None	Yes	Threat to influence	Political threat
393	Gulf War	2 Aug 1990–12 Apr 1991	Iraq	UN Coalition	Yes	Threat to influence	Threat of grave damage
408	N. Korea Nuclear I	Early Mar 1993–21 Oct 1994	North Korea	South Korea	no	Threat to influence	Threat to influence
411	Haiti Military Regime	Mid-Jul–15 Oct 1994	Haiti	None	Yes	Threat to influence	Political threat

412	Iraq Troop Deployment—Kuwait	7 Oct–10 Nov 1994	Iraq	Kuwait, Saudi Arabia, and others	No	Threat to influence	Threat to influence
419	Desert Strike	31 Aug–14 Sep 1996	Iraq	UN allies	Yes	Threat to influence	Territorial threat
422	UNSCOM I	13 Nov 1997–23 Feb 1998	Iraq	UN allies	Yes	Political threat	Threat of grave damage
427	US Embassy Bombings	7 Aug–20 Aug 1998	Afghanistan, Sudan	None	No	Limited military threat	Limited military threat, limited military threat
429	UNSCOM II: Op. Desert Fox	31 Oct 1998–20 Dec 1998	Iraq	UN allies	Yes	Political threat	Threat of grave damage
430	Kosovo	20 Feb–10 Jun 1999	Serbia (Yugoslavia)	NATO allies	Yes	Threat to influence	Threat of grave damage
434	Afghanistan—USA	11 Sep 2001–7 Dec 2001	Afghanistan	UK, Pakistan	Yes	Threat of grave damage	Threat of grave damage
440	Iraq Regime Change	12 Sep 2002–1 May 2003	Iraq	UK	Yes	Threat of grave damage	Threat to existence
441	North Korea Nuclear II	4 Oct 2002–6 Jan 2004	North Korea	South Korea, Russia, Japan, China	No	Threat to influence	Political threat
448	Iran Nuclear II	10 Jan 2006–4 Dec 2007	Iran	UK, France	No	Threat to influence	Threat to influence
450	North Korea Nuclear III	5 May 2006–3 Oct 2007	North Korea	None	No	Threat to influence	Political threat

Note: The crisis numbers, names, and dates were taken from the ICB data. For a more detailed description of the author's method, please see the appendix.

of military hostilities (*capitulation*) or not (*continued resistance*). The appendix describes these coding procedures in greater detail and presents a sample case to illustrate this process.

The target conceded to US demands before the application of force in eight of the nineteen crises in which the United States issued a compellent threat from 1945 to 2007. During the Cold War, the opponent conceded in six of eleven cases, for a threat success rate of roughly 55 percent. In the post–Cold War period, however, the target conceded to US demands in only two of eight crises in which the United States issued a compellent threat, yielding a post–Cold War success rate of 25 percent.[22] In other words, the United States' compellent threats were associated with target compliance in more than half of the Cold War–era crises and only one-quarter of the post–Cold War crises.

The target's reaction to the threat's execution also differs across the two periods. During the Cold War, when the target resisted and the United States executed its threat, the target responded with continued resistance in only one case out of four. By contrast, the target continued to resist in five of six cases in the post–Cold War period in which the United States executed its threat. These results are consistent with hypothesis 2 and with the logic of costly compellence. The fact that most post–Cold War US opponents have continued to resist after the initial application of force suggests that the United States' compellent threats do not lack immediate credibility.

Nor can the inability to bring sufficient force to bear on post–Cold War targets explain the willingness of weak states to resist US compellent threats. Schelling's theory of compellence suggests that the ability to deliver violence on the opponent should be an effective coercive tool, as long as the target does not doubt that the violence will be administered. The power-discrepancy variable constructed by the ICB Project demonstrates that the United States was more powerful than its opponent in all cases in which it issued a threat except the Cuban Missile Crisis.[23] In many of the post–Cold War crises, the United States was considerably more powerful than its target. This reflects both the United States' tendency to threaten force as part of a coalition in the post–Cold War period (a tendency that will be discussed in greater detail below) and the fact that targets of US compellent threats tended to be small, weak states. In fact, the average power-discrepancy score for the post–Cold War period (41.25) is considerably higher than the average for Cold War crises in which data are available and the United States had an advantage (19.14).[24] This variable is not a perfect measure of relative power, nor is the difference in the average power discrepancy across the two periods very meaningful. The data do suggest, however, that a lack of capability cannot explain why the United States' threats failed to compel weak targets in either period.

The findings are clear: US compellent threats are less effective on average in the post–Cold War period than they were before the rise of the cost-minimizing model of warfare. Table 2.2 presents the crises in which the United States issued a compellent threat, with the target's initial response highlighted. Table 2.4 at the end of this chapter provides a more extensive description of each of the crises in which the United States issued a compellent threat. Information about the sources used to construct all tables in this chapter is located in the appendix.

Additional Findings

The United States Does Not Bluff

If we define a "bluff" as a threat that the United States issues but does not intend to execute if and when the target resists, then one of the most surprising findings to emerge from these data and one with the greatest relevance to policymakers is that the United States does not bluff. There is no evidence that the United States ever issues an explicit threat with the intention of backing down if the target resists. In all crises in which the United States issued an explicit threat (types 3, 4, or 5) and the target resisted, the United States executed the threatened action. There were two Cold War cases in which the United States issued an *implicit* threat, the target resisted, and the United States failed to execute: the *Pueblo* Crisis and the Iran Hostage Crisis. Both cases were coded as *passive implicit* threats, however, because in each case the United States sent forces in response to the opponent's behavior but did not issue explicit demands of the target or specify the punishment for noncompliance.[25] It is possible that

Table 2.2. Effectiveness of US Compellent Threats in Crises, 1945–2007

Crisis #	Crisis Name	Opponent	Type of Threat	Threat by Coalition?	US Demands	Power Discrepancy	Response to Threat	Threat Executed?	If Threat Executed, Target's Reaction
111	Turkish Straits	USSR	Passive implicit	No	Accept agreement on Turkish Straits	10	**Concede**	No	n/a
140	Korean War III	China, North Korea	Vague	No	Accept armistice	n/a	**Concede**	No	n/a
180	Pathet Lao Offensive	Pathet Lao, USSR	Vague	No	Cease-fire	n/a	**Concede**	No	n/a
196	Cuban Missile	USSR	Ultimatum	No	Remove missiles from Cuba	–9	**Concede**	No	n/a
213	Pleiku	North Vietnam	Active implicit	Yes	Cease-fire	n/a	**Resist**	Yes	Continued resistance
224	Pueblo	North Korea	Passive implicit	No	Release ship	16	**Resist**	No	n/a
238	Black September	Syria, USSR	Passive implicit	No	Withdraw from Jordan	34	**Concede**	No	n/a
249	Christmas Bombing	North Vietnam	Active implicit	Yes	Return to negotiations	27	**Concede**	Yes	Capitulation
259	Mayaguez	Cambodia	Vague	No	Release ship	18	**Resist**	Yes	Capitulation
309	US Hostages in Iran	Iran	Passive implicit	No	Release hostages	10	**Resist**	No	n/a
391	Invasion of Panama	Panama	Vague	No	Regime change	19	**Resist**	Yes	Capitulation

Crisis #	Crisis Name	Opponent	Type of Threat	Threat by Coalition?	US Demands	Power Discrepancy	Response to Threat	Threat Executed?	If Threat Executed, Target's Reaction
393	Gulf War	Iraq	Ultimatum	Yes	Withdraw from Kuwait	11	**Resist**	Yes	Continued resistance
411	Haiti Military Regime	Haiti	Open-ended	Yes	Regime change	19	**Resist**	Yes	Capitulation
419	Desert Strike	Iraq	Vague	Yes	Withdraw from northern zone	15	**Concede**	No	n/a
422	UNSCOM I	Iraq	Vague	Yes	Readmit weapons inspectors	15	**Concede**	No	n/a
429	UNSCOM II: Operation Desert Fox	Iraq	Open-ended	Yes	Readmit weapons inspectors	15	**Resist**	Yes	Continued resistance
430	Kosovo	Serbia (Yugoslavia)	Open-ended	Yes	Accept peace agreement	179	**Resist**	Yes	Continued resistance
434	Afghanistan—USA	Afghanistan	Open-ended	Yes	Surrender terrorists and close training camps	39	**Resist**	Yes	Continued resistance
440	Iraq Regime Change	Iraq	Ultimatum	Yes	Regime change	37	**Resist**	Yes	Continued resistance

Note: The crisis numbers and names were taken from the ICB data. For a more detailed description of the author's method, please see the appendix.

there were crises in which the United States issued a threat and would not have followed through if the target had not conceded, but we cannot observe such cases.

There were, however, no crises in either the Cold War or post–Cold War periods in which the United States issued an explicit threat and was exposed as bluffing. This both deepens the puzzle of why weak states choose to resist the United States' threats and suggests that immediate credibility is a necessary but not sufficient condition for the successful use of compellent threats. In fact, the finding that the United States does not bluff is consistent with the rationalist theory of target-state behavior advanced by costly compellence. The theory asserts that targets do not doubt the immediate credibility of the United States' cheap threats, which makes sense given that the United States always follows through on the threatened action. Instead, when a target observes the United States issuing a cheap threat, it doubts that the unipole has the will to apply decisive force against it after the threatened action fails to induce compliance.

The Type of Threat Issued

All of the compellent threats that the United States issued in post–Cold War crises were communicated explicitly.[26] Although the United States employed an implicit threat in six of eleven Cold War crises, it did not issue any implicit threats (types 1 and 2) in post–Cold War cases. This does not mean that in the post–Cold War period the United States has never maneuvered its forces to influence international political events without issuing an explicit threat. Rather, in post-1989 crises in which it wished to compel its opponents, the United States explicitly articulated its demands and the punishment for noncompliance.

The observation that the United States exclusively employs explicit threats in the post–Cold War period is consistent with the logic of costly compellence. The theory suggests that a bipole is more restrained than a unipole in issuing compellent threats because the bipole must consider its fellow superpower's reaction to any threat. Opting for an implicit threat gives the United States and its opponent more room to maneuver and also allows the target to "save face." The fact that the United States employed implicit threats during the Cold

War is not surprising, then, because the risks of escalation under bipolarity were much higher than they are now. In the absence of a peer competitor, the United States can be less restrained in its use of compellence, and thus it is not surprising that its threats have been more explicit in the post–Cold War period.[27]

Allies

The United States issued two compellent threats on behalf of an ally during the Cold War. Both were active implicit threats administered by the United States as part of its war in Vietnam. By contrast, in all post–Cold War crises in which it issued a compellent threat, the United States did so in conjunction with or on behalf of at least one other state. If we examine table 2.1, we find that the United States also worked in conjunction with allies on several other post–Cold War crises in which it did not issue a compellent threat, including the nuclear crises with North Korea and Iran.

That allies have been more involved in the United States' compellence in the post–Cold War period than they were under bipolarity seems surprising. The United States is a unipole, and therefore it can execute military action around the world without assistance. The fact that the United States employs threats in conjunction with allies in the post–Cold War period is consistent, however, with the argument that the United States is pursuing a war-fighting model that minimizes the costs of military action. By sharing coercive duties with its allies, the United States can lower its own costs for executing compellent threats.[28]

The Influence of Demand Type

In addition to being more likely to issue an explicit threat and to coerce its targets in conjunction with allies, the United States also seems to be more expansive in its demands in the post–Cold War period. Several of the Cold War threats demanded that the target reverse some action that it had recently undertaken; others were intended to end or to resume negotiations in an ongoing military conflict. Some of the post–Cold War threats demanded a reversal of a recent challenge to the status quo; some demanded territorial revision or infringements on state sovereignty. There were also two post–Cold War crises in which the United States demanded regime change (Haiti Military Regime, Iraq Regime Change), but only one during the late Cold War period (Panama). Table 2.3 presents the United States' demands in each crisis in which it issued a compellent threat and the target's initial response, with the cases involving regime change highlighted.

It does seem, therefore, that the United States' demands were more expansive on average in the post–Cold War crises than they were during bipolarity.[29] Some might argue that an increased propensity to make impossible demands is responsible for the decline in US compellent-threat effectiveness that we observe after 1990. If we exclude from the analysis those cases in which the United States threatened regime change, however, the relative success rates for the two periods remain largely unchanged. Excluding the regime-change cases, US compellent threats were associated with compliance in six out of ten Cold War crises (60 percent) and in two of six post–Cold War crises (33 percent). These success rates are very similar to those we observe for the entire data set. Furthermore, it is not the case that targets resisted *only* in the face of expansive post–Cold War threats. There were Cold War cases (e.g., *Pueblo, Mayaguez*) and post–Cold War cases (e.g., Kosovo, Desert Strike) in which targets resisted in the face of relatively modest demands. The argument that expansive demands cause compellent-threat failure cannot explain the overall patterns in compellent-threat effectiveness across the two periods. We will explore the logic of this theory of compellent-threat failure in greater detail in the case chapters.

Dating the Cost-Minimizing Model of Warfare

The United States has adopted a model of warfare that dramatically limits the human, political, and financial costs of employing force. Many of the trends that make up this military model date roughly to the end of the Cold War. The costly compellence theory predicts that threats would be more likely to fail in the post–Cold War period because the use of force has become relatively cheap for the United States. For this reason, we have compared targets' willingness to resist US compellent threats during the Cold War and post–Cold War periods.

Table 2.3. US Demands

Crisis #	Crisis Name	Opponent	Demand	Target's Initial Response to Threat
Cold War Cases:				
111	Turkish Straits	USSR	Accept agreement on Turkish Straits	Concede
140	Korean War III	China, North Korea	Accept armistice	Concede
180	Pathet Lao Offensive	Pathet Lao (USSR)	Cease-fire	Concede
196	Cuban Missile	USSR	Remove missiles	Concede
213	Pleiku	North Vietnam	Cease-fire	Resist
224	Pueblo	North Korea	Release ship	Resist
238	Black September	Syria (USSR)	Withdraw from Jordan	Concede
249	Christmas Bombing	North Vietnam	Return to negotiations	Concede
259	Mayaguez	Cambodia	Release ship	Resist
309	US Hostages in Iran	Iran	Release hostages	Resist
391	**Invasion of Panama**	**Panama**	**Regime change**	**Resist**
Post–Cold War Cases:				
393	Gulf War	Iraq	Withdraw from Kuwait	Resist
411	**Haiti Military Regime**	**Haiti**	**Regime change**	**Resist**
419	Desert Strike	Iraq	Withdraw from excluded northern zone	Concede
422	UNSCOM I	Iraq	Readmit weapons inspectors	Concede
429	UNSCOM II: Operation Desert Fox	Iraq	Readmit weapons inspectors	Resist
430	Kosovo	Serbia (Yugoslavia)	Accept territorial revision / peace agreement	Resist
434	Afghanistan—USA	Afghanistan	Surrender terrorists, close terrorist training camps, give US access to camps, etc.	Resist
440	**Iraq Regime Change**	**Iraq**	**Regime change**	**Resist**

Note: The crisis numbers and names were taken from the ICB data. For a more detailed description of the author's method, please see the appendix.

We could, however, date the rise of this model to the end of direct US military involvement in Vietnam in 1973. As previously noted, the United States ended conscription that year, and the specter of high casualties during the Vietnam War shaped the decision making of both civilian and military leaders in the following decades. By reviewing tables 2.1 and 2.2, we find that the *Mayaguez* Crisis of May 1975 is the first post-Vietnam crisis in which the United States issued a compellent threat. If we divide the data in this way, then we find that targets conceded to the United States' demands in six of eight crises during the period 1945 to 1973 (75 percent) and in only two of eleven post-Vietnam crises (18 percent). In other words, if we date the start of the cost-minimizing model to 1973, then the historical record is even more strongly in line with the expectations of the costly compellence theory, which predicts that threats will be less effective when the use of force is relatively cheap. Although there are compelling reasons to date the United States' cost-minimizing model to the end of the Cold War, because some of these trends date to the end of the Vietnam War we should be able to observe a decline in threat effectiveness starting from that point.

Whether we date the rise of the cost-minimizing model of warfare to 1973 or to the end of the Cold War, the evidence is clear: The United States' compellent threats have been less effective on average since it adopted a model that limits the human, political, and financial costs of employing force.

Limits of the Data Set

This data set is not without limits. It is based on a list of international crises, which is not a random sample of events in international politics. In fact, crises are characterized by a high degree of hostility and a heightened risk that military force will be used. For this reason, the list of international crises constitutes a collection of situations in which compellent threats are highly likely to be employed. It is unlikely but possible that the United States has employed a compellent threat outside the context of an international crisis. Starting from the list of crises does, however, allow us to consider the conditions associated with the choice to issue a compellent threat when the stakes are relatively high. Starting from a list of compellent threats would not allow us to compare cases in which threats were employed with those in which they were not.

The size of the data set does not permit us to isolate the relative impact of different factors associated with effective compellence. We cannot test, for example, whether the rise of the RMA thesis or the elimination of conscription has had a greater impact on US compellent threat effectiveness. We should not discount the possibility that factors other than those described in this study may have contributed to the difference in the United States' use of compellent threats in the post–Cold War period. The data set does, however, allow us to examine the frequency with which the United States has issued compellent threats as a bipole and as a unipole and the rate at which the United States' threats have been effective in coercing target-state behavior during the two periods. Thus, the data set provides the best means available to evaluate the patterns predicted by the costly compellence theory.

The Record of US Compellent Threats: Summary

The costly compellence theory asserts that expensive compellent threats are more effective than cheap threats in coercing target states. It suggests that the United States would issue threats more frequently as a unipole than as a bipole and that these compellent threats would be less effective, on average, in the post–Cold War period when the use of force is relatively cheap. This chapter presents a new data set on the United States' use of compellent threats in international crises from 1945 to 2007. The data demonstrate that the United States has, in fact, issued threats more frequently as a unipole than as a bipole: The United States issued a compellent threat in eleven of forty-nine crises during the Cold War (22.4 percent) and in eight of fourteen crises (57.1 percent) in the post–Cold War period. These results are consistent with hypothesis 1(a). Furthermore, the data show that the United States does not bluff. The United States never failed to execute an explicit threat in the face of a target's resistance. This makes the willingness of target states to resist the United States' demands even more surprising.

The target resisted US demands in five of eleven cases (45 percent) in which the United States issued a threat during the Cold War. In the post–Cold War period, the target resisted in six of the eight crises (75 percent) in which the United States issued a threat. These results are consistent with hypothesis 2, which asserts that threats issued by a unipole that minimizes the costs of force are less effective than those issued by a unipole with a more costly model of war-fighting. In only one Cold War crisis in which the United States executed its threat did the target continue to resist after the application of force. By contrast, the target continued to resist US demands in five of six cases in the post–Cold War period in which the United States executed its compellent threat. The willingness of targets to continue to resist US demands, even after threats have been executed, suggests that the United States' compellent threats do not fail because they lack immediate credibility. Rather, it suggests that they fail because targets doubt the ultimate credibility of the United States' compellent threats. They doubt that the United States is willing to apply additional, decisive force against targets that continue to resist its demands.

The data set on US compellent threats in crises demonstrates that the historical record is consistent with the predictions of costly compellence. This evidence is not enough on its own, however, to convince us of the theory's validity for explaining the decline in US compellent threat effectiveness that we have observed since the end of the Cold War. Collapsing individual cases of coercion into single data points for the purposes of a data set allows us to make general observations, but it also flattens a lot of complexity. The data are structured so that we may observe whether a threat is associated with a target's resistance or compliance in a particular case, but this does not allow us to conclude with certainty that a particular threat caused the target's subsequent behavior. This would be a problem even if we had enough data to permit the use of sophisticated regression techniques. For this reason, the evaluation of overall trends in threat effectiveness must be accompanied by careful examination of individual cases to determine whether and to what extent a threat was responsible for the target's resistance or concession.

Case Chapters: Method

In the following chapters, I evaluate four cases in which the United States issued a compellent threat: the 1962 Cuban Missile Crisis, the

2011 threat against Libya, and the 1991 and 2003 threats against Iraq. First, I evaluate each case with the congruence method of within-case analysis.[30] This method is attractive for the cases in question because we can interview neither Nikita Khrushchev nor Muammar Qaddafi to determine how the costliness of the United States' threat influenced their decisions. Instead, I employ the variables dictated by the costly compellence theory and by each of the alternative theories under investigation to make a prediction about the target's response to the threat and then evaluate whether the evidence from the case is consistent with these predictions.

The fact that the congruence method does not require us to evaluate the causal mechanism at work in each case is also one of its greatest limitations. We cannot establish a causal relationship between the independent and dependent variables simply because a case's outcome is consistent with the theory's prediction. To attempt to compensate for this weakness in the congruence method, I combine it with process tracing. That is, for each case I attempt to identify the logic that the target employed in deciding whether to concede to the United States' demands before the application of force.[31] Although the evidence appropriate for process tracing is relatively scarce in some cases, this combination of the congruence method and process tracing provides the best opportunity to test the plausibility of the costly compellence theory. The congruence method allows us to evaluate whether the theory can predict the outcome of individual cases and not only the aggregate trends demonstrated in this chapter. The addition of process tracing allows us to identify the logic of the target's decision to concede or resist and to determine whether we can eliminate other possible explanations.

Although it has its limits, the congruence method does point to a potentially useful way of evaluating cases prospectively, particularly for policymakers. In the heat of a crisis, a US policymaker does not have the ability to tap into the target leader's thought processes to determine how he or she evaluates a US compellent threat. If the congruence method demonstrates that the costly compellence theory can be a reliable predictor of the target's response to a compellent threat, then the framework can be useful for policymakers considering how to formulate a compellent campaign with the greatest likelihood of coercing a target state.

Case Chapters: Competing Theories

In addition to evaluating the power of the costly compellence theory, for each case I also evaluate three competing explanations of compellent threat failure. The first, which I call the *reputation theory*, asserts that a threat's credibility (and, therefore, its effectiveness) depends on the coercer's record for following through on past threats.[32] This theory predicts that a target will concede to a unipole's threat when the unipole has followed through on its recent commitments. The unipole's failure to follow through on past threats, or the lack of a record for following through on past threats, will render the unipole's threat ineffective.[33] If this causal mechanism is at work in a particular case, we would expect a target to claim that it resisted because it did not believe that the unipole would execute its threat and that the target harbored those beliefs because of the unipole's record of bluffing. Or the target would claim that it conceded because it inferred from the unipole's willingness to follow through on past threats that it would follow through in the present.

Although Jonathan Mercer's work undermines this straightforward view of state reputation,[34] this theory plays a prominent role in debates about foreign policy in the United States and has done so since the Cold War. For example, the argument that "face" was worth fighting for was often employed to justify the United States' involvement in Vietnam. Secretary of State Dean Rusk and Secretary of Defense Robert McNamara sent President John F. Kennedy a joint memorandum in 1961 arguing that "the loss of South Vietnam to Communism would . . . undermine the credibility of American commitments elsewhere."[35] More recently, some have argued that the 2003 invasion of Iraq would convince leaders of other "rogue" states that they could be next. That is, the United States could not fail to take action against Saddam without undermining its ability to deal with other members of the "axis of evil." For example, Amitai Etzioni draws a direct link between Operation Iraqi Freedom and Qaddafi's decision in late 2003 to relinquish his programs to develop weapons of mass destruction (WMDs).[36] Because the reputation theory is so prominent in contemporary debates on both theory and policy, it is important to consider it as an alternative explanation for the target's behavior.

The second competitor is the *preponderant power* theory, which asserts that successful compellence is a function of the coercer's overwhelming advantage in relative power over the target. The preponderant power theory is at the heart of both realist theories of compellence and hegemonic stability theory. Hegemonic stability theory suggests that a state that is at a disadvantage in relative power would not willingly submit to war with an overwhelmingly powerful opponent.[37] A state that commands more power than its target will be able to get what it wants without fighting because the weaker opponent will not risk a fight that it would lose. Similarly, Art argues that "lurking behind the scenes, unstated but explicit, lies the military muscle that gives meaning to the posturing of the diplomats . . . . Military power undergirds the other instruments of statecraft."[38] In this view, military power or force affects the outcome of interstate disputes even when it is not actively employed. This theory will likely play an important role in the debate about the United States' role in the international system in coming decades, and so it merits examination as an alternative to the costly compellence theory.

Thus, the preponderant power theory asserts that the threatener's ability to inflict pain is the mechanism that causes the target to yield. It predicts that the target will yield to a compellent threat when the threatener is so powerful that engaging it in combat would be disastrous. While the reputation theory focuses on the perceived willingness of the threatening state to use force, the preponderant power theory focuses on the threatener's capability to execute the threatened action.

The third and final alternative is one that I will refer to as the *expansive demands* theory of compellent threat failure. This theory asserts that a compellent threat is likely to fail when the threatener makes extreme demands of the target—for example, when it demands regime change. The target is more likely to concede to the threatener's demands when they are limited. The logic of the expansive demands theory dictates that targets will claim to resist because the coercer demands too much. Conversely, we would expect targets to concede to a threat because the threatener's demands were moderate.

The logic of the expansive demands theory is consistent with Sechser's argument that targets resist when they are not compensated sufficiently for the loss in reputation they would suffer for conceding.[39]

The theory also has a high degree of intuitive appeal: Why would a target concede when the threatener demands that the target surrender everything it has? As demonstrated earlier in this chapter, however, the aggregate trends in compellent-threat effectiveness are not consistent with the argument that targets will resist expansive demands and concede to more limited demands. Nevertheless, it is important to consider the expansive demands theory as a possible explanation for the outcomes of individual cases.

Case Selection

Chapters 3 and 4 present the Cuban Missile Crisis and the 2011 crisis with Libya, respectively. These two cases constitute a pair of "most likely" cases for the costly compellence theory, each with a different predicted outcome.[40] The theory strongly predicts that the target would concede in the Cuban Missile Crisis and strongly predicts resistance in the 2011 crisis with Libya. In this sense the costly compellence theory outperforms other theories that can explain compellent-threat failure but not success. The Cuban Missile Crisis is the only Cold War case among the four and arguably the most famous crisis of that period. The Libya intervention in 2011 was too recent to be included in the ICB Project and hence does not appear in the data set, but it provides an important and relatively current case in which the use of force was expected to be extremely cheap.

The second group of cases, the 1991 and 2003 crises with Iraq, occupies chapters 6 and 7, respectively. Each case is an important test for the theories under investigation. As a pair of cases, they also provide us with the ability to draw comparisons between two separate attempts to coerce the same target state and the same target leader. This allows us to focus on factors that differed across the two crises while letting factors related to the target state itself fade into the background. Finally, these two cases present a unique opportunity for scholars of coercion because we are able to evaluate new primary sources on the Iraqi regime's decision making that were uncovered after the 2003 invasion.

Table 2.4. Crises in Which the United States Issued a Compellent Threat

Crisis #	Crisis Name	Opponent	Type of Threat	Description
111	Turkish Straits	USSR	Passive implicit	The United States sent forces to the region on August 20, 1946, to compel the Soviet Union to accept the Turkish position on the postwar agreement for the straits. The threat was also intended to deter the Soviet Union from taking further action in the region. The Soviet Union backed down from the confrontation on October 26, ending the crisis without violence.
140	Korean War III	China, North Korea	Vague	In May 1953, the United States transmitted (through John Foster Dulles) a veiled threat to launch a tactical nuclear strike if an armistice were not reached to end the war in Korea. Although demands were specified, there was no deadline for compliance, and the US action to be taken was implied but not clearly specified. The Chinese responded by making concessions on June 8 to break the deadlock in negotiations, and an armistice agreement was reached on July 27. The threat is coded as a compellent threat and not an act of brute force because of the relatively limited size of the US nuclear arsenal in 1953 and the scale of the implied attack. There is considerable debate about whether the threat actually reached the Chinese. See Betts, *Nuclear Blackmail,* 42–47.
180	Pathet Lao Offensive	Pathet Lao, USSR	Vague	On March 23, 1961, Kennedy gave a televised press conference in which he demanded a cease-fire from the Pathet Lao. There was no deadline for compliance, and the response in case of noncompliance was not specified. This was also a tacit deterrent threat to prevent the Soviet Union from further intervention. On May 3, a cease-fire between the Pathet Lao and the Laotian government went into effect, and on the 16th the Geneva Conference on Laos commenced.
196	Cuban Missile	USSR	Ultimatum	The United States first issued a vague threat with the announcement of the blockade. On October 27, 1962, Robert Kennedy transmitted an ultimatum to Soviet ambassador Anatoly Dobrynin: The United States would launch an operation to remove the missiles from Cuba if the Soviet Union did not agree to do so itself. Soviet premier Khrushchev ordered a stop to construction of the missile sites in Cuba the following day. See chapter 3 for a detailed discussion of this case.

Table 2.4. *continued*

Crisis #	Crisis Name	Opponent	Type of Threat	Description
213	Pleiku	North Vietnam	Active implicit	After attacks on US installations at Pleiku, the United States launched Operation Rolling Thunder on March 2, 1965. The campaign was designed to coerce the North Vietnamese into accepting a cease-fire, but US policymakers were careful to retain a degree of ambiguity about their motives and demands. There was disagreement within the US administration about the goals of the bombing campaign. The actual targeting of the bombing campaign suggests that it was intended to coerce, at least at the beginning. The campaign was also intended to deny the enemy the ability to pursue its strategy. The threat-execution variable was coded in the affirmative because the bombing proceeded over a long period of time—that is, it was not an isolated raid against the target. The North Vietnamese continued to resist during and after the campaign.
224	Pueblo	North Korea	Passive implicit	After North Korea seized the USS *Pueblo* on January 22, 1968, the United States called up the reserves and sent naval forces (including nuclear forces) to the Sea of Japan. Although the United States did demand the release of the ship, it did not explicitly threaten force or issue an ultimatum (hence the "passive implicit" coding). The North Koreans resisted releasing the ship over ten months of negotiations. The United States never used the forces it moved to the region. North Korea agreed to release the crew in December 1968, but the United States never recovered the ship.
238	Black September	Syria, USSR	Passive implicit	In response to Syria's invasion of Jordan on September 19, 1970, the United States placed airborne divisions on alert and sent naval forces to the eastern Mediterranean as an implicit threat to compel Syria to withdraw. The United States also issued a blanket deterrent threat to prevent the Soviet Union and Egypt from intervening directly. The United States did not employ the force it sent to the region, and a peace agreement was reached between Jordan and Syria on September 27 after a meeting of the League of Arab States in Cairo.

Crisis #	Crisis Name	Opponent	Type of Threat	Description
249	Christmas Bombing	North Vietnam	Active implicit	The United States launched the Linebacker II bombing campaign on December 18, 1972, after the breakdown of the Paris peace talks. The campaign was intended to coerce the North Vietnamese to return to negotiations, and it was intended to compel through fear, not to deny the North Vietnamese the ability to continue to pursue their strategy. On January 8, 1973, North Vietnam proposed a meeting in Paris, and the Paris Peace Accords were signed on the 27th. This response is coded as both concession and capitulation because the threat was an active compellent threat communicated through the application of force.
259	Mayaguez	Cambodia	Vague	The Khmer Rouge seized a US-registered cargo ship on May 12, 1975. The next day, the United States issued a nonspecific military threat demanding the release of the ship and its crew. The threat did not specify the action to be taken (simply "serious consequences") and did not set a deadline, hence the coding of a "vague" threat. US forces launched the first of two attacks to recover the ship late on the 13th. The Khmer Rouge agreed to release the ship and crew the following day, just as the United States launched the second attack, which included the landing of marines on Tang Island and further bombing of targets on the mainland.
309	US Hostages in Iran	Iran	Passive implicit	The United States conducted naval exercises on November 13, 1979, in the Arabian Sea following the seizure of hostages at the US embassy in Tehran on the 4th. The exercise was an implicit threat both to compel the release of the hostages and to deter the Iranians from harming them. No explicit threat was issued. A raid to rescue the hostages failed in April 1980, but this denial mission was not intended to coerce the Iranians into changing their behavior. A compellent threat was never executed, and the Iranians retained many of the hostages until President Ronald Reagan's inauguration.

Table 2.4. *continued*

Crisis #	Crisis Name	Opponent	Type of Threat	Description
391	Invasion of Panama	Panama	Vague	US military personnel in Panama were attacked, and Panama declared war against the United States in December 1989. In the run-up to the invasion, the United States beefed up forces in the region (a passive implicit threat); government officials also made public statements in which they refused to rule in or rule out the use of force against Manuel Noriega's regime. US demands were not very clear, nor was there a deadline for compliance, but the United States launched an invasion with twenty-six thousand troops on December 20. Noriega surrendered on January 3.
393	Gulf War	Iraq	Ultimatum	The United States began sending forces to the Persian Gulf region in November 1990 in response to Iraq's invasion of Kuwait on August 2. President George H. W. Bush issued a vague threat against Iraq on January 9, 1991. The US-led UN coalition then issued an ultimatum: Iraq must leave Kuwait by January 15 or face military action. This threat was affirmed by Secretary of State James Baker in talks with Iraq's foreign minister and was carried out on the 17th. See chapter 5.
411	Haiti Military Regime	Haiti	Open-ended	On September 15, 1994, President Clinton made a public address in which he demanded that the Haitian regime step down or face a US invasion. Although the demand was for an immediate withdrawal, there was no specific deadline for compliance. US forces were also moved to the region in anticipation of the threatened invasion. The crisis was resolved only after US forces had been launched and were preparing to land on the island on the 19th. See the discussion of this case in the appendix.
419	Desert Strike	Iraq	Vague	Iraqi troops crossed into the excluded northern zone to intervene in the Kurdish Civil War on August 31, 1996. The US-led UN coalition initially responded with an active implicit threat (air strikes on September 3, 1996). By September 12, the United States explicitly threatened additional air strikes but did not specify the terms or deadline for compliance—hence the coding of a "vague" threat. Iraq backed down and agreed to observe the exclusion zones on the 14th, before this second threat was executed.

Crisis #	Crisis Name	Opponent	Type of Threat	Description
422	UNSCOM I	Iraq	Vague	Iraq expelled US weapons inspectors working with the United Nations Special Commission (UNSCOM) on November 13, 1997. On the 15th, President Clinton assured Iraq that the United States had the forces to carry out an attack if it did not readmit weapons inspectors. He also authorized the movement of additional forces to the region but stopped short of issuing a specific deadline for compliance or threatening a specific attack on Iraq. Iraq agreed to readmit weapons inspectors on November 19, but the crisis was reignited on January 13, 1998, when it halted inspections led by American Scott Ritter. The crisis was finally defused on February 23, 1998, after the United States had sought support for military action in the UN and after negotiations brokered by Kofi Annan. Iraqi action was coded as concession, and the United States did not execute its threat.
429	UNSCOM II: Op. Desert Fox	Iraq	Open-ended	Iraq suspended cooperation with UNSCOM inspectors again in August 1998. On November 14, 1998, Iraq announced it would readmit inspectors as US planes were in the air and preparing to bomb Iraq (an active implicit threat). In the following days, the US administration issued an open-ended threat of future air strikes if Iraq did not comply with the renewed inspections. This threat was executed by joint US-British action beginning on December 16, after Iraqi officials had resumed disruption of inspections in late November and early December. The strikes ended on December 20, but there was no agreement reached on future inspections. Iraq continued to resist after the threat was executed.

Table 2.4. *continued*

Crisis #	Crisis Name	Opponent	Type of Threat	Description
430	Kosovo	Serbia (Yugoslavia)	Open-ended	NATO initially threatened to attack if a peace agreement in the war between Serbia (the Federal Republic of Yugoslavia) and the Kosovar Albanian forces were not reached by February 23, 1999. The deadline passed with a tentative peace agreement that quickly broke down. President Clinton then issued an open-ended threat in a news conference on March 19 in which he threatened NATO air strikes if Milošević did not stop the attacks on Kosovo and if he did not accept a new peace agreement already signed by the Kosovar Albanians. Clinton avoided articulating a specific deadline for compliance. The NATO bombing campaign began on March 24, and Milošević continued to resist for more than three months.
434	Afghanistan–USA	Afghanistan	Open-ended	In response to the terrorist attacks of September 11, President George W. Bush made a speech on September 20 in which he demanded that the Taliban turn over Osama bin Laden and other al-Qaeda leaders (in addition to several other demands), or else they would "share in [the terrorists'] fate." Although this statement did not initially specify the action to be taken, later in the speech he outlined the diplomatic and military action that the United States was prepared to execute in its campaign against al-Qaeda worldwide. The Taliban resisted US demands, and the joint US-UK attack began on October 7.
440	Iraq Regime Change	Iraq	Ultimatum	The UN issued a vague threat on September 12, 2002, demanding that Iraq readmit weapons inspectors, which it did on September 16. The United States rejected the disclosures that Iraq made about its weapons programs over the following months. The United States issued an ultimatum on March 17, 2003, giving Saddam and his sons forty-eight hours to leave Iraq or face invasion. The threat was executed on March 20. Saddam continued to resist even after the launch of the invasion and was finally hunted down and captured on December 13, 2003. See chapter 6.

Note: The crisis numbers and names were taken from the ICB data. For a more detailed description of the author's method, please see the appendix.

Notes

1. We will see later in this chapter that if we date the model to the end of the Vietnam War, the findings are even more consistent with costly compellence.

2. See, for example, George, Hall, and Simons, *Limits of Coercive Diplomacy: Laos, Cuba, Vietnam*; George and Simons, *Limits of Coercive Diplomacy*, 2nd ed.; and Art and Cronin, *United States and Coercive Diplomacy*.

3. See, for example, Blechman and Kaplan, *Force without War*; Zelikow, "Force without War, 1975–1982"; and Blechman and Wittes, "Defining Moment."

4. Sullivan and Koch, "Military Intervention by Powerful States." The data set is available at http://www.prio.no/jpr/datasets.

5. Sechser, "Militarized Compellent Threats, 1918–2001."

6. The project's website is maintained by the Center for International Development and Conflict Management at the University of Maryland and can be accessed at http://www.cidcm.umd.edu/icb/.

7. Background information on the latest release of the ICB data is available at "ICB Project Information," http://www.cidcm.umd.edu/icb/info/project_information.aspx.

8. The ICB Project has published its data and crisis histories periodically since 1988. The most recent print volume was Brecher and Wilkenfeld, *Study of Crisis*. The online resource updates and replaces this updated volume published in 2000. The data sets and codebooks are available for download at http://www.cidcm.umd.edu/icb/data/. The online ICB data viewer displays information about individual crises, including an event summary and the coding of each variable in the data set. The data viewer also allows the user to search for crises based on actor or crisis attributes. The data viewer is accessible at http://www.cidcm.umd.edu/icb/dataviewer/.

9. For the sake of consistency, I adopt the definition of "crisis" employed by the ICB Project: "There are two defining conditions of an *international crisis*: (1) a change in type and/or an increase in intensity of *disruptive*, that is, hostile verbal or physical, *interactions* between two or more states, with a heightened probability of *military hostilities*; that, in turn, (2) destabilizes their relationship and *challenges* the *structure* of an international system—global, dominant, or subsystem." From Brecher and Wilkenfeld, *Study of Crisis*, 4–5, emphasis in original. The specific definition of what constitutes a crisis does not affect the logic or implications of costly compellence.

10. Blechman and Kaplan, *Force without War*, 23.

11. All figures attributed to the ICB Project were calculated with data downloaded from http://www.cidcm.umd.edu/icb/data/.

12. Correlates of War (COW) Project, "Chronological List of All Wars." The COW Militarized Interstate Disputes (MIDs) data set was considered and

rejected as a starting point for the US compellent-threat data set. Detailed summaries are not available for the pre-1993 MIDs, and many of the existing post-1993 summaries are not detailed enough to ascertain whether a threat was issued. This data set does code for the highest action taken by each actor in the dispute. The possible actions include various types of threats. Because this variable ("HiAct") codes the highest action only, however, it is in many cases impossible to ascertain from it whether a threat was issued.

13. More detailed information about the coding process for each variable can be found in the appendix.

14. Note that threats that were intended both to compel change in the present and deter future behavior were counted as compellent threats in this data set.

15. Although implicit threats depend on the movement of forces to communicate with the target, forces may also be moved in support of explicit threats.

16. The invasion of Panama was included in the Cold War period because the crisis began in 1989.

17. There were also several cases during the Cold War in which the United States issued implicit and/or explicit deterrent threats. Table 2.1 does not report these threats.

18. A simple logit regression confirms that the United States issues threats more frequently in the post–Cold War period and that this difference is statistically significant. The results of this model are presented in the appendix.

19. The variable concerning crisis stakes was taken from the ICB coding, as described in the appendix.

20. The fact that the United States' vital interests have rarely been threatened in the post–Cold War period poses a major challenge to the evaluation of its coercive success. It is difficult to identify any post-1990 crisis in which the United States' major material interests were seriously at risk. The terrorist attacks of September 11 were horrific, put a drag on the US economy, and drove the United States to war in the Middle East. It would be difficult to argue, however, that transnational terrorists can inflict the damage that the Soviet Union could have inflicted on the United States during the Cold War. Similarly, although the wars in Iraq and Afghanistan were major military undertakings, they were wars of choice. The failure to prevail in either campaign would not have exposed US territory to invasion or put the United States at risk of an all-out nuclear exchange, as would have been possible if a Cold War–era crisis had escalated. The nuclear crisis with (prenuclear) North Korea in the mid-1990s seems to be the closest that the United States came to involvement in a devastating war in the post–Cold War period. Even if that confrontation had spiraled out of control, however, it would have been devastating for South Korea and a major blow to the US military, but it would not have posed an existential threat to the United States.

21. Drennan, "Nuclear Weapons and North Korea," 171.

22. As described in the appendix, I counted the Haiti Military Regime Crisis as one in which the target initially resisted and capitulated after the threat was executed. This case was the most challenging of the post–Cold War crises to code. One could argue that this represents a case in which the target conceded before the application of force, since US forces landed on but never actually attacked the island. Even if we code the Haiti case as one in which the target concedes to the initial threat, the difference in effectiveness is still considerable across the two periods: 55 percent during the Cold War and 38 percent during the post–Cold War period. Given this coding, the target continued to resist in all cases in which the United States executed a post–Cold War threat (five of five).

23. This variable is described in greater detail in the appendix.

24. If we exclude the Kosovo Crisis, which has a power-discrepancy score of 179, then the average for the post–Cold War period is 21.57. This is still 13 percent higher than the average power-discrepancy score for the Cold War crises in which the United States enjoyed an advantage over its opponent.

25. In the *Pueblo* Crisis, the United States moved forces to the region both to compel the North Koreans to release the ship and to deter them from taking any future action. During the Iran Hostage Crisis, the United States undertook a naval exercise as an implicit threat to compel the release of the hostages and to deter the Iranians from hurting the hostages or taking further action. The United States did launch a failed mission to rescue the hostages, but this would be classified as a denial mission. It was aimed at denying the target the ability to achieve its objectives rather than being an attempt at coercion.

26. In cases where the United States issued more than one threat, only the final threat was coded. During the Iraq Regime Crisis, the United Nations demanded on September 12, 2002, that Iraq readmit weapons inspectors, which it did. The United States later issued an ultimatum on March 17, 2003, giving Saddam Hussein and his sons forty-eight hours to leave or face attack by coalition forces. I employed this second and final threat to code the Iraq Regime Crisis. We will explore this case in greater detail in chapter 6.

27. The United States may be starting to realize, however, that even small states that feel angry and humiliated can generate significant costs. One of the by-products of US involvement in post–Cold War international politics has been the rise of transnational terrorism aimed at the United States. The United States will have to incorporate the costs of such terrorism into its calculations moving forward.

28. The logic of collective action also suggests that it will be more difficult for a coalition to follow through on its threat than it would be for a single state, since all the actors have incentives to free-ride. If the United States issues a

threat in conjunction with an ally or on behalf of a preexisting alliance, then the target may believe that the coalition arrayed against it will splinter. The finding that the United States does not bluff, however, would seem to undermine such an argument.

29. It is worth noting that the United States pursued regime change during the Cold War without employing compellent threats—for example, in Iran in 1953. In other words, the United States may have been more willing to seize "expansive demands" through brute force or covert action during the Cold War, rather than employing compellent threats as it has in the post–Cold War period.

30. For a complete description of the congruence method, see chapter 9, "The Congruence Method," in George and Bennett, *Case Studies and Theory Development*.

31. See ibid., 206.

32. These theories imply, but rarely stipulate, the belief that threat *effectiveness* is a simple function of threat *credibility*. The first chapter demonstrates why it is important to distinguish between these two concepts and why the costly compellence theory is built on this distinction. Arguments that relate credibility to reputation usually assume that credibility is a sufficient cause of threat effectiveness, so I employ such logic when generating predictions with the reputation theory but not with the costly compellence theory.

33. The general logic of the reputation theory does not stipulate whether the unipole's willingness to execute threats against the same state, or in the same issue area, is necessary for credibility or whether the record of credibility is wiped away with a change in the coercer's leadership. We will explore this logic in greater detail in the case chapters.

34. Mercer, *Reputation and International Politics*.

35. Rusk, *As I Saw It*, 433.

36. Etzioni, "Coming Test," 3–4.

37. See, for example, Blainey, *Causes of War*, 122.

38. Art, "American Foreign Policy," 10.

39. Sechser, "Goliath's Curse." Sechser's theory seems to generate an invariant prediction of the target's response: Targets resist powerful coercers because they demand too much. It is not clear how this theory would ever permit a target facing a unipole to concede to a compellent threat.

40. For a discussion of most-likely and least-likely case analysis, see George and Bennett, *Case Studies and Theory Development*, 120–23.

Chapter 3

The 1962 Cuban Missile Crisis

The Cuban Missile Crisis was perhaps the closest that the United States and the Soviet Union came to nuclear catastrophe during the Cold War. During the crisis, the United States announced and implemented a blockade of Cuba and transmitted a private ultimatum to Soviet premier Nikita Khrushchev to compel him to reverse the installation of nuclear missiles on the island. Both actions meet the definition of a compellent threat. Khrushchev ultimately agreed to reverse the installation of the missiles in exchange for a noninvasion pledge and a secret agreement to remove Jupiter missiles from Turkey, and a potential nuclear war was averted.

The Cuban Missile Crisis has generated a wealth of scholarship, and the case has figured prominently in studies of crisis management and coercive diplomacy.[1] The purpose of this analysis is not to contribute new historical evidence on the case. Instead, I employ existing sources and scholarship on the crisis to evaluate the predictive power of the theory developed in this study. Because of the costliness of the United States' threats against the Soviet Union, the costly compellence argument strongly predicts that these threats would be effective in convincing the Soviets to remove the missiles from the island. Competing theories of threat effectiveness perform poorly in predicting the outcome of this case. The evidence from process tracing is also consistent with costly compellence: Khrushchev believed that the United States was highly motivated to achieve its goals because it was willing to run such a high risk and pay such potentially high costs to achieve them.

Crisis Overview

In July 1962, the Soviet Union decided to covertly install nuclear missiles on the island of Cuba. This installation would proceed over two stages. First, Cuba's defensive capabilities would be augmented

95

by the addition of surface-to-air missile (SAM) stations. Second, the nuclear warheads would be shipped to the island and installed at launch pads in secret. The first shipments began to arrive in late July, and the Central Intelligence Agency (CIA) concluded that they were intended to fortify Cuba's defenses. Few in the US intelligence community anticipated that the Soviets would install offensive weapons on the island.[2]

An American U-2 flight on August 29 revealed the construction of SAM sites on Cuba, prompting a statement by President Kennedy on September 4.[3] In this statement, the president noted, "There is no evidence . . . of offensive ground-to-ground missiles; or of other significant offensive capability. . . . Were it to be otherwise, the gravest issues would arise."[4] Three days later, President Kennedy submitted a request to Congress for the authority to call up the reserves.[5] He also doubled the frequency of U-2 flights over Cuba. Through September and early October, these flights continued to find evidence of construction on the island. At this time, the Kennedy administration still believed that these installations were defensive in character.[6] Secretary of State Dean Rusk noted in an interview on September 29 that "any weapon is offensive if you are on the wrong end of it. But the configuration of the military forces in Cuba is a configuration of defensive capability."[7]

The crisis began on Tuesday, October 16, 1962, when President Kennedy was informed that photographs taken during a U-2 flight on the 14th revealed "a launching pad, a series of buildings for ballistic missiles and even one missile on the ground in San Cristobal."[8] Kennedy immediately decided that the missiles would have to go. That morning was the first meeting of the group that became known as the Executive Committee, or ExComm. This group of advisers would meet throughout the crisis while its members maintained their normal schedules as much as possible so as not to alert the Soviets that anything was amiss.[9] As ExComm debated the US response, the U-2 flights continued. Flights on the 17th uncovered several other installations, and analysts estimated that there were between sixteen and thirty-two missiles that could be operational within a week. Armed with nuclear warheads, these missiles could have killed eighty million Americans.[10]

From the start, the debate within ExComm revolved around how to achieve the removal of the missiles without risking a wider confrontation and without sacrificing the American position in Berlin. Arthur M. Schlesinger notes that discussions on the first day of the crisis focused on two options: acquiescence or an air strike. Given that Kennedy had made it clear that allowing the missiles to remain on the island was unacceptable, the group searched for more alternatives. On Wednesday the 17th, Secretary of Defense Robert McNamara proposed an idea that had been mentioned briefly in the previous day's discussion: a blockade of Cuba. The blockade would be intended to prevent the delivery of additional missiles to the island and convince the Soviets to reverse the installations already under way. It also gave the president an option between inaction and an assault on the island.[11]

Attorney General Robert Kennedy noted in his memoir of the crisis that the Joint Chiefs of Staff were unanimous in calling for military action to take out the missiles.[12] Over the first week, the military concluded that a limited, "surgical" strike to attack the installations would be risky. Such a strike would not necessarily eliminate all the missile sites and might invite retaliation. A larger strike that would target all sources of danger emanating from Cuba, including the Castro regime itself, would be more prudent.[13] Air Force chief of staff Curtis LeMay led the way in urging the president to choose the military option. The Joint Chiefs felt that a blockade would not convince the Soviets to remove the missiles from the island.[14] Although the president opposed a strike, preparations were nonetheless initiated for an attack on Cuba. A previously scheduled naval exercise in the Caribbean provided cover for the assembly of an amphibious task force of forty thousand marines (plus five thousand at Guantánamo), and the army would assemble more than a hundred thousand troops in Florida. Tactical fighters were flown to Florida airfields from all over the country.[15]

By Friday, October 19, the debate within ExComm had coalesced around two options: a blockade or a military strike to destroy the missiles and launch sites. McNamara and Robert Kennedy favored the blockade, while the military (and some civilians) favored a strike. Robert Kennedy argued forcefully that a surprise attack on Cuba would violate the United States' values and traditions. Returning from a campaign stop the following day, President Kennedy presided over a final vote among the ExComm members. Eleven favored a blockade, and six favored an immediate strike. President Kennedy issued orders to prepare for the blockade, which would be called a "quarantine" because a "blockade" would constitute an act of war.[16]

As President Kennedy prepared to address the nation on Monday evening, further military preparations were made in anticipation of the quarantine. In addition to the movements of troops described above, missile crews were placed on alert, 180 ships were deployed to the Caribbean, and the B-52 bomber force, loaded with nuclear weapons, was ordered into the air. The United States was also consulting its allies and making preparations for a retaliatory blockade of Soviet-occupied Berlin.[17] In his address to the American people on the evening of the 22nd, Kennedy announced that the United States had uncovered "unmistakable evidence . . . that a series of offensive missile sites is now in preparation on [Cuba]. The purposes of these bases can be none other than to provide a nuclear strike capability against the Western Hemisphere." He then described the plan for the quarantine and asserted that "it shall be the policy of this nation to regard any nuclear missile launched from Cuba against any nation in the Western Hemisphere as an attack by the Soviet Union on the United States, requiring a full retaliatory response upon the Soviet Union."[18]

Tensions were high as the quarantine went into effect on Wednesday, October 24. That morning, several Soviet ships bound for Cuba turned back. The tanker *Bucharest* identified itself to a US ship and was allowed to pass through to the island. On Friday the 26th, the first Soviet ship was stopped and boarded but was allowed to continue to Cuba after an inspection. In the meantime, evidence continued to mount that the missile installations were nearing completion. The members of ExComm waited nervously for a response to a message President Kennedy sent to Premier Khrushchev on the 25th.[19] They received the first of two responses the following evening. In this letter, Khrushchev assured the president that the missiles were intended solely for defensive purposes. Referring to the launch of a nuclear attack, he avowed that "only lunatics or suicides, who themselves want to perish and to destroy the whole world before they die, could do this."[20] Most important, he agreed to remove the missiles in exchange for an end to the quarantine and an American promise not to invade Cuba. Khrushchev's offer was met with an initial feeling of relief by the members of ExComm, who for the first time saw "light at the end of the cave."[21]

The following morning, however, President Kennedy received a second letter from Khrushchev. In addition to the noninvasion pledge and the end of the quarantine, Khrushchev demanded the removal of Jupiter missiles stationed in Turkey in exchange for removing the missiles from Cuba. Robert Kennedy characterized this second letter as much more formal than the first.[22] On the subject of the NATO missiles stationed in Turkey, Khrushchev asked, "Do you believe that you have the right to demand security for your country and the removal of such weapons that you qualify as offensive, while not recognizing this right for us?" He further offered to pledge that the Soviet Union would not interfere in Turkey's domestic affairs if the United States would do the same for Cuba.[23] Robert Kennedy felt that the demand for the swap was reasonable, and this possibility had been raised within ExComm earlier in the crisis. The president was, however, reluctant to agree to such a trade under pressure from the Soviet Union. While debating the United States' next move that afternoon, the members of ExComm learned that a U-2 had been shot down over Cuba, and that the pilot, Maj. Rudolf Anderson Jr., had been killed. Although this incident prompted renewed pleas to take military action against the installations, the president was adamant about the need for restraint.[24]

After several hours of tense deliberation with his advisers that afternoon, Kennedy sent a message to the Soviet premier, accepting the terms presented in the first of Khrushchev's two letters.[25] In exchange for the cessation of work on the launch sites and the removal of missiles from Cuba, the United States would end the quarantine and pledge not to invade the island. Kennedy's letter makes no mention of the message he had received from Khrushchev that morning, nor does it offer to remove the Jupiter missiles from Turkey.[26] That evening, Robert Kennedy met privately with Soviet ambassador Anatoly Dobrynin at the Justice Department, carrying with him a copy of the president's letter to Khrushchev. During this meeting,

Robert Kennedy delivered an ultimatum: If the Soviet Union did not agree within twenty-four hours to remove the missiles, the United States would invade Cuba. Kennedy recalled in his memoir, "We had to have a commitment by tomorrow that those bases would be removed. . . . He [Dobrynin] should understand that if they did not remove those bases, we would remove them."[27] The following day, Khrushchev sent a message in which he informed the president that he had "given a new order to dismantle the arms which you described as offensive, and to crate and return them to the Soviet Union."[28]

Characterizing the Threat

The United States' response to the introduction of Soviet missiles on Cuba consisted of two compellent threats: the blockade and the announcement thereof, which was a vague threat, and the ultimatum transmitted by Robert Kennedy to the Soviet ambassador on October 27.[29] Kennedy's speech from October 22, quoted above, announced the start of the quarantine and demanded the removal of the missiles from Cuba. US ground, air, and naval forces were positioned both to enforce the blockade and to communicate the gravity of the United States' interest. The president mentioned but did not describe in detail the military buildup that the United States was undertaking. Referring to the justification for the quarantine, Kennedy asserted that "further action is required—and it is underway; and these actions may only be the beginning." The president then announced that, if the missiles were not removed, "further action will be justified. I have directed the Armed Forces to prepare for any eventualities."[30]

Thus, in his announcement of the quarantine, President Kennedy specified the United States' demands—the removal of the missiles from Cuba—and hinted at the military action that would follow in the event that compliance was not forthcoming. This announcement meets the criteria for a vague threat. Without this speech from President Kennedy, the blockade itself and the movement of US forces in preparation for a potential invasion would have qualified as a passive implicit threat.[31] We also know that the Soviet premier did interpret the quarantine and Kennedy's speech as a threat. In response to Kennedy's speech, Khrushchev concluded that "this is not a war against Cuba but some kind of ultimatum."[32] Although Kennedy's speech does not qualify as an ultimatum in the terms of this study, it is clear from this statement that Khrushchev did interpret the quarantine as a compellent threat.

The chief advantage of relying on a vague threat at this stage of the crisis was presumably the fact that doing so gave the Soviet premier room to maneuver rather than backing him into a corner at the outset. As the crisis progressed, however, the president evidently became more willing to employ a stricter variant of compellence. In his meeting with the Soviet ambassador on the night of October 27th, Robert Kennedy asserted that the Soviet Union had twenty-four hours to agree to remove the missiles from Cuba, or else the United States would launch an invasion of the island. This private, explicit communication meets the classic definition of an ultimatum: a clear demand for a change in the status quo, a specified punishment for noncompliance, and a deadline.[33]

Contextual Variables

The costly compellence theory suggests that the United States' threats against the Soviet Union would be ultimately credible and hence effective if issuing and executing the threats were costly for the United States. First, we will consider the contextual variables that defined both the vague threat and the ultimatum. The Cuban Missile Crisis occurred at the height of the Cold War, when the United States was one of two superpowers dominating a bipolar system. In 1962, the United States still employed conscription and had not yet begun to hire private contractors to conduct its military operations. The United States had not yet transitioned to a technology-intensive, casualty-avoiding military strategy based on the RMA thesis.

These contextual variables all suggest that issuing and executing the 1962 threats would be very costly for the United States. The use of any type of military force, either to enforce the blockade or to carry out an invasion of Cuba, would have risked the lives of conscripted troops not supported by the type of sophisticated technology that enables standoff strike operations in the era of the RMA. Thus, both the structure of the international system and the character of the US military in 1962 suggest that it would be costly for the United States to issue and to execute a compellent military threat during the Cuban Missile Crisis. Table 3.1 summarizes the contextual variables for the 1962 threats against the Soviet Union and how these variables affected the costliness of US action.

Threat-Specific Variables

Both the vague threat and the ultimatum entailed the use of the same basic package of force in the event that the Soviet Union failed to heed the United States' demands. According to Robert Kennedy's account, the plan for an attack on Cuba, had the quarantine failed, called for both air strikes against targets in Cuba and an invasion force of ninety thousand troops. Although the use of airpower is a cornerstone of the modern casualty-avoidant military model, the plan to attack Cuba depended on a major contingent of ground troops and envisioned twenty-five thousand American casualties.[34] In this case, airpower was intended to attack missile sites and support the ground invasion, not to serve as a substitute for a high-casualty ground assault.

Although President Kennedy's vague threat on October 22 did not explicitly specify that the United States was planning to invade the island if the Soviet Union did not agree to remove the missiles (a threat that Robert Kennedy spelled out for the Soviet ambassador on the 27th), the Soviets were aware of the preparations that the United States was making. In a letter addressed to the president of the UN Security Council on October 23, the Soviet government characterized the quarantine as a "naval blockade," which constituted a violation of international law. The letter also acknowledged the "landing of additional United States troops at the United States Guantanamo base . . . and the United States armed forces . . . being placed in a state of combat readiness."[35] In other words, the Soviet government was aware that the United States was preparing ground and other forces for imminent military action.

Although the United States' allies responded positively to the quarantine, they did not share the burden of coercing the Soviet Union or

Table 3.1. Contextual Variables, Cuban Missile Crisis

Contextual Variables		Effect on US Military Action
Polarity:	Bipolar	More costly
Conscription?	Yes	More costly
Contractors?	No	More costly
RMA?	No	More costly

otherwise reduce the United States' costs for the planned invasion of Cuba. The Organization of American States (OAS) unanimously approved the US quarantine plan in a meeting on October 23.[36] French president Charles de Gaulle lent his support and waved away offers to view the U-2 photographs of missile sites.[37] There was a televised showdown at a meeting of the UN Security Council between US ambassador Adlai Stevenson, armed with surveillance photographs of the installations on Cuba, and Soviet ambassador V. A. Zorin. They shared several heated exchanges but made no progress on the missiles.[38] Despite some attempts at mediation by UN secretary-general U Thant, the Security Council did not issue any resolutions on the conflict (which is not surprising, given that both the United States and the Soviet Union wielded a veto in that body), nor did the United States present itself as acting on behalf of the UN.[39]

For the purposes of evaluating the likely success of the threats, the fact that many of the United States' allies approved of the quarantine is irrelevant. The US ultimatum was delivered privately, and neither it nor the vague threat was issued on behalf of or in conjunction with US allies. The United States bore the full brunt of responsibility for executing its threat and for the consequences that would follow.[40] Nor did the United States solicit contributions from its allies to offset the costs of the quarantine or the threatened invasion. The crisis unfolded quickly, and there were no calls for increased taxes to pay for the operation.

The final variable to consider is the extent to which civilian casualties resulting from an invasion would have been politically costly for the United States. The costly compellence theory focuses on the extent to which casualties inflicted on target-state civilians are politically costly for the unipole. Cuban civilians would have been vulnerable in the event of a ground invasion, but these casualties would not have been broadcast in 1962 in the way that collateral damage is publicized in the post–Cold war period. Consequently, the willingness to inflict violence on Cuban civilians would have been less politically costly for the United States in 1962 than it has been in the post–Cold War period.[41]

The civilians most at risk in the event of escalation between the Soviet Union and the United States were, however, the American and Soviet civilians who would have perished in an all-out nuclear exchange. In this sense, the Cuban Missile Crisis is unique among the cases this study examines. Unlike most other compellent threats issued by the United States, which may endanger the target state's civilians, the 1962 threats also put US (and Soviet) civilians at risk. At the time of the crisis, US declaratory nuclear policy was focused on city-avoidance. Even if such a strategy of city-avoidance could have been implemented successfully, however, it would have been devastatingly costly for both the United States and the Soviet Union. The Pentagon estimated that US casualties would still have numbered ten million in a city-avoidant exchange.[42] Although casualties suffered by Cuban civilians would have been only moderately costly for the United States in 1962, executing the invasion of Cuba would have been extremely costly for US and Soviet civilians if the conflict had escalated to a nuclear exchange. In this sense, the vulnerability of American civilians made the United States' 1962 threats extremely costly to execute.

In sum, the independent variables of interest all suggest that issuing and executing the threatened invasion of Cuba would have been very costly for the United States. The United States was threatening a ground invasion in conjunction with air strikes that would be executed unilaterally, that would not be paid for by increased taxes or allies' contributions, and that would have placed Cuban, American, and Soviet civilians at risk. Because executing the threat would have been so costly for the United States in 1962, the costly compellence theory strongly predicts that the Soviet Union would concede to US demands. Table 3.2 summarizes the variables associated with the threat against the Soviet Union and indicates whether each variable makes the threat and execution of force more or less costly for the United States. We do not distinguish here between the vague threat

Table 3.2. Threat Variables, Cuban Missile Crisis

Threat Variables		Effect on US Military Action
Ground invasion?	Yes	More costly
Allies?	No: Ultimatum issued unilaterally	More costly
Payment	Allies not asked to contribute; no tax increases	More costly
Civilian vulnerability	US and Soviet civilians at high risk in nuclear exchange; Cuban civilians at moderate risk	Extremely costly

and the ultimatum because the package of force to be employed by the United States was the same for both threats.

Cuban Missiles: Alternative Theories

Reputation Theory

The reputation theory asserts that the credibility of today's threat depends on the threatener's record of following through on past threats. The theory's prediction for this case is not immediately clear. On the one hand, the United States had not yet followed through on any compellent threat issued in a post-1945 crisis. The data set presented in the second chapter demonstrates that the United States had issued compellent threats prior to the Cuban Missile Crisis, but no target had resisted US demands and tested the United States' determination to follow through on its threat. The fact that no target had resisted a post–World War II US compellent threat also means, however, that the United States had never *failed* to execute a compellent threat or been exposed as bluffing. In other words, the United States had developed neither a record for following through on its compellent threats nor a record for bluffing.

On the other hand, the United States had taken action to bolster its commitment to Berlin during a recent crisis. In July 1961, President Kennedy announced an increase in the draft, a reserves call-up, increased spending on civil defense, and an increased state of ground alert for Strategic Air Command (SAC) in response to escalating rhetoric from Moscow on Berlin.[43] When the Berlin Wall was under construction in August, the president sent the First Battle Group to reinforce the US garrison and to deter the Soviets from severing access to West Berlin.[44] The crisis seemed to have been defused on October 17, however, when Khrushchev lifted the deadline for the separate peace treaty and for an end to the occupation of Berlin. Although there were additional confrontations in Berlin after this date, the United States' willingness to defend West Berlin was never actively tested.[45] Unlike the threats issued during the Cuban Missile Crisis, Kennedy's strategy in the summer of 1961 was intended to *deter* the Soviet Union from altering the status quo in Berlin. Complying with US demands in October 1962 entailed a very public reversal for Khrushchev, in a way that US efforts to prevent a change in Berlin did not.

In sum, the reputation theory yields an inconclusive prediction for the 1962 crisis. The strictest variant of the theory asserts that credibility today is a function of the willingness to execute yesterday's threat. Because the United States had not yet been tested on a compellent threat in a Cold War crisis, a strict interpretation of the theory suggests that the 1962 threats were likely to fail. A more relaxed view of the theory might suggest that the willingness to uphold commitments of any kind renders a threat credible. Thus, the United States' willingness to shore up deterrence in the 1961 Berlin Crisis suggests that the Soviets would be more likely to concede to US demands in the 1962 crisis. The United States did not, however, have to execute its deterrent threat in Berlin. Thus, the United States developed neither a reputation for following through on its threats nor a reputation for bluffing with its behavior in the 1961 crisis. Therefore, the relaxed variant of the reputation theory yields an indeterminate prediction of the Soviet response to the 1962 US ultimatum. As a whole, the reputation theory of credibility weakly predicts that the 1962 threats would fail and that Khrushchev would resist the demand to remove the missiles from Cuba.

Preponderant Power

The preponderant power theory of threat effectiveness asserts that a state that enjoys recognized superiority in military power will be able to coerce a weaker opponent without applying force. To determine what this theory would predict about the Cuban Missile Crisis, we must examine the actors' perceptions of the relative balance of power at the time of the crisis. In the case of the Cuban Missile Crisis, we must consider both the conventional and the nuclear balance.

President Kennedy came into office believing in a "missile gap" that favored the Soviet Union. By the end of 1961, however, this belief had been "definitively debunked."[46] Although the Soviets had few intercontinental ballistic missiles (ICBMs), estimates suggested that enough would survive a US first strike to kill between two million and fifteen million Americans. The Soviets also possessed enough short- and medium-range missiles to do serious damage to Western Europe in the event of nuclear escalation.[47] Reconnaissance photos confirmed in late September 1961 that the missile gap actually favored the United States. In October 1961, a year before the crisis over missiles in Cuba, Deputy Secretary of Defense Roswell Gilpatric announced in a speech that "the count of U.S. bombers, submarines, carrier strike forces, and theater nuclear forces favor[ed] the United States." The Soviets responded to this public denial of strategic parity by emphasizing the high yields of Soviet warheads and by testing two massive weapons in the Arctic later that month.[48]

In the fall of 1962, the Institute for Strategic Studies (ISS) estimated that the Soviets had roughly seventy-five ICBMs. The Western alliance had somewhere between 450 and 500. A Soviet ICBM carried a ten-megaton warhead, however, while ICBMs in the West were equipped with warheads of either three or four megatons.[49] In October 1962, American intelligence agreed with the IIS estimate of approximately seventy-five Soviet ICBMs. In a top-secret memorandum that he delivered to ExComm on October 27 (a day after he received the request to do so and rather late in the crisis), State Department official Raymond L. Garthoff argued that the additional missiles in Cuba would "increase the first-strike missile salvo which the USSR could place on targets in the continental United States by over 40 percent." He also noted that "approximately 40 percent of the SAC bomber force [was] now located on air bases within range of Soviet MRBMs [medium-range ballistic missiles] in Cuba, and almost all of it is in range of the IRBMs [intermediate-range ballistic missiles]."[50] According to Garthoff's estimate, the United States still had a relative advantage in strategic nuclear forces, but the installation in Cuba dramatically increased the Soviet first-strike capability.[51]

In 1962, total mobilized manpower was estimated at 8 million for the Western alliance, while the communist bloc's strength was estimated at 7.7 million. The communist bloc had more than twice the number of tanks as its Cold War opponent, with thirty-eight thousand compared to the Western bloc's sixteen thousand. If we isolate the two superpowers, the Soviet army had twenty thousand front-line tanks and fifteen thousand second-line tanks, while the US Army had roughly twenty-five hundred battle tanks. The Western allies held the lead in long-range bombers (630 compared to 200), but the Soviets had nearly three times the number of MRBMs as did the West.[52]

According to the ISS, the Soviet Union itself had 3.6 million people in the armed forces in the fall of 1962. The Soviet military budget was set at $14.74 billion that year, an 8 percent increase over the previous year. The ISS report notes that Soviet policy in 1962 "continue[d] to place marked emphasis on the development of long and medium range missiles as a deterrent to aggression and a support to diplomacy."[53] The US armed forces numbered 2.815 million in the fall of 1962, while the defense budget was $52 billion.[54] US policy was focused on efforts to "enlarge the size of the American strategic retaliatory systems and to make them less vulnerable to surprise attack. This is partly with a view to retaining the option of using the deterrent in a controlled and selective fashion in response to any local Soviet aggression."[55] In addition, the "deployment of tactical nuclear weapons into NATO land forces" continued in the fall of 1962. The United States did, however, institute "double-key" arrangements so that US consent was required (at least in theory) before the host country could deploy a nuclear weapon based on its territory.[56]

Whether the United States or the Soviet Union enjoyed clear superiority in 1962 depends on the index of power that we examine. The Soviet Union clearly led the United States in global conventional ground capabilities, even when we add in the strength of the United States' allies. This meant that the US position in Berlin was very vulnerable to a conventional attack in 1962, a vulnerability that was on the minds of many American decision makers during the Cuban Missile Crisis. In terms of the local balance of power in the Caribbean, however, the United States obviously had the advantage in conventional capabilities. The United States also exceeded the Soviets in both long-range bombers and ICBMs. This seemed to leave the Soviet Union vulnerable to US strategic nuclear forces, even though NATO still feared a Soviet conventional attack on Western Europe.

Khrushchev's decision to station missiles in Cuba appears to have been motivated, at least in part, by a desire to equalize the nuclear balance between the two superpowers. This suggests that the Soviets acknowledged that the United States led the Soviet Union in strategic nuclear forces. Although he would deny this during the crisis, Khrushchev allegedly referred to the scheme to place missiles on Cuba as "an offensive policy."[57] According to Aleksandr Fursenko and Timothy Naftali, Khrushchev spoke "confidently of the growth in Soviet power that by 1963 would force the United States to accommodate Moscow's perceived needs in Central Europe and elsewhere. The Cuba ploy would ensure that this necessary change in the balance of power occurred."[58] Although Robert McNamara believed that the installation of nuclear weapons on Cuba did not change the balance of power, some of the other members of ExComm did believe that the Soviet move neutralized the US advantage in strategic nuclear forces.[59]

Khrushchev also claimed that installing nuclear weapons in Cuba would increase his leverage over the United States in a final push to resolve the Berlin issue after the conclusion of US elections on November 6.[60] It is clear that President Kennedy and other members of ExComm were also preoccupied by the effect of the missile crisis on Berlin. In a meeting on the first day of the crisis, Secretary Rusk expressed concern that the Soviets might have been "thinking that they can either bargain Berlin and Cuba against each other, or that they could provoke us into a kind of action in Cuba which would give an umbrella for them to take action with respect to Berlin."[61] President Kennedy also believed, from the outset, that the crisis over missiles on Cuba was directly tied to the question of Berlin.[62] Later in the crisis, as the quarantine was being put into place, President Kennedy "ordered preparations to proceed for a possible blockade of Berlin" and contacted the United States' European allies to prepare for such a contingency.[63] Because the two sides believed that the crisis over Cuba threatened the status quo in Berlin, the conventional balance of power in Europe at the time of the Cuban Missile Crisis must be taken into account in an assessment of the relative balance of power. Although both sides seem to have acknowledged that the United States led the Soviet Union in long-range nuclear delivery capability in 1962 and in local conventional capabilities in the Caribbean, the Soviet Union still outmatched the Western allies in conventional military capability in Europe.

To further complicate our assessment, we now know that the Soviets had delivered nuclear warheads to Cuba by October 1962. At the time, the CIA reported that there were no warheads on the island. The Soviets had 43,000 troops on Cuba, which was 33,000 more than the CIA had estimated, in addition to 270,000 Cuban troops prepared to "fight to the death." These troops were armed with tactical nuclear warheads to repel a US invasion.[64] In fact, by October 22, several tactical missiles had already been deployed to Soviet infantry units on the island and were operational, while the nuclear warheads remained under Soviet control at a nearby facility.[65] US decision makers were unaware of these facts at the time, so we cannot conclude that they affected their calculations. We can expect, however, that these facts influenced Soviet calculations during the crisis and that they would have led the Soviets to conclude that the United States did not, in fact, command an overwhelming advantage in nuclear capability that could be brought to bear on the crisis.

The fact that it is difficult to identify a clear leader in relative power means that the necessary condition for the preponderant power theory of compellent-threat effectiveness—an obvious imbalance of relative power favoring the United States—did not exist at the time of the Cuban Missile Crisis. The United States led the Soviets in long-range nuclear-delivery capabilities and had the advantage in conventional capabilities in the Caribbean, but the Soviet Union had more MRBMs than the United States and outmatched the Western allies in conventional capabilities in Europe. Furthermore, the Soviets had installed nuclear weapons on Cuba by October 1962, which would have led them to discount even further the US lead in nuclear capability. Because the United States lacked a clear advantage in relative power, the preponderant power theory predicts that the United States' threats during the Cuban Missile Crisis would fail.

Expansive Demands

It is clear that the demand to remove the missiles from Cuba was not as extreme a demand as a change in regime or the surrender of a piece of Soviet territory. It is equally clear, however, that complying with the United States' demands would have entailed a very public reversal for the Soviet regime. The United States had made very high-profile declarations in the UN Security Council and in the media, accusing the Soviet Union of installing offensive weapons on Cuba and demanding their immediate removal. If Khrushchev chose to concede, it would be difficult for him to claim that he had not done so in response to pressure from the United States. This is not, however, a unique feature of the Cuban Missile Crisis. By definition, a compellent threat demands a change in the status quo.

The key decision makers on the US side did not view the missiles on Cuba as central to the Soviet Union's interests. After the crisis, President Kennedy and others acknowledged that they could not necessarily hope to prevail over the Soviet Union in a future crisis simply because it had yielded over the missiles, precisely because the United States' demands in the crisis had not targeted the Soviet Union's core interests.[66] This does not mean that the Soviet Union viewed the demands in that way, but it does indicate that the US decision makers did not believe that their demands posed an existential threat to the Soviet Union.

In public statements and in requests to the UN, Soviet representatives characterized the United States' decision to implement the quarantine as aggressive and in violation of international law. These statements offer few hints, however, about how the demand for the missiles' removal was viewed by Soviet leaders in terms of the Soviet Union's goals and interests. To the extent that they acknowledged the motivation for the missiles' installations, Soviet representatives emphasized that the missiles were intended to enhance Cuba's defense. All states, in their view, should be entitled to make provision for their own defense without interference from an outside power:

> The United States is demanding that the military equipment Cuba needs for its own defense should be withdrawn from its territory,

a step to which no State prizing its independence can, of course, agree. . . . The United States Government is assuming the right to demand that States should account to it for the way in which they organize their defence, and should notify it of what their ships are carrying on the high seas. The Soviet Government firmly repudiates such claims.[67]

In other words, in their public statements on the crisis, the Soviet government framed the United States' demand in terms of how it would infringe on Cuba's sovereignty.[68] Soviet representatives also evaluated the United States' demands in terms of how they would erode the rights enjoyed by states in general. In his statement to the UN Security Council on October 23 on the demand for the missiles' removal and the quarantine of Cuba, Ambassador Zorin asserted that "it is not a trivial matter that is involved; it is a matter of a unilateral and arbitrary action by a great Power which constitutes a direct infringement of the freedom and independence of a small country."[69]

There is some evidence about how the Soviet premier understood the United States' demand. In deliberations at the Kremlin, Khrushchev asserted that, even if the missiles were removed from the island, "we can [still] defeat the USA from USSR territory."[70] On the decision to remove the missiles from the island, he asserted that "this is not cowardice. . . . It is a prudent move. . . . The future does not depend on Cuba, but on our country."[71] Although he might have preferred to keep the missiles on the island, Khrushchev asserted that removing them would not require the sacrifice of the Soviet Union's ability to defend itself. In other words, the United States' demands were not trivial, but they were not so great as to challenge core Soviet security interests.

It is possible that the Soviet leader viewed the demand to remove the missiles from Cuba as one that threatened core Soviet interests but chose not to voice that opinion or did so in documents or conversations to which we do not have access. Once the Soviet leader had decided to remove the missiles, claiming that the demand to do so attacked his core interests would not have enhanced his standing, either at home or abroad. Khrushchev did frame his motivation for installing the missiles in terms of Cuba's defense and in terms of his objectives in Berlin. He did not claim that the move was intended to guarantee Soviet security, and thus the removal of the missiles would not have posed a dire threat. Furthermore, the fact that Khrushchev was so eager to trade the missiles in Cuba for the Jupiter missiles in Turkey suggests that he did view the United States' demands as not entirely outrageous, since he requested that the United States make a similar sacrifice.

On the spectrum of demand expansiveness, the United States' request that the Soviets remove their missiles from Cuba falls somewhere in the middle. The United States was not demanding a trivial concession, nor was it demanding that the Soviet Union surrender a vital component of its national security. Given that the demand was not excessive, the expansive demands theory does not predict that the threat was highly likely to fail. The demand was not so limited, however, that the theory would strongly predict concession. Accepting the United States' terms in the crisis would have entailed a very public reversal for the Soviet regime, even if the missiles were not viewed as a vital component of Soviet security. In other words, the expansive demands theory predicts neither that the United States' 1962 threats were highly likely to succeed nor that they were highly likely to fail. In the case of moderate demands, the theory is indeterminate.

In sum, both the contextual variables and the threat characteristics suggest that threatening and executing military action against the Soviet Union would have been highly costly for the United States. For this reason, the costly compellence theory strongly predicts that the Soviet Union would concede to US demands before the use of force. The reputation theory weakly predicts that the threat would fail: Although the United States had not been revealed as bluffing in any Cold War crisis, it had not yet followed through on any compellent threat either, particularly against an opponent as fearsome as the Soviet Union. The preponderant power theory predicts that the threat would fail because the United States did not enjoy a clear and obvious advantage in relative power over the Soviet Union. Finally, because the United States' demands in the crisis were relatively moderate, the expansive demands theory yields no prediction about the Soviet Union's response. Table 3.3 summarizes the four theories' predictions.

Table 3.3. Predictions, Cuban Missile Crisis

Theory	USSR's Predicted Response	Strength of Prediction
Costly compellence	Concede	Strong
Reputation	Resist	Weak
Preponderant power	Resist	Moderate
Expansive demands	Indeterminate	n/a

The Outcome: Missiles on Cuba

On the morning of Sunday, October 28, the day after Robert Kennedy delivered his brother's letter and the United States' ultimatum, Khrushchev sent a message to the president. In it Khrushchev announced that "in addition to earlier instructions on the discontinuation of further work on weapons construction sites, [the Soviet government] has given a new order to dismantle the arms which you described as offensive, and to crate and return them to the Soviet Union." He reminded the president of his pledge not to attack Cuba and consented to monitoring by UN representatives to verify the removal of the missiles.[72] The United States achieved its objectives without having to execute its threat to invade Cuba. Had the invasion been launched, Soviet forces might have employed the tactical nuclear weapons at their disposal, and an all-out nuclear exchange might have ensued.

The question, then, is why Khrushchev chose to concede to the United States' demands. Although Khrushchev's letter agreeing to remove the missiles arrived on Sunday the 28th, the day after Robert Kennedy communicated the ultimatum to the Soviet ambassador, this does not mean that the ultimatum was necessarily responsible for his concession.[73] As noted earlier in this chapter, Khrushchev considered President Kennedy's speech on October 22 announcing the quarantine to be an ultimatum, although it meets only the definition of a vague threat. Nonetheless, it is clear that in combination with the quarantine itself, President Kennedy delivered a compellent threat to the Soviet premier and that he understood it as such. The Soviet embassy in Washington also took the announcement of the quarantine seriously: In the hours after the speech, its staff destroyed sensitive materials and made preparations for war.[74]

It is also clear that the Soviet Union characterized the US decision to implement the quarantine as dangerous and aggressive. In a letter to the British philosopher Bertrand Russell on the 25th, Khrushchev assured him that the Soviet Union "will not take any reckless decisions. . . . We are fully aware of the fact that if this war is unleashed, from the very first hour it will become a thermonuclear and world war."[75] He recognized that the situation was extremely dangerous, and this seems to have been a powerful motivator in the decision to concede to the United States' demands. In deliberations at the Kremlin that same day, Khrushchev asserted that he needed to act to prevent the situation from "spiral[ing] out of control."[76] According to Fursenko and Naftali's account, at this point Khrushchev "came to admit the terror that he and the others had felt since Kennedy's October 22 speech."[77] As a result of that speech, the Soviets were terrified that they could find themselves in a nuclear war if they did not agree to resolve the crisis. In other words, the Soviet leadership understood the quarantine and the announcement thereof as a compellent threat and recognized the high level of danger that the United States had introduced to the crisis.

We now know that the Soviet premier's decision to remove the missiles from Cuba preceded the delivery of the final ultimatum on the 27th. Fursenko and Naftali assert that Khrushchev had decided to reverse course as early as October 25: "Khrushchev was now convinced that the Soviet Union could not keep ballistic missiles in Cuba without going to war."[78] The Soviet leader hoped, however, to extract something from the Americans in exchange for this concession. Fursenko and Naftali also assert that Khrushchev was probably unaware that SAC had been put on nuclear alert the previous day. They argue instead that Khrushchev's sense that the Soviet Union could not win a war in the Caribbean contributed to his decision to concede.[79] This consideration would not have mattered if the Soviet premier did not believe that the United States was prepared to use force to remove the missiles. It is interesting to note, however, that Khrushchev assured his advisers as late as October 27 that he did not believe that an American attack on the island was imminent, despite intelligence reports to the contrary. As time passed without an attack, he became increasingly confident that Kennedy had reined in the hawks in his own administration and would not risk an invasion.[80] Still, he noted in meetings on Saturday that "there was no guarantee" that the United States would not attack.[81] Having already sent one message indicating that the Soviet Union would agree to remove the missiles in exchange for a noninvasion pledge (the message that the Kennedy administration received on Friday, the 26th), Khrushchev now focused on the Jupiter missiles in Turkey as a way to seize a concession from the Americans in exchange for his own compliance.

In fact, Khrushchev was already in a meeting on Sunday morning preparing the response to Kennedy's letter from October 27 when he learned about Robert Kennedy's secret meeting with Dobrynin. Khrushchev had already decided to concede, but the additional pressure of the ultimatum seems to have convinced the Soviet leader that "there was no time to waste."[82] He proceeded with the message, agreeing to discontinue work on the missile sites, and instructed Dobrynin to inform Robert Kennedy that he expected that the Jupiter missiles would be removed from Turkey in exchange for these public concessions.[83] The ultimatum seems to have affected the timing and urgency of the Soviet leader's response but not the content.

The Logic of Khrushchev's Response

The fact that Khrushchev seems to have been motivated to concede by fear of the crisis spiraling out of control (a fear generated by the United States' threat) is not consistent with the logic of any of the alternatives to the costly compellence theory. Recall that the reputation theory weakly predicted that the threat would fail because the United States' lack of record for following through on its threat convinced the Soviet leader that the threat was a bluff. This does not seem to have been the case with the Cuban Missile Crisis. Although at times Khrushchev questioned whether Kennedy would launch an attack on Cuba, according to Fursenko and Naftali these doubts did not arise from a belief that Kennedy had a reputation for inaction. Indeed, Khrushchev decided to install missiles on Cuba after the failed Bay of Pigs Invasion and after recent deployments of US troops to Southeast Asia.[84]

The preponderant power theory also predicts that the threat would fail, due to the United States' lack of a clear advantage in relative power. There is some evidence that knowledge of the United States' local superiority in conventional power affected Khrushchev's decision to remove the missiles. Given that Khrushchev knew that there were nuclear weapons on Cuba and the Americans did not, and given his determination to obtain the removal of the Jupiter missiles, it does not seem likely that a perception of American superiority was the driving force behind Khrushchev's decision to concede. Most important, the preponderant power theory predicted that the threat would *fail* to obtain concessions from the Soviets. Finally, the prediction of the expansive demands theory was indeterminate, but there is nothing in Khrushchev's decision to suggest that he conceded only because the demands were minor, as the logic of that theory would dictate.

Instead, Khrushchev conceded because the United States' threat effectively communicated the devastation that could follow from a failure to concede. In this sense, the logic of Khrushchev's decision is consistent with the logic of the costly compellence theory. It was the willingness to issue a compellent military threat in such a highly charged and dangerous situation—that is, the United States' willingness to put its own safety at risk to issue the threat and to enforce the quarantine—that communicated how strongly committed the United States was to obtaining its demands from the Soviet Union. The willingness to send troops to Cuba in the face of possible nuclear weapon use lent the United States' threat ultimate credibility. The ultimatum came after Khrushchev had already decided to remove the missiles from Cuba, a decision spurred by the vague threat contained in the quarantine and the announcement thereof. Clearly, Khrushchev was also concerned about the costs that his own country would suffer in the event that the United States executed its threat, but it was the perceived costliness of issuing and executing the threatened invasion of Cuba that convinced Khrushchev that the United States was committed to achieving its demands.

The 1962 Cuban Missile Crisis: Summary

During the course of the Cuban Missile Crisis, the United States issued two compellent threats, both demanding that the Soviet Union remove offensive missiles from Cuba. The first was a vague threat communicated by President Kennedy on October 22 when he announced the quarantine of Cuba, and the second was a secret ultimatum passed from Robert Kennedy to the Soviet ambassador on the evening of October 27. The costly compellence theory accurately predicts Khrushchev's decision to remove the missiles from Cuba. Both issuing and executing the United States' compellent threats in the 1962 crisis would have been very costly. Consequently, these threats were highly likely to succeed in coercing the Soviets to remove their missiles from Cuba.

The evidence on Khrushchev's decision making is also generally consistent with the mechanism proposed by the theory. None of the competing theories predict that the United States' threats were likely to succeed, nor is the evidence for why Khrushchev conceded to the United States' demands consistent with the causal logic proposed by these theories. Although this chapter was not intended to be an exhaustive or groundbreaking history of what was arguably the most dangerous crisis during the Cold War, it does demonstrate that the costly compellence theory can accurately predict a case in which the stakes were high and the target conceded.

Notes

1. See, for example, Betts, *Nuclear Blackmail*, chapter 3; George, "Cuban Missile Crisis"; Allison and Zelikow, *Essence of Decision*; and Press, *Calculating Credibility*, chapter 4.

2. Schlesinger, *Thousand Days*, 795–98.

3. Ibid., 798.

4. "Statement by President John F. Kennedy on Cuba, September 4, 1962," in Larson, *"Cuban Crisis,"* 3.

5. "Request by President Kennedy to Congress for Standby Authority to Call Up Reserves, September 7, 1962," in ibid., 6–7.

6. Schlesinger, *Thousand Days*, 799.

7. "Interview of Secretary of State Dean Rusk by John Scali of ABC News, September 29, 1962," in Larson, *"Cuban Crisis,"* 28–32.

8. Schlesinger, *Thousand Days*, 801.

9. Ibid., 801–2.

10. Kennedy, *Thirteen Days*, 28.

11. Schlesinger, *Thousand Days*, 804–5.

12. Kennedy, *Thirteen Days*, 28.

13. Schlesinger, *Thousand Days*, 803–4.

14. Kennedy, *Thirteen Days*, 28–29.

15. Schlesinger, *Thousand Days*, 803.

16. Ibid., 806–8.

17. Kennedy, *Thirteen Days*, 41, 46.

18. "Address by President Kennedy, October 22, 1962," in Larson, *"Cuban Crisis,"* 41, 44.

19. Kennedy, *Thirteen Days,* 52–63.

20. Quoted in Kennedy, *Thirteen Days*, 67.

21. Schlesinger, *Thousand Days*, 827.

22. Kennedy, *Thirteen Days*, 71.

23. "Letter from Chairman Khrushchev to President Kennedy, October 27, 1962," in Larson, *"Cuban Crisis,"* 156, 157.

24. Kennedy, *Thirteen Days*, 71–75.

25. Ibid., 77–79.

26. "Letter from President Kennedy to Chairman Khrushchev, October 27, 1962," in Larson, *"Cuban Crisis,"* 159–60.

27. Kennedy, *Thirteen Days*, 82. This conversation was evidently kept secret until April 1963, when Robert Kennedy described it during a speech in Columbia, South Carolina. See "U.S. Threat Cited." Several individuals involved in crisis deliberations were apparently also unaware of this secret ultimatum, but Kennedy described it in his memoir, which he wrote in 1967. Schlesinger's account from 1965 also mentions the meeting on the night of October 27 and the terms of the message that Kennedy conveyed to the Soviet ambassador (*Thousand Days*, 829–30). George provides a survey of sources on the ultimatum itself. See note 65 in "Cuban Missile Crisis," 140.

28. "Letter from Chairman Khrushchev to President Kennedy, October 28, 1962," in Larson, *"Cuban Crisis,"* 162.

29. See the appendix for a complete description of the criteria used to code threat types.

30. "Address by President Kennedy, October 22, 1962," in Larson, *"Cuban Crisis,"* 43.

31. One could argue that the establishment of the quarantine and the movement of forces into Florida were also intended to deter additional Soviet missile installations.

32. Quoted in Fursenko and Naftali, *Khrushchev's Cold War*, 474.

33. The data set records the threat type for the Cuban Missile Crisis as an "ultimatum" because the coding rules dictate that I employ the last threat issued in the crisis to evaluate the case.

34. Kennedy, *Thirteen Days*, 43. According to Schlesinger, the Pentagon anticipated forty to fifty thousand US casualties in the event of an invasion

(*Thousand Days*, 831). Regardless of whether the actual estimate was twenty-five thousand or fifty thousand, it is clear that the decision makers anticipated that the invasion would cause a significant number of US casualties.

35. "Soviet Request for Convening the U.N. Security Council and Statement by the Soviet Government, October 23, 1962," in Larson, *"Cuban Crisis,"* 50.

36. "Resolution Adopted by OAS, October 23, 1962," in ibid., 64–66.

37. Kennedy, *Thirteen Days*, 40–41.

38. Ibid., 57–59.

39. See Larson, *"Cuban Crisis,"* for communications with U Thant and statements by the American and Soviet ambassadors.

40. President Kennedy did claim in the public and private statements quoted in this chapter that the Soviet installations on Cuba threatened world stability, but he did not claim to be acting as an agent of any alliance.

41. It is clear, however, that President Kennedy and his brother were concerned about killing innocent Cuban civilians in the event of an attack on the island. See Kennedy, *Thirteen Days*, 29.

42. Freedman, *Evolution of Nuclear Strategy*, 225.

43. Betts, *Nuclear Blackmail*, 102–3.

44. Ibid., 98.

45. There were, however, additional confrontations after this date between US and Soviet tanks at Checkpoint Charlie. We now know that the Soviets considered American behavior during this standoff deliberately provocative. Decision makers in Washington were apparently unaware of the extent of American actions on the ground during this standoff. See Garthoff, "Berlin 1961."

46. Betts, *Nuclear Blackmail*, 99.

47. Ibid., 102.

48. Ibid., 105–6.

49. Institute for Strategic Studies (ISS), *Communist Bloc*, 26–28. This work was published in the fall of 1962 and therefore provides an estimate of what was publicly known at the time of the crisis.

50. Garthoff, *Intelligence Assessment and Policymaking*, 32. McGeorge Bundy notes that Garthoff's memo had little impact on the thinking of most of the major decision makers involved in the deliberations over how to respond to the missiles in Cuba, with the exception of Paul Nitze and the Joint Chiefs of Staff. Bundy argues that most of the decision makers did not feel that the installation radically altered the strategic balance and that this consideration was irrelevant given President Kennedy's assessment that the missiles could not be tolerated due to the "political damage" they would cause the United States. See Bundy, *Danger and Survival*, 451–52.

51. In addition, we now know that the estimate of seventy-five Soviet ICBMs

was too high. In 1962, the Soviets had "forty-four operational launchers, plus six test and training launchers." The installations in Cuba would have increased Soviet first-strike capability by 80 percent, not the 40 percent that Garthoff asserted in his 1962 memo. See Garthoff, *Intelligence Assessment and Policymaking*, 29.

52. ISS, *Communist Bloc*, 6, 19, 26–28.

53. Ibid., 3.

54. Ibid., 19.

55. Ibid., 9.

56. Ibid., 11.

57. Quoted in Fursenko and Naftali, *Khrushchev's Cold War*, 435.

58. Ibid.

59. "Excerpts from Off-the-Record Meeting on Cuba, October 16, 1962, 6:30–7:55 PM," in "Documentation: White House Tapes," 184. Garthoff's estimate, described earlier in this chapter, also seems to disagree with McNamara's assessment. See Garthoff, *Intelligence Assessment and Policymaking*, 32–33.

60. Fursenko and Naftali, *Khrushchev's Cold War*, 436, 455–59.

61. "Excerpts from Off-the-Record Meeting on Cuba, October 16, 1962, 11:50 AM–12:57 PM," in "Documentation: White House Tapes," 178.

62. "Excerpts from Off-the-Record Meeting on Cuba, October 16, 1962, 6:30–7:55 PM," in ibid., 185.

63. Kennedy, *Thirteen Days*, 46–47.

64. McNamara, "Reflections on War," 130.

65. Fursenko and Naftali, *Khrushchev's Cold War*, 469.

66. Schlesinger, *Thousand Days*, 831, 841.

67. "Soviet Request for Convening the U.N. Security Council and Statement by the Soviet Government, October 23, 1962," in Larson, *"Cuban Crisis,"* 53–54.

68. The irony, of course, is that it was an outside power—the Soviet Union—that had placed the missiles there in the first place.

69. "Excerpt from Statement by Soviet Ambassador Valerian A. Zorin to U.N. Security Council, October 23, 1962," in Larson, *"Cuban Crisis,"* 91.

70. Quoted in Fursenko and Naftali, *Khrushchev's Cold War*, 483. The authors assert that Khrushchev was not entirely convinced of this.

71. Quoted in ibid., 484.

72. "Letter from Chairman Khrushchev to President Kennedy, October 28, 1962," in Larson, *"Cuban Crisis,"* 161–62, 163.

73. We will see later in this chapter that the evidence suggests that Khrushchev had decided to remove the missiles as early as the 25th. Bundy's account of the crisis suggests that the Soviets made overtures about a peaceful settlement as early as Friday, the 26th. See Bundy, *Danger and Survival*, 405–7.

74. Fursenko and Naftali, *"One Hell of a Gamble,"* 247–49.

75. "Letter from Chairman Khrushchev to Lord Bertrand Russell, October 25, 1962," in Larson, *"Cuban Crisis,"* 125–26.

76. Fursenko and Naftali, *Khrushchev's Cold War,* 483.

77. Ibid., 484.

78. Fursenko and Naftali, *"One Hell of a Gamble,"* 259.

79. Ibid., 260.

80. Ibid., 273–74.

81. Quoted in Fursenko and Naftali, *"One Hell of a Gamble,"* 274.

82. Ibid., 285. Interestingly, Dobrynin was careful to stress that Robert Kennedy's communication had constituted "a request . . . not an ultimatum" (quoted on p. 285). Dobrynin conveyed the United States' demand, the likelihood of an invasion in the event of noncompliance, and the deadline for the Soviet decision. Although he did not label it as such, it is clear that Dobrynin understood and communicated to Khrushchev all the key points of an ultimatum. We can imagine that there would have been strong incentives not to explicitly characterize Robert Kennedy's communication in such a way, given that the Soviet premier had already decided to concede.

83. Ibid., 285–86.

84. Fursenko and Naftali, *Khrushchev's Cold War,* 431–44.

Chapter 4
The 2011 Libya Crisis

In early 2011, a rebellion broke out in Libya against longtime leader Muammar Qaddafi. Amid reports of escalating violence, on March 18, 2011, President Obama issued a statement demanding that the regime halt its advance on the rebel-held city of Benghazi and threatening military action. When Qaddafi resisted, the United States and its allies implemented a no-fly zone over Libya. Although the rebel forces on the ground eventually captured Qaddafi, the United States' compellent threat failed: Despite facing a coalition of the world's strongest military powers, the Libyan leader was defeated only through the use of brute force and only by indigenous ground forces.

This case is too recent to be counted by the International Crisis Behavior Project list of international crises, which stops in 2007, and thus it does not appear in the data set on US compellent threats presented in the second chapter. The United States' threat against Libya in early 2011 is, however, a perfect example of the phenomenon under investigation in this study. The costly compellence theory strongly predicts that Qaddafi would resist the United States' demands in March 2011. The use of force was so cheap for the United States, and the risks associated with issuing and executing the threat so low, that the threat lacked ultimate credibility. This case is thus very different from the Cuban Missile Crisis, in which issuing and executing the United States' compellent threat was so dangerous that the costly compellence theory strongly predicted that the Soviet Union would concede.

There is even less information available about Qaddafi's decision making than there is about Khrushchev's during the Cuban Missile Crisis. I draw on the public statements that Qaddafi made prior to and during the crisis, in addition to statements made by individuals with whom he associated in the months prior to his death, to evaluate whether the logic of Qaddafi's decision is consistent with that described by the costly compellence theory or by the other theories

123

under investigation. From what we know, Qaddafi resisted not because he doubted the United States' ability or willingness to use force against him, or because the United States' demands were too great, but because he believed he could outlast a coercer that lacked the will to muscle him into compliance after the limited use of force failed.

Likely to Resist: The 2011 Threat against Qaddafi

On March 17, 2011, the UN Security Council issued a resolution authorizing the use of force to halt violence against Libyan civilians rebelling against Qaddafi's rule. The next day, President Obama issued a public statement in which he condemned the Qaddafi regime and threatened military action if the United States' demands were not met:

> Now, once more, Moammar Qaddafi has a choice. The [UN] resolution that passed lays out very clear conditions that must be met. The United States, the United Kingdom, France, and Arab states agree that a cease-fire must be implemented immediately. That means all attacks against civilians must stop. Qaddafi must stop his troops from advancing on Benghazi, pull them back from Ajdabiya, Misrata, and Zawiya, and establish water, electricity and gas supplies to all areas. . . . These terms are not subject to negotiation. If Qaddafi does not comply with the resolution, the international community will impose consequences, and the resolution will be enforced through military action.[1]

In this statement, Obama demanded that Qaddafi halt the advance on rebel-held Benghazi. He also asserted that the United States would "provide the unique capabilities that we can bring to bear to stop the violence against civilians, including enabling our European allies and Arab partners to effectively enforce a no fly zone."[2] Finally, Obama described what the United States would *not* undertake in its campaign against Qaddafi: "I also want to be clear about what we will not be doing. The United States is not going to deploy ground troops into Libya."[3] The United States would limit its involvement to the enforcement of a no-fly zone in partnership with its allies.

Obama's threat against Qaddafi in March 2011 meets all of the terms of an open-ended compellent military threat. The president made a clear demand of the Libyan leader—a halt in the advance on Benghazi—and promised that the United States and its allies would implement a no-fly zone over Libya if he chose not to comply. Obama's threat did not, however, specify a deadline for compliance, and thus it does not meet the terms of a classic ultimatum.[4]

2011 Threat against Libya: Contextual Variables

In 2011, the United States remained the world's sole superpower. Because there was no other power capable of checking the United States' behavior or capable of damaging its interests elsewhere in the event that the crisis escalated, it would not be very risky for the United States to issue a threat against Libya in early 2011. In other words, it would be relatively cheap for the United States to issue the threat against Qaddafi.

The United States' military model also suggests that the use of force against Qaddafi would be relatively cheap. The United States ended the draft in 1973 and has since relied on an all-volunteer force. Although Obama promised that the United States would not be sending ground troops into Libya, the individuals responsible for enforcing the no-fly zone would be volunteers, not conscripts that had been compelled to serve. Obama did not explicitly threaten Qaddafi with an army of contractors, but the United States was relying heavily on private military contractors in 2011 to prosecute its wars.[5] Without the ability to employ these contractors in Iraq and Afghanistan, the United States might have been unable to threaten and execute military action against Qaddafi in the spring of 2011, at a time when the AVF clearly lacked the manpower to meet all of the United States' overseas commitments.

Although the campaigns in Iraq and Afghanistan had temporarily shifted the US military's focus onto counterinsurgency operations, the Obama administration was not eager to abandon the technology-heavy, RMA-based model of warfare that dominated American war-fighting before 2001. For example, the use of drone strikes in Pakistan accelerated dramatically during the first Obama administration.[6] Most important, the actual threat against Qaddafi promised an air campaign to implement a no-fly zone over Libya, in keeping with the RMA's emphasis on technology over costly manpower. All of the contextual variables suggest that issuing and executing the threat

Table 4.1. Contextual Variables, 2011 Libya Crisis

Contextual Variables		Effect on US Military Action
Polarity:	Unipolar	Less costly
Conscription?	No	Less costly
Contractors?	Yes	Less costly
RMA?	Yes	Less costly

against Qaddafi would not be very costly for the United States. Table 4.1 summarizes the contextual variables and indicates how each variable affects the costliness of threatening and executing military action against Libya in 2011.

Threat-Specific Variables

Obama's threat against Qaddafi specifically mentions many of the variables of interest to the costly compellence theory. As noted above, the president promised not to send ground troops to Libya. The United States would be enforcing the no-fly zone exclusively from the air. In contrast to the 2001 invasion of Afghanistan, in which the United States assumed the bulk of responsibility for the actual attack, the 2011 intervention against Libya would be spearheaded by the United States' allies. As Obama stated, "American leadership is essential, but that does not mean acting alone—it means shaping the conditions for the international community to act together."[7] Dispersing the costs of coercing Libya among the United States' allies was particularly attractive in spring 2011, when the unipole was already embroiled in two other major military operations. Although Obama's threat did not indicate how the United States would pay for the campaign against Libya (beyond relying on its allies), there were no subsequent proposals to levy a "Libya tax" to cover the operating costs for US forces.

The extent to which the target state would be vulnerable to politically costly collateral damage is the final independent variable of interest. The explicit goal of the threatened intervention was to protect Libyan civilians: "Left unchecked, we have every reason to believe that Qaddafi would commit atrocities against his people. Many thousands could die. A humanitarian crisis would ensue. . . . Our focus has been clear: protecting innocent civilians within Libya, and holding the Qaddafi regime accountable."[8] Libyan civilians might be somewhat vulnerable to air strikes undertaken to enforce the no-fly zone, but they were explicitly excluded from targeting by the conditions of the United States' threat. In terms of civilian casualties, the United States' costs for intervening in Libya in spring 2011 would be low. Table 4.2 summarizes the characteristics of the 2011 threat against Libya and indicates whether each variable makes the use of force more or less costly for the United States.

Both the contextual variables and the conditions associated with the threat itself suggest that issuing and executing the threat against Libya would be relatively cheap for the United States. The unipole's military was composed entirely of volunteers, and the no-fly zone would be enforced exclusively from the air, allowing the United States to exploit its advantages in high-tech warfare and to minimize its own casualties. Furthermore, the United States was threatening action on behalf of a coalition that would share the costs of enforcing UN Security Council Resolution 1973 and was shying away from a strong leadership role in an operation designed to protect Libyan civilians. Because the threat against Libya in March 2011 was so cheap for the United States, the costly compellence theory strongly predicts that the target would resist the United States' demands.

2011 Libya Crisis: Alternative Theories

Reputation Theory

The reputation theory asserts that a compellent threat's effectiveness depends on the threatener's willingness to follow through on past threats. The data set on US compellent threats presented in the second chapter demonstrates that the United States has followed

Table 4.2. Threat Variables, 2011 Libya Crisis

Threat Variables		Effect on US Military Action
Ground invasion?	No; enforcing no-fly zone from the air	Less costly
Allies?	Yes; they would assume control of operation	Less costly
Payment	No tax increases; allies bearing brunt of the burden	Less costly
Civilian vulnerability	Intervention explicitly undertaken to protect Libyan civilians	Less costly

through on its explicit threats in all cases in which the target resisted US demands. This suggests, according to the reputation theory, that the United States' threat would be highly effective in coercing the Libyan regime. The United States had also demonstrated a willingness to execute military action against Libya over several decades of contentious relations. In 1986, the United States launched a bombing raid that failed to kill Qaddafi and failed to deter his sponsorship of the Lockerbie bombing. When it invaded Iraq in 2003, the United States had also demonstrated that it was willing to overthrow a dictator who resisted in the face of a US compellent threat.[9] Because the United States had consistently demonstrated a willingness to follow through on its compellent threats, the strictest variant of the reputation theory—that credibility today depends on the willingness to follow through on yesterday's threats—strongly predicts that the target would concede to the United States' demands.

The more relaxed variant of the reputation theory holds that credibility is a function of a state's reputation for upholding its commitments in general, and it also suggests that Qaddafi was likely to concede to the United States' demands. The interconnectedness of the Berlin Crisis and the Cuban Missile Crisis presented an obvious point of reference for the United States' reputation in 1962. There does not seem to be a similar link between the 2011 Libya Crisis and any other event. The United States had not become involved in any of the other uprisings during the 2011 Arab Spring, but it had not committed itself to doing so. In early 2011, the United States was still involved in the wars in Iraq and Afghanistan and had been waging a drone campaign against al-Qaeda leaders in Pakistan and Yemen. There was no obvious or stated connection, however, between these commitments and the 2011 Libya Crisis. In other words, the United States had demonstrated a willingness to execute its post–Cold War compellent threats and had not failed to follow through on any related commitments. The reputation theory strongly predicts that Qaddafi would yield to the United States' threat in March 2011.

Preponderant Power

The preponderant power theory suggests that a large and recognized imbalance in relative power favoring the coercer should convince the target of a threat to yield to the coercer's demands. Because of Libya's relative weakness in the 2011 crisis, the theory strongly predicts that Qaddafi would yield to the United States' threat. The World Bank records a GDP of $62.4 billion for Libya in 2009, the last year for which data are available.[10] According to the International Institute for Strategic Studies (IISS), Libya spent $1.7 billion on defense that year. This figure amounted to 2.84 percent of Libya's GDP and spending of $266 per capita.[11] Libya's population was estimated at 6.5 million in 2011. The IISS estimates that Libya had seventy-six thousand personnel in the active armed forces in 2011, with forty thousand in reserve. The army comprised fifty thousand of these soldiers, half of which were conscripts.[12] These figures do not include foreign mercenaries, of which the number in Libya in early 2011 is unknown. About ten thousand troops were believed to be concentrated in the elite brigades drawn from tribes loyal to Qaddafi. Libya had amassed an impressive amount of military hardware after Qaddafi seized power in 1969.[13] This Soviet equipment was, however, largely obsolete and "unusable for lack of parts, skilled technicians, and maintenance" by the spring of 2011.[14]

Libya's air defenses were a key factor for the United States and its allies in planning and implementing the no-fly zone. A report by the US Congressional Research Service noted that "Libya's air defense system relie[d] on Soviet and Russian systems, most 20–30 years old and at least two generations behind current technology." Although Libya possessed 180 fighter and attack aircraft and 100 helicopters, most were believed inoperable or antiquated, and Libyan pilots were poorly trained. Because Libya's air defenses were concentrated along the Mediterranean coast, carrier-based forces could be used to enforce the no-fly zone.[15] Finally, Libya had given up its program to develop nuclear weapons in 2003.

Even if we exclude the NATO allies from our analysis, there is a clear imbalance of power favoring the United States. The United States recorded a GDP of $14.04 trillion in 2009, the last year before the intervention for which data are also available on Libya's economy.[16] The United States spent $661 billion on defense that year, a figure that amounted to 4.68 percent of US GDP and spending of more than $2,100 per capita. US defense spending amounted to nearly half of total global defense spending in 2009.[17] In 2011, the United States had 1.564 million in the active armed forces and 871,000 reservists, out of a total population of 318 million.[18] These figures exclude the private military contractors employed by the United States in Iraq and Afghanistan. In early 2011, the Libyan military fielded mostly rundown, Soviet-era equipment. By contrast, the US military boasted eleven aircraft carriers, seventy-one submarines, and thousands of aircraft and tanks.[19] The US military was also widely acknowledged as the most proficient and technologically advanced conventional force in the world.

When it issued a threat against Libya's leader in 2011, the United States did so from a position of overwhelming strength. Although many of the United States' troops were tied down in Iraq and Afghanistan in the spring of 2011, the threat against Libya explicitly excluded the use of US ground troops. Attacking Qaddafi's forces from the air would allow the United States and its allies to capitalize on their superiority in technology over Qaddafi's outdated defenses. The preponderant power theory strongly predicts that Qaddafi would concede to the United States' threat before the application of force.

Expansive Demands

The expansive demands theory predicts that the threat against Qaddafi would succeed if the United States' demands were limited and fail if the demands were too extensive. The demand specified by Obama's threat was clear: a halt in the advance on rebel-held Benghazi. How do we rank this demand in terms of severity? First, it is clear that the United States was not seeking trivial concessions. Qaddafi was acting to quash a rebellion that he likely believed threatened his tenure as leader of Libya, and the demand to halt the advance likely would have been viewed as a demand to stop fighting the rebellion. Qaddafi had seized power in a coup in 1969, and there would have been no reason for him to expect that he could have negotiated a peaceful political transition with the rebels if he had agreed to lay down his arms.[20]

On the other hand, Obama's threat did not contain an explicit demand for regime change, and the United States was not threatening an invasion to effect one in the event that Qaddafi chose to resist. In

fact, the United States had been sending a number of mixed messages in the weeks leading up to the threat. In early March, Secretary
of Defense Robert Gates asserted that imposing a no-fly zone over
Libya would be "a big operation in a big country." He was responding to critics from both the left and the right urging the president
to take a harder line against the Libyan dictatorship. At the time, an
administration official explicitly backed away from a call for regime
change, arguing that Obama viewed the uprisings of the Arab Spring
and any changes they might cause as "organic to the region," rather
than requiring a US-imposed solution.[21]

Although the United States had implemented some economic
sanctions and called for Qaddafi to resign, in the weeks leading up to
Obama's final threat there was little consensus in the administration
on the preferred outcome of the crisis.[22] Furthermore, the Obama
administration was very deliberately restrained in its response to the
uprisings that were erupting in several other countries. At the same
time that international attention was focused on the potential plight
of civilians in Benghazi, protesters were being mowed down in the
streets in Yemen and Bahrain, and the Obama administration (and
its European allies) deliberately refrained from calling for regime
change or threatening an attack against those countries.[23]

In addition, the United States' 1986 raid had failed to dislodge the
Libyan leader, and thus he may have doubted that the United States
was implicitly demanding and willing to facilitate regime change. In
fact, the very unwillingness of the United States to send in ground
troops, as outlined in President Obama's threat, may have encouraged Qaddafi to believe at the time of the threat that the United
States would have been satisfied with an outcome short of regime
change.[24]

Given both the history of abandoned regime-change attempts and
the inconsistencies emanating from the Obama administration, we
should not assume that Qaddafi understood Obama's speech as a
veiled threat of regime change. Had the administration been calling
for Qaddafi's overthrow in the early days of the crisis, then it would
be reasonable to assume that he read Obama's demands as an implicit
demand that he relinquish control of the country. As we will see later
in this chapter, Qaddafi may have had good reason to believe that
the United States lacked the will to prosecute a campaign necessary

to unseat him, but this does not bear directly on the logic of the expansive demands theory. The United States' demand for a halt in the advance on Benghazi falls somewhere between the demand for the removal of missiles from Cuba and regime change. Although we should not assume that Qaddafi believed the United States was demanding an end to his tenure as ruler of Libya, the United States was still demanding substantial concessions. For this reason, the expansive demands theory predicts with moderate strength that the Libyan leader would resist the United States' demands in March 2011.

Four Predictions, One Threat against Libya

The costly compellence theory strongly predicts that the Libyan dictator would resist the United States' threat in March 2011. All the independent variables of interest indicate that issuing and executing a compellent military threat against Libya would be a low-cost undertaking for the United States. Because of the United States' record of following through on its compellent threats, the reputation theory predicts that the target would yield to US demands before the actual application of force. The United States' relative power vastly exceeded Libya's in the spring of 2011, and thus the preponderant power theory also predicts that Qaddafi was likely to concede to the United States' demands. Finally, the expansive demands theory predicts with moderate strength that Qaddafi would resist. Table 4.3 summarizes the theories' predictions.

The 2011 Threat against Libya: Outcome

On March 17, 2011, the UN Security Council passed Resolution 1973, which demanded an immediate cease-fire in Libya. The resolution expressed great concern for the risks to Libyan civilians from the escalating violence and from attacks threatened by forces loyal to Qaddafi. The resolution authorized the freezing of Libyan assets and an arms embargo. Most important, Resolution 1973 authorized member states "to take all necessary measures" to enforce a no-fly zone over Libya.[25] The same day, Qaddafi warned that loyalist forces were moving toward the rebel stronghold of Benghazi and that those who resisted his forces would be shown "no mercy."[26]

Table 4.3. Predictions, 2011 Libya Crisis

Theory	Libya's Predicted Response	Strength of Prediction
Costly compellence	Resist	Strong
Reputation	Concede	Strong
Preponderant power	Concede	Strong
Expansive demands	Resist	Moderate

The following day, Libyan foreign minister Moussa Koussa announced an immediate cease-fire. Reports from inside Libya indicated, however, that loyalist forces continued to advance on Benghazi and to shell the city.[27] The same day, Obama issued his speech threatening Qaddafi with a no-fly zone and demanding a halt in the advance. The *New York Times* reported on March 19 that witnesses claimed government tanks had rolled into Benghazi after a heavy artillery barrage.[28] There was no evidence that the announced cease-fire was being upheld or that the loyalist forces had stopped their advance—that is, there was no evidence that Qaddafi had conceded to the United States' demands. That same day, a Libyan government spokesman quoted a letter to France, Britain, and the UN in which Qaddafi warned that an intervention in Libya would be "clear aggression." In a separate letter to the United States, Qaddafi asserted that Libyans were "prepared to die" for their country in the event of a military attack.[29]

Operation Odyssey Dawn began on Saturday, March 19, with strikes by French warplanes intended to prevent loyalist forces from attacking Benghazi. These strikes were not coordinated with France's partners, and they caused considerable friction at the meeting of NATO allies in Paris that morning. The main assault, which consisted of missile strikes, began at around two o'clock in the afternoon, Washington time. The US Navy fired several rounds of Tomahawk missiles to knock out missile, radar, and communication facilities around Tripoli, Misurata, and Syrte. At the outset of the campaign, US officials stressed that the mission was under British and French leadership. The United States would limit its participation and would transfer command to one of its European allies within days.[30] On the morning after the launch of Odyssey Dawn, Adm. Mike Mullen, the chairman of the Joint Chiefs of Staff, declared that a no-fly zone was "effectively" in place and that the advance on Benghazi had been stopped.[31]

Qaddafi's Response

Qaddafi remained defiant even as the first missiles rained down on his country. Had he resisted because he doubted the will of the United States to use force, then we would have expected Qaddafi to back down shortly after the initiation of military action—that is, shortly after the United States demonstrated the willingness to execute its threat. Instead, Qaddafi continued to resist demands for a cease-fire and issued bold statements of defiance. Speaking via telephone to state television on Sunday morning, the day after the launch of Odyssey Dawn, Qaddafi promised a "long war" of resistance to Western attack. He announced that he was making weapons available to the Libyan population. The leader promised, "We will not leave our land and we will liberate it. . . . Those who are on the land will win the battle."[32] The latter point contrasts with the coalition's decision not to employ ground troops and to attack Libya exclusively from the air. It suggests that Qaddafi viewed the refusal to send troops as a sign that the United States was not committed to its objectives.

On Monday, March 28, more than a week after the establishment of the no-fly zone, Qaddafi issued a statement in which he denied that Libya was undergoing an internal "crisis of any kind," and he compared Libya's government to the Athenian democracy. He blamed the upheaval on "elements of al-Qaeda [that had] infiltrated . . . [and] attacked . . . military compounds and police stations with the aim of getting arms." Qaddafi then argued that the NATO allies were "supporting and backing . . . al-Qaeda through air cover and missile cover to enable it to control north Africa, thus becomes [sic] a second Afghanistan." He then claimed that "hundreds" of Libyans were being killed by the "brutal unjust aggression" perpetrated by the United States and its allies.[33]

In other words, Qaddafi resisted the United States' compellent threat, and he continued to resist after NATO launched the operation against him. In fact, Qaddafi would continue to defy the demands of the international community and of the Libyan rebels until he was tracked down and killed in October 2011. The costly compellence theory correctly predicts Qaddafi's resistance. Qaddafi's refusal to comply with US demands is also consistent with the expansive demands theory, but it is inconsistent with the predictions generated by the reputation and the preponderant power theories.

Although Qaddafi's resistance fits with the predictions of both the costly compellence and expansive demands theories, we cannot evaluate the relative explanatory power of these theories without considering the available evidence on why Qaddafi decided to resist. Since we cannot interview the late Libyan leader, let us consider public statements Qaddafi made before and during the intervention and statements imputed to him by his associates. As noted above, Qaddafi's immediate reaction to the intervention was to assert that he and his people would fight a long campaign on the ground to prevail over the foreign aggressors. This is consistent with the causal mechanism proposed by the costly compellence theory, which asserts that the target of a US threat resists not because it doubts the threat's immediate credibility, but because it believes that it can outlast a coercer that lacks the motivation to apply sufficient force to achieve a brute force victory after coercion fails. Many other elements of Qaddafi's behavior and his statements following the intervention are also consistent with the argument that the cheapness of the United States' threat convinced the Libyan leader that he could outlast the unipole.

Civilian Casualties

The costly compellence theory asserts that compellent threats that do not target civilians or that explicitly exclude civilians from attack are less costly to implement than threats that do target civilians, and hence such threats are less effective in inducing target-state compliance. The issue of civilian casualties figured prominently in the framing of the crisis by both the Obama administration and the Libyan regime. Qaddafi's media strategy suggested a belief that highlighting casualties caused by NATO air strikes would increase the costs of the operation and enable him to outlast his coercers.

At the start of Operation Odyssey Dawn, Qaddafi claimed that the foreign air strikes were inflicting a large number of casualties on Libyan civilians, even as witnesses reported that Qaddafi's forces were continuing to bomb rebel-held cities. In response to reports of casualties resulting from the no-fly zone, Secretary of Defense Robert Gates claimed that "it's perfectly evident that the vast majority—if not nearly all—of civilian casualties have been inflicted by Gaddafi. . . . We've been very careful about this. It's almost as though some people here are taking at face value Gaddafi's claims about the number of civilian casualties, which as far as I'm concerned are just outright lies."[34] This statement suggests that the Obama administration was very aware of the political costs of inflicting casualties on Libyan civilians. If the United States did not care about these casualties, or if they were not politically costly, then Secretary Gates would not have responded to accusations about collateral damage inflicted by the bombing. Instead, he felt it necessary to reassure both domestic and international observers that the United States and its allies were taking pains to minimize risks to civilians.

It is also clear that Qaddafi was aware of the role of civilian casualties in undermining support for the no-fly zone. The first report of a Libyan civilian death deemed credible by the Western media came ten days after the launch of Operation Odyssey Dawn. A NATO air strike hit an ammunition depot, and the explosion sent a tank shell into the bedroom of a nearby home, killing an eighteen-month-old child. Qaddafi had been claiming throughout the operation that the no-fly zone was inflicting heavy civilian casualties. Upon learning of the baby's death, the Libyan government press office transported journalists seventy miles outside Tripoli to observe the damaged house and the child's grave.[35]

Qaddafi's efforts to publicize the baby's death suggest that he was very aware that heavy civilian casualties could undermine support for NATO's intervention. In fact, representatives from both Russia and China expressed concerns about the level of casualties inflicted by the no-fly zone.[36] If it were not costly for the architects of Operation Odyssey Dawn to inflict such casualties, then Qaddafi would have had no reason to emphasize them or to fabricate reports about deaths caused by the air strikes. In fact, his behavior suggests that Qaddafi hoped to erode the motivation of the coalition aligned against him by raising the political costs of the air campaign, consistent with the logic of costly compellence.

Strains within the NATO Alliance

NATO assumed sole command of air operations over Libya twelve days after the start of Operation Odyssey Dawn, on March 31. NATO would now be responsible for Operation Unified Protector, which included the maintenance of "the arms embargo, no-fly zone and actions to protect civilians and civilian centres."[37] The US Department of Defense announcement of the transfer of power asserted that the operation would focus on protecting civilians. The chairman of the NATO military committee, Adm. Giampaolo Di Paola, stressed that "NATO is not engaged in Libya to decide the future of the Libyan people. . . . That is up to Libyans themselves. We are helping enforce the will of the international community to protect them from attacks so that they can start shaping and deciding of [*sic*] their future."[38] In other words, the United States avoided sending ground troops into Libya and transferred control of the Libyan intervention to its allies as quickly as possible, just as Obama had promised. This suggests that the United States viewed working with allies as a way to minimize the costs of executing its threat.[39]

As NATO air strikes against Qaddafi and his forces continued in the spring and summer of 2011, the alliance began to show signs of strain. In mid-April, shortly before NATO stepped up its attacks on regime targets, Qaddafi could be seen on state television riding through Tripoli in an open vehicle. At that time, US Secretary of State Hillary Clinton noted, "As our mission continues, maintaining our resolve and unity only grows more important. . . . Qaddafi is testing our determination."[40] Indeed, as the intervention dragged on, disagreements arose about its scope and duration. Only fourteen of NATO's twenty-eight members were actively participating in Operation Unified Protector, and only six of these were attacking targets in Libya. Britain was responsible for most of the air strikes, but leaders from both France and Britain were calling for greater contributions from their allies. Clinton asserted that the alliance had all the resources necessary to carry out its mission, but Adm. James Stavridis, the Supreme Allied Commander in Europe, argued that more sophisticated attack aircraft "were needed to strike Libyan military equipment deliberately operating in heavily populated areas."[41]

We do not have any testimony from Qaddafi on how he viewed

these disagreements within NATO. The facts that the United States had threatened to execute military action in conjunction with an alliance and had then transferred control of that action to its allies as quickly as possible likely would have contributed to Qaddafi's belief that the United States lacked the motivation to secure a costly brute-force victory. In fact, much of the evidence we have on Qaddafi's last few months suggests that he did, in fact, doubt the ultimate credibility of the United States' threat and believed that he could outlast his coercers.

Qaddafi's Final Weeks

NATO air strikes continued in the spring and summer of 2011, and the focus shifted from simply enforcing the no-fly zone to directly targeting loyalist forces and aiding rebel operations. In late April, NATO began bombing loyalist forces in and around Misurata, which had been under siege by Qaddafi's forces for months. The strikes targeted Qaddafi's artillery and tanks, and they enabled the rebels to launch a counteroffensive on April 25. After several bloody months of fighting, the rebels finally declared the Battle of Misurata over on May 15. The rebels' progress was uneven in the following months, as their momentum slowed in the east after the siege of Misurata was broken. They launched a campaign from the western mountains in early June and made steady gains before halting in early July outside Qawalish,[42] a town roughly eighty miles south of Tripoli.[43] The initial attempts to seize the town were hampered by ammunition shortages, suggesting that the lack of a formal supply network hindered the rebels' ability to attack Qaddafi's troops.

Qaddafi remained defiant in the summer of 2011, even as NATO inflicted its heaviest bombing to date on Tripoli in early June. After strikes on the Bab al-Aziziya compound, Qaddafi vowed on state television that "we [Libyans] will stay in our land dead or alive." President Obama, meanwhile, asserted that it was "just a matter of time" before Qaddafi would be ousted from power.[44] By late July, the rebels were closing in on Tripoli from the south and west. They were moving out of the Nafusa Mountains and into towns along the road to Tripoli. The rebels also gained control of roads delivering critical supplies to Qaddafi and his forces from Tunisia. By the beginning of August, after months of inconclusive fighting and the accumulation of NATO air strikes on Qaddafi and his forces, the rebels began to make rapid gains in their advance on Tripoli. By August 15, they had gained control of all the major highways leading into Tripoli and had surrounded the city. Over the next few days, the rebels consolidated their control of the area around the capital. On August 18, they gained control of the key city of Zawiyah, home to a major oil refinery.[45] On August 20, fighting erupted in the Libyan capital. Rebels surrounded the city and claimed credit for a new uprising in Tripoli. Witnesses reported frequent overflights and air strikes by NATO jets.[46] The following day, rebels surged into the capital, where they encountered only limited resistance. The rebels claimed control of the city, with the exception of Qaddafi's compound, and arrested two of the Libyan leader's sons.[47]

The Libyan rebels overran Qaddafi's Tripoli compound on August 23, but it would take another month before they quashed the remnants of Qaddafi's forces. After a two-month siege of Qaddafi's hometown of Syrte, the rebels surrounded Qaddafi and his forces, roughly a hundred men. When Qaddafi's convoy attempted to flee the city on the morning of October 20, they were spotted and attacked by an American Predator drone and French warplane. The strike did not kill Qaddafi, who escaped to a drainpipe along with a handful of supporters. Cell phone video footage shows the bleeding dictator being pulled from the drainpipe and set upon by angry rebels. The official account given by Libya's transitional council blames Qaddafi's death on wounds sustained "in a crossfire," but the injuries visible in the cell phone footage, including a gunshot wound to the head, suggest that the rebels executed the Libyan dictator.[48]

Failed Compellence: Qaddafi's Defiance

Although the rebels finally succeeded in ousting Qaddafi from power with the help of NATO air strikes, the campaign to coerce the Libyan leader was a total failure. Qaddafi never conceded willingly. The rebels and their NATO supporters achieved their objectives through brute force only after coercion failed.

Qaddafi maintained his public defiance until he met his grim demise in the desert outside of Syrte. In a statement aired by a Syrian television station on September 1, more than a week after the fall of Tripoli, Qaddafi had branded the rebel forces "traitors" and vowed to "keep fighting" until he had turned Libya "into a hell." Presumably addressing the NATO allies still launching air strikes against his forces, Qaddafi had promised that the Libyan people "cannot be brought to their knees. You cannot even pass through their soil, can you imagine ruling them?"[49] This statement seems to suggest that the unwillingness of the so-called occupiers to put boots on the ground made them unfit to prevail in the struggle for Libya's future. Qaddafi also called the NATO allies "weak," and he promised that Libyans would "stand up to them from city to city, mountain to mountain, valley to valley. It will continue to be a long battle."[50]

Qaddafi's characterization of the "occupiers" as weak and unmotivated and his continued insistence that Libyans would outlast the NATO allies are consistent with the causal logic developed in this study. The costly compellence theory asserts that the target of a cheap US compellent threat resists not because it doubts the threat's immediate credibility, but because it doubts the United States' willingness to apply decisive force in order to exact compliance after coercion fails. In a campaign of violence against his own people, Qaddafi had an incentive to characterize the struggle for Libya as a battle between loyal citizens and foreign invaders. The NATO allies were in fact providing critical air support to the rebels, but it is doubtful that the air strikes on their own would have been enough to dislodge the dictator from power.

We will probably never know exactly what Qaddafi was thinking as the rebels overran Tripoli and closed in on him in Syrte. A member of Qaddafi's forces claimed that Qaddafi was "very afraid of NATO" and more open to the idea of relinquishing power than his sons. In his final weeks, Qaddafi was apparently largely cut off from the world, without access to the internet. Despite his fiery rhetoric in statements to a Syrian television station, Qaddafi apparently took no part in the fighting.[51] In his final public statements, however, Qaddafi remained defiant and characterized the forces arrayed against him either as weak occupiers or despicable traitors who would be defeated by highly motivated Libyans.

The Logic of Qaddafi's Resistance

Qaddafi's decision to resist the United States' demands in March 2011 is consistent with the prediction of the costly compellence theory. The use of force against Libya would be so cheap for the United States that the threat lacked ultimate credibility. Qaddafi's statements and behavior during the crisis are also consistent with the causal logic proposed by costly compellence. Qaddafi did not back down after the international community launched its operation, which suggests that he did not doubt the threat's immediate credibility. Instead, Qaddafi remained defiant throughout the spring and summer of 2011, even after the fall of Tripoli in August.

Furthermore, Qaddafi's actions and statements suggest that he believed he could outlast his less-motivated opponents. At the launch of Operation Odyssey Dawn, Qaddafi promised his opponents a long war, and he characterized his NATO opponents as weak and cowardly. Throughout the conflict, Qaddafi continued to assert that his loyal subjects would fight to the death in a long war for their country. He characterized the conflict as a battle of wills between NATO allies attacking from the air and Libyans dying on the ground to protect their homeland. This characterization is consistent with the argument that Qaddafi persisted in the belief that his opponents lacked the motivation to defeat him and would abandon their objectives if they were not obtained quickly. It also suggests that the relative cheapness of the intervention—air strikes that the United States would be passing off to its allies as quickly as possible—convinced Qaddafi that the United States lacked the will to defeat him.

Qaddafi also employed the international media as a tool to try to erode the will of the United States and its allies. From the start of NATO's campaign, Qaddafi and his spokesmen vigorously claimed that the air strikes were killing innocent civilians. US government officials asserted that these claims were greatly exaggerated and that Qaddafi and his forces were responsible for Libyans' suffering. When the first death by air strike was confirmed, international journalists were hustled to the victim's grave. This is strong evidence that Qaddafi believed he could erode support for the NATO campaign by publicizing casualties inflicted by the air strikes.

Qaddafi's characterization of the conflict and his justifications for continuing to resist are inconsistent with the causal mechanisms proposed by the alternative theories under investigation. Neither the reputation theory nor the preponderant power theory predicted that Qaddafi would resist, but the Libyan leader's refusal to concede is consistent with the expansive demands theory. It is possible that the Libyan leader decided to resist because the United States' demands were too great. There is no evidence from his public statements to suggest that this was the case, but neither is there evidence indicating that the demand did *not* influence Qaddafi's decision to resist. In the absence of such evidence on either side, we cannot definitively rule out the logic of the expansive demands theory. It is clear, however, that the limited information that we do have about Qaddafi's decision suggests that he resisted not because he doubted that the United States would launch air strikes against him (a prospect he had faced and survived in the past), but because he thought that he could withstand the initial attack and then outlast the United States' motivation—the limits of which were signaled by the relative cheapness of the threatened action.

The US Model of Cheap Force

The campaign against Libya in 2011 was a perfect example of the low-cost model of US force described in the first chapter: The United States attacked a target from the air, in conjunction with its allies, and with minimal risk to US soldiers. Obama commented on Qaddafi's death at a press conference on October 20, 2011. He praised the "courageous Libyan people [who] fought for their own future," and he denounced Qaddafi's tenure as leader. Obama also stressed that "without putting a single U.S. service member on the ground, we achieved our objectives." Most important, the president hinted that the Libyan intervention would serve as a model for future US action. Obama noted the gains made in the campaign against al-Qaeda, then emphasized the "winding down" of the war in Iraq and "transition" under way in Afghanistan. He argued that "working in Libya with friends and allies, we've demonstrated what collective action can achieve in the 21st century."[52]

What Obama and other observers who hailed the mission as a triumph miss, however, is the fact that the effort to coerce Qaddafi was a complete and total failure. Despite threatening Qaddafi, the leader of a poor and weak state, with the world's most formidable military, the United States never convinced him to back down. Qaddafi's advance was halted by and he was ultimately captured by indigenous troops on the ground—that is, by forces that the United States and its European allies were explicitly unwilling to contribute. The United States secured its preferred outcome in the short term only because there were local forces willing and able to do the more dangerous and costly work of tracking down the Libyan leader.

The 2011 Libya intervention should not be held up as a model of the effective use of local forces to fight the United States' battles. The cycle of violence that persisted in Libya after Qaddafi's death,[53] the subsequent attack on the American embassy in Benghazi,[54] and the role of Libyan munitions in fueling ongoing conflicts in North Africa and Syria[55] should indicate that low-cost interventions are not likely to yield high-quality outcomes over the long term, even if brute force "succeeds" after coercion fails. Kuperman may be correct in calling the 2011 Libya intervention "an abject failure."[56] As we will discuss in the concluding chapter, however, these seemingly cheap interventions are likely to remain popular with policymakers for the foreseeable future.

Summary

In March 2011, the United States demanded that Qaddafi halt his advance on rebel-held Benghazi or face a no-fly zone enforced from the air. All the independent variables associated with the costly compellence theory indicate that issuing and executing the threat against him would be relatively low-cost: The United States was the unipole in 2011, it employed an all-volunteer force supplemented with private contractors, it had adopted many elements of the RMA thesis to substitute technology for manpower, it threatened an air campaign and explicitly excluded the use of ground troops, it threatened action in conjunction with several allies that would later assume control of the operation, and it acted to protect Libyan civilians. Consequently, the costly compellence theory predicts that the threat against Qaddafi would fail, and this is exactly what happened.

By contrast, two competing theories predict that the threat against

Qaddafi would succeed. The reputation theory predicts that the US threat would be effective because the United States had never failed to execute an explicit compellent threat in a post–World War II crisis in which a target resisted and because the United States had demonstrated a willingness to execute military action against recent targets and against Libya in past conflicts. The United States enjoyed such an overwhelming advantage over Libya in all measures of state power that the preponderant power theory strongly predicts the threat's success. Qaddafi's resistance is consistent, however, with the prediction of the expansive demands theory. The demand that Qaddafi halt his attacks on Libyan civilians and rebel forces posed a serious challenge to his rule. There is no evidence, however, to either confirm or deny the causal mechanism for threat failure proposed by this theory.

Qaddafi's statements and behavior, both before and during the intervention, are consistent in many ways with the logic of the costly compellence theory. He argued that the conflict with NATO would drag into a long war of attrition and that the Libyan people were prepared to fight on the ground to protect their country from aggressors attacking from the air. He also took great pains to highlight the civilian casualties inflicted by the no-fly zone in an effort to raise the political costs of the intervention and thereby erode the will of his coercers. Although we cannot know the exact reason why Qaddafi chose to resist the United States' threat in 2011, much of the limited evidence from Qaddafi's statements and behavior, both before and during the crisis, is consistent with the logic of costly compellence.

Notes

1. Obama, "Remarks by the President."
2. Ibid.
3. Ibid.
4. International outcry in early 2011 focused on allegations that the Qaddafi regime and its forces were indiscriminately attacking civilians. In "A Model Humanitarian Intervention?," Kuperman presents a very persuasive case that the Qaddafi regime was not slaughtering Libyan civilians indiscriminately, that there was no reason to expect a massacre if his forces had taken Benghazi, and that the NATO intervention actually prolonged the rebellion in Libya and increased the suffering of Libyan civilians. These arguments are vitally important to an assessment of whether the intervention was necessary and successful,

but they do not alter our ability to classify Obama's strategy as a compellent threat. Later in this chapter, we will see that reports from the time asserted that Qaddafi chose not to halt the advance on the city (as dictated by Obama's threat) and thus that he did not comply with the United States' demands. We can make this assessment regardless of whether Qaddafi's forces were likely to massacre civilians had they taken Benghazi in March 2011.

5. A definitive count of the number of contractors in Iraq at the height of the war is difficult to obtain. Estimates on the number of contract personnel in Iraq in 2007 ranged from 100,000 to 180,000. Singer notes that even conservative estimates put the number of contractors at or above 100 percent of the US military presence in Iraq and well above the combined contributions of all US allies. See Singer, *Corporate Warriors*, 247.

6. See Mazzetti, Schmitt, and Worth, "Two-Year Manhunt."

7. Obama, "Remarks by the President."

8. Ibid. As noted above, Kuperman presents a convincing case that Qaddafi's forces would not have inflicted such violence on the population, but this does not alter the fact that the intervention was justified and sold as a measure to protect civilians. See Kuperman, "A Model Humanitarian Intervention?"

9. In the years immediately preceding the 2011 threat, the United States had also had a rapprochement with the Libyan regime. Qaddafi renounced his programs to develop weapons of mass destruction in 2003, and in October 2008, he resolved all outstanding terrorist claims with the United States (sees "Libya Pays to End Terrorism Cases"). The United States' decision to implement sanctions against Qaddafi's regime in February 2011 and to enforce UN Security Council Resolution 1973 was a dramatic shift away from more constructive relations. The reputation theory cannot incorporate these shifts into its prediction.

10. Figures are in current US dollars, and the figure for Libya was calculated using the official exchange rate. Data are from the World Bank, "GDP (current US$)."

11. International Institute for Strategic Studies (IISS), *Military Balance 2011*, 474.

12. Ibid., 320.

13. Poggioli, "Gadhafi's Military Muscle."

14. Koring, "Libyan Military Widely Regarded."

15. Gertler et al., *No-Fly Zones*, 15–16.

16. World Bank, "GDP (current US$)."

17. IISS, *Military Balance 2011*, 477.

18. Ibid., 56.

19. For figures on US military equipment, see IISS, *Military Balance 2011*, 56–67.

20. The coup in which he seized power was not bloody, but there is no recent history of peaceful regime transition in Libya on which Qaddafi might have hoped to base a plan for succession.

21. Sanger and Shanker, "Gates Warns of Risks."

22. On the sanctions imposed on the Libyan regime in February 2011, see "US Imposes Sanctions on Libya" and "US Issues Travel Ban."

23. Bumiller and Kirkpatrick, "Obama Warns Libya."

24. Whether the Obama administration actually would have accepted a continuation of the Qaddafi regime or a less bloody power transition if he had halted the attacks in March is irrelevant. For the purposes of the expansive demands theory, what is relevant is what Qaddafi believed, or what we can infer he might have believed, about the United States' demands in March 2011.

25. United Nations Security Council (UNSC), "Resolution 1973 (2011)," 3. Interestingly, the resolution explicitly rules out a foreign occupation force.

26. Kirkpatrick and Fahim, "Qaddafi Warns of Assault."

27. "Libya Declares Ceasefire."

28. Kirkpatrick, Erlanger, and Bumiller, "Allies Open Air Assault."

29. "Gaddafi Warns West."

30. Kirkpatrick, Erlanger, and Bumiller, "Allies Open Air Assault."

31. Kirkpatrick, Erlanger and Bumiller, "Qaddafi Pledges 'Long War.'"

32. Ibid.

33. "Gaddafi Statement: Response to Coalition."

34. Sly, Wilgoren, and Whitlock, "U.S. Jet Crashes."

35. Kirkpatrick, "Libyans Offer Credible Case."

36. Neither Russia nor China was participating in the no-fly zone, but they were in a position to block future UN Security Council resolutions on the crisis.

37. "NATO Takes Command."

38. Garamone, "NATO Assumes Command."

39. The disagreements within NATO, which I describe below, also suggest that multilateralism makes the attack both less costly and less operationally effective. This suggests that unilateral coercion is more effective not only because it is more costly (and thus because the associated threat may be more likely to be perceived as ultimately credible), but also because an operation undertaken by the United States alone should be more militarily effective than the same operation undertaken by an alliance.

40. Quoted in Myers and Dempsey, "NATO Showing Strain."

41. Ibid.

42. Information on the timeline of the rebels' campaign from "Battle for Libya" and "Libya—Revolution and Aftermath (2011)."

43. Estimate derived by the author from Google Maps, available at https://maps.google.com/maps.

44. Graff, "Gaddafi Defiant as NATO Intensifies."

45. "Battle for Libya."

46. Fahim and Kirkpatrick, "Heavy Fighting Reported in Tripoli."

47. Fahim and Kirkpatrick, "Jubilant Rebels Control Much of Tripoli."

48. Anderson, "King of Kings"; Fahim, Shadid, and Gladstone, "Violent End to an Era."

49. "Muammar Gaddafi Urges Followers."

50. Ibid.

51. Fahim, "In His Last Days."

52. "Obama on Muammar Gaddafi Death."

53. A very few examples of the continuing unrest and violence in Libya: At a November 2013 demonstration against armed groups in Tripoli, twenty-seven were killed and more than two hundred wounded when gunmen opened fire on the protesters; see "Anti-Militia Protest Turns Deadly." On the assassination of Libya's deputy industry minister by gunmen in January 2014, see "Gunmen Assassinate Libya's Deputy." On the militia that had been enforcing a blockade of three oil export ports, see, "Militia Holding Libyan Port."

54. For continuing coverage of the Benghazi attack and its aftermath, see "Benghazi Attack under Microscope."

55. Nichols, "Libya Arms Fueling Conflicts."

56. Kuperman, "Obama's Libya Debacle."

Chapter 5

The 1991 Threat against Iraq

In this chapter, I evaluate the United States' failed threat against Saddam Hussein in 1991. In the following chapter, I evaluate the threats that preceded the 2003 invasion. The circumstances surrounding each case were unique. The threats were separated by more than ten years and by many other attempts to coerce the Iraqi regime. Both cases involved several attempts to coerce Saddam before the final threat and before the onset of military action. Comparing two threats that targeted the same regime does, however, give us additional leverage on the question of whether and to what extent the cheapness of the United States' threat affects a target's decision to resist.

I begin this chapter by surveying the events leading up to the 1991 Gulf War, including the United States' efforts to employ compellent threats to coerce Saddam to evacuate Kuwait. I draw on news accounts, memoirs of key US decision makers, and various secondary sources to determine what the costly compellence theory and the alternative theories under investigation predict about Saddam's response to the United States' threat. I then examine recently released primary sources on Saddam and his regime to evaluate his decision making.[1] These sources consist of declassified, translated documents and transcripts of recordings seized after the 2003 invasion and interviews of Iraqi military and political leaders, including Saddam himself. They are an invaluable source of information about his decision making and views of the United States. We cannot assume that these materials constitute a random sample of all those held by the US government or all those generated by the Iraqis, but they do provide unique insight into the mind of one of the most notorious targets of the post–Cold War period.

August 1991: Iraq Invades Kuwait

Following a dispute over oil revenues, Iraq invaded neighboring Kuwait on August 2, 1990. By the end of the day, Iraqi tanks had rolled into the capital, Kuwait City, and Iraqi troops occupied the emir's palace.[2] That day, the UN Security Council passed Resolution 660, which condemned the invasion and demanded the immediate withdrawal of Iraqi forces from Kuwait.[3]

The United States was also quick to denounce the invasion. President George H. W. Bush declared that "there is no place for this sort of naked aggression in today's world."[4] Bush quickly froze Iraqi and Kuwaiti assets in the United States, valued at $30 billion in 1990. He declared a "virtual trade embargo" against Iraq and urged other countries to do the same.[5] An American naval task force, led by the carrier *Independence*, headed from the Indian Ocean to the mouth of the Persian Gulf "in a show of strength." On August 3, the United States House of Representatives voted unanimously to impose trade sanctions, and the Senate approved a resolution calling for multilateral action under the UN Charter to restore peace in the Persian Gulf region.[6] The Arab League also convened an emergency meeting within a week of the invasion. By a majority vote, it passed a resolution demanding that Iraq withdraw its forces from Kuwait.[7]

The day before the invasion, the *New York Times* had reported on the Pentagon's new defense strategy for the 1990s. The plan would cut a half million of the military's 2.1 million troops, reducing the force by roughly 25 percent. It also acknowledged that defense budgets would be shrinking in the coming years. Interestingly, the strategy anticipated that "third world powers like Iraq, which is already regarded as a formidable opponent, [would] become more powerful." The United States would emphasize "tactical air forces, instead of ground troops," in dealing with such "regional threats."[8]

This "formidable opponent" presented President Bush with a major foreign policy challenge when it invaded Kuwait the following day—a challenge that would set a precedent for future UN action and for the United States' use of force in the post–Cold War period. Bush unveiled this new defense strategy in a speech at the Aspen Institute on the day of the Iraqi invasion. In his speech, the president acknowledged the invasion, but he focused on the new vision for the US military: a smaller, more agile force to address regional threats rather than a large conventional military aimed at the now-defunct Soviet Union in Europe. Bush's remarks demonstrate that US planners were already envisioning a force that would allow the United States to attack its foes from a distance while saving US lives and dollars.[9] In a session with British prime minister Margaret Thatcher before his speech, Bush asserted that "we're not ruling any options in but we're not ruling any options out" for responding to the invasion of Kuwait.[10]

Returning from Camp David on August 5, Bush was similarly noncommittal on the United States' response to the crisis in the Persian Gulf. He began his remarks by highlighting the consensus among the United States' allies about the invasion: "There seems to be a united front out there that says Iraq, having committed brutal, naked aggression, ought to get out, and that this concept of their installing some puppet . . . will not be acceptable." Bush then asserted that the invasion of Kuwait "would not stand." Although he admitted that he was consulting military officials, the president promised that the United States would be "pushing forward on diplomacy" in the coming days. When pressed by reporters about whether he was preparing to launch military action, Bush reaffirmed his conviction that the United States and its allies would not accept the installation of a puppet regime in Kuwait, but he refused to commit to a specific course of action.[11] In other words, in the days immediately following the invasion, Bush condemned Iraq's behavior but would neither publicly commit to nor publicly rule out the use of force.

Despite the ambiguous rhetoric that he employed in his first public statements about the invasion, President Bush had "decided in [his] own mind in the first hours that the Iraqi aggression could not be tolerated."[12] In the days immediately following the invasion, the White House and senior military officials focused on protecting US ally Saudi Arabia. By August 6, there were eleven Iraqi divisions in or deploying to Kuwait, and reports indicated that forces were being positioned along the Saudi border.[13] That same day, Defense Secretary Dick Cheney, US Central Command (CENTCOM) commander Gen. H. Norman Schwarzkopf, and Director of Central Intelligence

Robert Gates arrived in Jiddah, Saudi Arabia. They were charged with obtaining approval from the Saudi king for an American military deployment on his soil. The American delegation promised that the United States was not interested in permanent bases. The king gave his consent, and on the following day the United States began to deploy forces to the region for Operation Desert Shield.[14]

In addition to laying the groundwork for a deployment to the Persian Gulf, the United States also began to implement economic sanctions against Iraq in conjunction with the United Nations. On August 6, the UN Security Council passed Resolution 661, which imposed comprehensive trade and financial sanctions on Iraq and occupied Kuwait.[15] On August 8, Iraq announced that it had annexed Kuwait as its nineteenth province. The UN Security Council deemed this declaration "null and void" on the following day.[16] On August 12, President Bush ordered the US Navy to block the export of Iraqi oil and to prevent the import of all goods into Iraq except food. It was the first naval blockade administered by the United States since the Vietnam War, and it recalled the "quarantine" imposed during the 1962 Cuban Missile Crisis.[17] Bush's press secretary claimed in a statement that afternoon that the United States was taking action against Iraq at the behest of the exiled emir of Kuwait and in accordance with Article 51 of the UN Charter, which grants the right to individual and collective self-defense.[18] The United States and the UN would continue to maintain these and additional economic, financial, and diplomatic sanctions as the United States built up its forces in the region over the coming months. Most notably, Bush signed the Iraq Sanctions Act of 1990 on November 5. The act endorsed the sanctions that had been implemented by executive order and imposed additional financial and trade sanctions on Iraq.[19]

In the days immediately following the annexation of Kuwait, President Bush condemned Iraq's behavior, but he refrained from issuing an explicit threat against the Iraqi regime. The simple declaration that the invasion was "unacceptable" does not meet the definition of a compellent military threat. The initial deployment of US forces to the Persian Gulf could be classified as an implicit deterrent threat intended to convince the Iraqi leader not to invade Saudi Arabia. At the start of the crisis, however, efforts to coerce Saddam were limited to economic sanctions while the United States steadily built up its forces in the Gulf and secured the support of its allies for a campaign to expel Iraqi forces from Kuwait.

Military Preparations: Desert Shield and Desert Storm

Operation Desert Shield began on August 7, 1990. The operation was intended to deter an Iraqi attack on Saudi Arabia and to defend Saudi Arabia in the event that deterrence failed.[20] Two carrier battle groups had been directed to the region on August 2, and additional naval forces soon began to patrol the waters of the Persian Gulf and to enforce the blockade unveiled by President Bush on the 12th. Fighters from the First Tactical Fighter Wing arrived in Saudi Arabia within a day and began patrolling the border with Iraq by August 9.[21] The 101st Airborne Division dispatched three thousand troops and 117 helicopters on the 17th.[22] Bush also signed Executive Order 12727 on the 22nd to activate nearly fifty thousand reservists across the four branches.[23] US forces would continue to arrive in Saudi Arabia through the autumn of 1990. By early October, there were twenty-seven Iraqi divisions sitting across the Saudi border in Kuwait, including all eight of the elite Republican Guard divisions.[24]

Although the United States' first official move against the Iraqi regime had been to implement economic sanctions, within days of the invasion the secretary of defense had instructed Powell and Schwarzkopf to begin planning for an offensive to expel Iraqi forces from Kuwait.[25] As the defensive Desert Shield buildup continued through the autumn of 1990, one of the biggest debates in the Bush administration concerned the role that airpower would play in the offensive.[26] President Bush authorized the deployment of two hundred thousand additional troops to the region on October 31, which would double the strength of coalition forces in Saudi Arabia.[27] In a news conference on November 8, the president announced that the United States would be sending additional forces to the Persian Gulf "to ensure that the coalition has an adequate offensive military option should that be necessary to achieve our common goals." He argued that the failure to reverse Iraq's aggression would undermine "the better world that we all have hoped to build in the wake of the Cold War."[28]

The plan for the offensive was refined and revised over the following months. Operation Desert Storm would begin with massive, simultaneous air attacks on targets in Iraq and the Kuwait Theater of Operations (KTO). Cheney and Powell reviewed the detailed plan at CENTCOM headquarters in Riyadh on December 19 and 20, at which time the secretary of defense approved it. They briefed President Bush on the plan when they returned to Washington, at which time he also approved it.[29]

The Coalition

The Bush administration decided that the American public would support the use of force against Iraq only if the United States had pursued all other options first and if it had obtained international support for military action. To that end, the administration sought to build a coalition of allies that would provide military and financial assistance to offset the United States' costs for expelling Iraqi forces from Kuwait.[30] Many of the United States' closest allies reacted as swiftly as did the United States in condemning the annexation. The United Kingdom froze Iraqi and Kuwaiti assets on the day of the invasion. In public remarks at the Aspen Institute, Prime Minister Thatcher asserted that the United Kingdom would "support in the Security Council those measures which collectively we can agree to and which collectively we can make effective."[31] Both the United Kingdom and France augmented their naval presence in the Gulf by August 6. In response to a request from King Fahd, the United Kingdom began a major deployment of air and naval units to Saudi Arabia on the 8th, and France announced that it would send ground units and advisers to Saudi Arabia the following day.[32] On August 10, the Arab League convened an emergency meeting in Cairo, where it passed a resolution condemning Iraq's invasion and annexation of Kuwait and pledged to send troops to Saudi Arabia.[33] The Bush administration also coordinated closely with the Soviet Union throughout the crisis. With the fallout from their war in Afghanistan still fresh in their minds, the Soviets opted not to send forces to the Gulf. They were, however, consulted on the terms for the UN Resolution that would be passed in November.[34]

In early September, Secretary of State James Baker embarked on an eleven-day trip around the world to solicit pledges of support from nine of the United States' allies for a sustained military operation in the Gulf.[35] The Bush administration's diplomatic offensive assembled an impressive coalition for the campaign against Iraq. Germany, Italy, Spain, and Greece agreed to allow the United States to use their air and naval bases, while Turkey shut down a critical pipeline through which Iraq exported much of its oil. Turkey also deployed fifty thousand troops to its border with Iraq and allowed the coalition to station troops on its soil in preparation for Desert Storm.[36] In keeping with the Arab League's pledge, several Arab states also contributed troops and financial support to the operation. Egypt sent two heavy divisions to Saudi Arabia, and President Hosni Mubarak worked closely with King Fahd and the Bush administration throughout the crisis.[37] In total, nearly fifty countries contributed to the effort to oust Iraqi forces from Kuwait. Thirty-eight of them sent air, sea, or ground forces, for a combined total of two hundred thousand troops, 60 ships, 750 aircraft, and 1,200 tanks.[38]

Just as important as the contributions of troops and equipment were the pledges of financial support that the Bush administration secured from its allies in the run-up to Operation Desert Storm. The Department of Defense dubbed the seeking of financial support for US operations "responsibility sharing." Total incremental costs for Operations Desert Shield and Desert Storm were estimated at $61 billion in 1991 dollars. The United States' coalition partners would pledge $54 billion to offset these costs. Saudi Arabia, Kuwait, Japan, and Germany made the largest contributions. The Department of Defense report notes that "without responsibility sharing, the US would have had to pay these costs either through a tax increase or through deficit spending, adding to the nations' [sic] fiscal difficulties."[39]

In addition to supporting the ground operation, these allies also proved particularly helpful in enforcing UN sanctions. With the assistance of nineteen coalition partners, the US Navy essentially halted commerce through Iraqi and Kuwaiti ports. Coalition forces stopped and boarded nearly one thousand ships for inspection over the seven months of the Persian Gulf crisis and diverted more than one million tons of cargo that violated the sanctions. The blockade succeeded in halting virtually all of Iraq's oil exports and cut off nearly 95 percent of Iraq's preinvasion revenues.[40]

Mixed Messages of Coercion

To secure the votes necessary to pass a UN Security Council resolution authorizing military action, Secretary Baker flew to twelve countries over eighteen days in November 1990.[41] With Baker chairing the meeting, on November 29 the Security Council passed its twelfth resolution on the Iraqi invasion of Kuwait.[42] Resolution 678 authorized member states "to use all necessary means to uphold and implement resolution 660 (1990) and all subsequent relevant resolutions and to restore international peace and security in the area." The resolution passed with a vote of 12–2. Cuba and Yemen opposed the resolution, and China abstained.[43]

With the passage of Resolution 678, the UN Security Council handed Saddam an ultimatum. He had until January 15 to remove Iraqi forces from Kuwait, or he would face the wrath of the UN-sanctioned coalition assembling in the Gulf. At a news conference the day after the passage of Resolution 678, President Bush demanded Iraq's "immediate and unconditional withdrawal from Kuwait" and the release of all foreign hostages still held in Iraq and Kuwait. He emphasized that Saddam faced an international coalition arrayed against him, not just the wrath of the United States. He expressed doubts about the ability of the economic sanctions to obtain Saddam's compliance. Bush also asserted that "if force is required, we and the other 26 countries who have troops in the area will have enough power to get the job done." Furthermore, "if there must be war, we will not permit our troops to have their hands tied behind their backs. . . . If one American soldier has to go into battle, that soldier will have enough force behind him to win and then get out as soon as possible. . . . I will never—ever—agree to a halfway effort." Bush told Saddam that "time is running out. You must leave Kuwait. And we've given you time to do just exactly that." Finally, the president presented another opportunity to resolve the crisis peacefully. He invited Iraq's foreign minister, Tariq Aziz, to come to Washington, and he offered to send Baker to Baghdad to meet with Saddam between December 15 and January 15.[44]

Bush's remarks contain several mixed messages about the United States' commitments. On the one hand, he stressed that Iraqi forces must evacuate Kuwait, and he asserted that the United States and its allies had the ability to expel them if they chose not to leave voluntarily. The president was also careful to emphasize that an operation to expel Iraqi forces from Kuwait would not be another Vietnam: US and coalition forces would hit the Iraqis hard, and they would evacuate their own forces from the area as quickly as possible after securing the UN's objectives.

On the other hand, in an exchange with reporters following these remarks, Bush was careful not to commit the United States to the automatic use of force in the event that the deadline passed without a withdrawal. When asked whether he had committed to use force on January 15, Bush replied, "No, the date was not a date at which point force had to be used." Later in the session, when pressed again on whether the United States would have to act on January 15, Bush asserted, "I don't think there will ever be a perception that the United States is going to blink in this situation." Finally, the president expressed reservations about the ability of the UN resolutions and sanctions regime to work: "I'm not all that hopeful that we'll get big results out of all of this. It's going the extra mile. It's taking the extra step."[45] These final remarks suggest that Bush had already decided to take action against the Iraqis but was allowing extra time for the development of a peaceful solution.

By offering to send Baker to negotiate with the Iraqi leader, President Bush also suggested that there was still an opportunity for Saddam to negotiate an end to the crisis. In fact, Baker believes that the Iraqis "mistook [this] initiative as a sign of weakness."[46] The UN resolution and the offer for negotiations were also intended to get Congress on board with the administration's plans. At the time Resolution 678 was passed, Congress was divided about the need to pass a resolution authorizing the use of force. New York senator Daniel Patrick Moynihan argued that Baker would struggle to convince Aziz that the United States was serious about using force without a congressional resolution. Several other members of Congress were urging the president to allow time for the resolutions and the sanctions regime to work.[47]

A week after Bush's press conference on Resolution 678, Saddam made a move of his own. On December 6, in a message to the Iraqi National Assembly, the Iraqi leader announced that he was releasing the remaining hostages held in Iraq and Kuwait. He also asserted that "Bush's invitation for talks, as far as we can discern, has continued to bear the possibilities or the inclination toward aggression and war. The buildup is growing." He called the US-led coalition of forces in Saudi Arabia the "armies of aggression," waiting for "the opportunity to invade the holy land."[48] Saddam had made a gesture by releasing the remaining hostages, but he seemed resistant about Bush's offer for additional negotiations.

As the remaining hostages were being evacuated from Iraq and Kuwait in December, the Bush administration struggled to reach an agreement with their Iraqi counterparts about the date for direct negotiations. Saddam agreed to send Aziz to Washington, but he claimed he was too busy to meet with Secretary Baker before January 12. Bush then demanded that the meeting with Baker take place before the third.[49] As the dispute about the date for negotiations continued, the Bush administration worried that Saddam would initiate a partial withdrawal from Kuwait around the time of the January 15 deadline in an effort to erode the will of the coalition to take action against him.[50]

Clarifying the Ultimatum: Baker Meets with Aziz

Secretary Baker finally met with Iraq's foreign minister in Geneva for a discussion that lasted eight hours on January 9, 1991. Since declassified, the Department of State's transcript of this meeting is worth examining in detail as a window into the decision making of the Iraqi regime before Desert Storm. At the start of the meeting, Baker gave Aziz a letter from Bush to Saddam. It assured Saddam that Iraq would face a "certain calamity" if he did not demonstrate "full and unconditional compliance with UN Security Council Resolution 678." Complying with the resolution was the only way that "the Iraqi military establishment will escape destruction." Bush assured Saddam that Iraq would not be able to exact a price for evacuating Kuwait. Referring to the January 15 deadline set by Resolution 678, the president's letter assured the Iraqi leader that the outcome of the crisis "is in your hands, and yours alone."[51] In other words, Iraq had a choice to make: It could comply with the demands of the United States and the international community, or it could choose to resist. If Iraq chose to resist, then it would meet with military action designed to destroy the Iraqi military, and possibly more.

Aziz read a copy of the letter. He then refused to deliver the sealed copy to his president. He argued that the letter was "full of expressions of threat. Indeed, it is worded in a manner which is foreign or alien to the usual manner used between heads of states."[52] Baker objected to this characterization, but he assured Aziz that "the only question is by what path you leave Kuwait—a peaceful withdrawal, or withdrawal by force."[53] He urged the Iraqis not to miscalculate the United States' will to enforce the resolution. Baker then reminded the foreign minister of the terms of Resolution 678 and argued that Iraqi troops would be vastly outclassed by the superior technology and firepower that the coalition forces would bring to bear in the event of war. The attack might even destroy the regime's ability to govern: "War will destroy everything you fought to build in Iraq, and it will trigger, thanks to your unwillingness to withdraw from Kuwait, a conflict that will turn Iraq into a weak and backward country."[54] Baker also promised that the United States would not attack Iraq or its military if it evacuated Kuwait voluntarily.

In response, Aziz told Baker, "We have no illusions about your intentions."[55] Iraq had been expecting US military action since the invasion of Kuwait and was aware of the nature of the buildup in Saudi Arabia. Aziz referred to Iraq's 1980–88 war with Iran and assured Baker that the Iraqis understood and were prepared to meet the costs of war. All of Iraq's people were convinced that "once war breaks out between us . . . we will be victorious."[56] He told Baker, "I hope you won't miscalculate our capability to endure the costs of war."[57] Baker and Aziz also spent a considerable amount of time discussing the Israeli–Palestinian dispute and Iraq's use of weapons of mass destruction.

After a lengthy discussion of these issues, Baker reminded Aziz of the United States' "request" that Iraqi forces evacuate Kuwait: "This request comes six days before the UN deadline, one you don't accept, but one I must say in all candor is very real in the eyes of the rest of the world community. So consider yourself tested."[58] Later in their exchange, Baker urged the Iraqi foreign minister not to believe that Iraq could absorb the costs of war or that the United States could not withstand casualties. He then assured Aziz that "midnight January 15th is very real. Time runs out six days from now. We can't and won't agree to an extension or postponement. Whether you choose to believe this or not is your business."[59] Aziz acknowledged that the deadline existed, but he argued that it would be the United States' choice to act after that date in deciding whether to attack or to continue negotiations. He then offered to meet with President Bush himself, a suggestion Baker rebuffed as intended to manipulate the deadline.[60] By the end of the meeting, Aziz had made no promise to withdraw.

In his memoirs, Baker claims that he never expected these negotiations to be successful, but the administration felt this final effort at diplomacy was necessary to secure congressional support.[61] Three days after Baker's meeting with Aziz, Congress did pass a resolution authorizing the use of military force to eject Iraqi forces from Kuwait under the authority of UN Security Council Resolution 678.[62] President Bush gave senior commanders a "tentative go ahead" for the offensive on January 11.[63] The January 15 deadline came and went, and Iraqi forces remained in Kuwait. Operation Desert Storm commenced on January 17 with an air campaign that lasted more than a month before the launch of the ground operations on February 23. In roughly a hundred hours of fighting, the US-led coalition routed the Iraqi forces, advanced into Iraqi territory, and declared a ceasefire. The coalition succeeded in expelling the Iraqis from Kuwait but only after the effort to coerce Saddam had failed.

The Failed 1991 Ultimatum

The statements made by President Bush and Secretary Baker in the run-up to Desert Storm bear the classic hallmarks of an ultimatum. The demand was clear: Iraqi forces must evacuate Kuwait, and there would be no negotiation on the terms of this evacuation. Baker's meeting with Aziz clarified the United States' position on the deadline. Although Baker avoided calling the terms of his communication a "threat," it is clear from Aziz's protestations, from the content of

Baker's statements, and from Bush's letter to Saddam that the United States was, in fact, threatening the Iraqi leader with military force if he did not comply with the UN resolutions by January 15.

Bush's willingness to continue with negotiations through January may, however, have led the Iraqi leader to doubt the sincerity of this ultimatum. Aziz urged Baker to allow him to meet with President Bush, but Baker denied this request because he believed it was intended to manipulate the January 15 deadline.[64] This suggests that the Iraqi minister may have been testing the United States' willingness to continue with negotiations in lieu of enforcing the deadline. Nevertheless, in his meeting with the foreign minister, Baker repeatedly referred to the deadline and urged Aziz to consider the defeat that the Iraqi military would suffer at the hands of coalition forces.

Costly Compellence: Contextual Variables

The United States was emerging as the world's sole superpower when it issued its ultimatum to Iraq. The Berlin Wall had fallen in 1989, and the Soviet Union was on the path to dissolution by the end of 1990. Although the Bush administration consulted with the Soviet Union during the buildup to Operation Desert Storm, there was no way for the dying bipole to limit the United States' ability to threaten and use force. In fact, the Soviet Union voted in favor of UN Security Council Resolution 678, which authorized member states to use force to expel the Iraqis from Kuwait.[65] In other words, the Bush administration's decision to adopt the deadline stipulated by the UN Security Council and to issue a US-backed compellent threat did not generate any danger for the United States, because doing so did not risk angering a peer competitor capable of checking US behavior.[66]

The United States fielded an all-volunteer military in 1991. Although reservists were called up for Operations Desert Shield and Desert Storm, there were no requests for a draft to augment the United States' presence in the Gulf. The United States would employ private contractors in the Gulf War but in an extremely limited capacity. Singer notes that "the ratio of uniformed military to contractors in the 1991 Gulf War was around 50:1." These contractors were involved in logistics and support activities. By contrast, the ratio would approach 1:1 in the 2001 war in Afghanistan, and private contractors would outnumber uniformed personnel in Iraq even at the height of the "surge" of 2007.[67] The limited role played by contractors in the 1991 campaign made the use of ground forces more politically costly for the United States than it would be in 2003, but overall the United States' military manpower structure was not very costly in 1991.

Despite the relatively low cost of the United States' military manpower structure, planners still worried about the effect of casualties on public support for the war. In 1991, Iraq commanded the world's fourth largest military. Early simulations of the ground campaign suggested that the offensive would generate ten thousand American casualties, and "it was well understood within the American military that holding down casualties was a political prerequisite for launching a military offensive."[68] From the earliest days of the crisis, Powell expressed doubts about the American public's willingness to tolerate casualties to liberate Kuwait. He argued consistently that public support was a necessary precondition for military action.[69] To limit casualties and to exploit the United States' advantages over the Iraqi military, Operation Desert Storm would employ key features of the RMA model of warfare: airpower and precision-guided munitions.[70] The operation began with a month-long air campaign to target Iraqi leadership and to soften up Iraqi forces in Kuwait before the start of the ground offensive. Attacking Iraq in this manner both allowed the United States to test its new vision of warfare and to limit casualties for US and coalition forces. Table 5.1 summarizes the contextual variables for the 1991 threat against Iraq. With the exception of the limited use of contractors, these conditions suggest that issuing and executing a threat against Iraq would not be very costly for the United States.

Table 5.1. Contextual Variables, Iraq 1991

Contextual Variables		Effect on US Military Action
Polarity:	Unipolar	Less costly
Conscription?	No	Less costly
Contractors?	Very limited	More costly
RMA?	Emerging	Less costly

Costly Compellence: Threat Variables

The manner in which the United States would carry out its ultimatum suggests that executing the 1991 threat against Iraq would be moderately costly for the United States. Most important, the United States was implicitly threatening Iraq with ground forces. Although Operation Desert Storm would begin with an intense air campaign, by January 1991 the United States and its allies had massed more than half a million troops in Saudi Arabia in preparation for the offensive. Employing troops in a ground offensive would be much more costly than attacking Iraqi forces solely from the air.

The human, political, and financial costs of conducting this ground campaign were mitigated, however, by the participation of the United States' allies in the campaign to expel Iraqi forces from Kuwait. As described above, the United States' allies sent a total of two hundred thousand troops to the region,[71] and they pledged $54 billion to offset the United States' $61 billion incremental costs for Operations Desert Shield and Desert Storm. This does not mean that it was easy for the United States to build and sustain the coalition opposing Iraq. Secretary Baker traveled around the world more than once to obtain guarantees of support from the United States' allies and from its erstwhile adversary, the Soviet Union. The purpose of assembling this coalition was, however, to minimize the United States' costs and thereby erode domestic political barriers to the use of force. By sharing responsibility for the threat's execution, the United States insulated itself from political fallout in a way that would not have been possible had the United States issued and executed its ultimatum unilaterally.

The vulnerability of Iraqi civilians and the political costs associated with inflicting collateral damage would vary according to the different phases of the campaign. In his January letter to Saddam, Bush asserted that "the people of the United States have no quarrel with the people of Iraq." Bush did not deliberately announce that Iraqi civilians would be spared, but he was careful to direct his ultimatum to the Iraqi regime.[72] In addition, the plan for Operation Desert Storm was designed to limit violence inflicted on Iraqi civilians. The aerial "decapitation" campaign that launched the war was intended to target key components of the Iraqi leadership infrastructure. It was not an area-bombing campaign designed to induce concessions by deliberately inflicting pain on civilians. US Air Force colonel John A. Warden III, author of the "Instant Thunder" campaign that would become the basis for the air attack that opened Desert Storm, estimated in December 1990 that the strategic bombing campaign would directly cause four hundred to two thousand civilian casualties. He noted that this number would constitute "a tiny fraction of the populace that was killed in the bombing of European and Japanese cities during air attacks in World War II. In terms of American and Iraqi lives lost, the campaign would be politically sustainable."[73]

The ground campaign to liberate Kuwait was not intended to liberate the Iraqi population. Had the United States planned to occupy Iraq, Iraqi civilians would have been put at risk by having a foreign army on their soil. This was not the case with the Gulf War, where the plan was limited to ejecting Iraqi forces from Kuwait and the coalition deliberately stopped short of overthrowing the Iraqi regime. In fact, Iraqi civilians would become vulnerable to violence inflicted by their *own* government after the cease-fire, when Saddam moved to crush rebellions against his rule.[74] Iraqi civilians faced a low (but not nonexistent) level of vulnerability during the air campaign that started Desert Storm. They were not, however, explicitly targeted by the United States' ultimatum. Table 5.2 summarizes the 1991 threat against the Iraqi regime and the associated costs for undertaking military action against Iraq. With the exception of the fact that the United States was threatening a ground campaign (in conjunction with a bombing campaign), the other characteristics reduced the United States' costs for carrying out the 1991 threat against Iraq.

In sum, the threatened ground attack would be moderately costly for the United States. In January 1991, hundreds of thousands of US troops were massed in Saudi Arabia and planning to launch a ground offensive, but the specific ways in which the United States was intending to use and pay for these forces helped to limit the United States' costs for executing military action against the Iraqis. Although the use of ground troops is relatively costly, the offensive would follow an air campaign that would soften up Iraqi ground forces by capitalizing on US advantages in technology and precision weaponry. The United States' allies would share some of the direct burdens of fighting, and they would also supply significant

Table 5.2. Threat Variables, Iraq 1991

Threat Variables		Effect on US Military Action
Ground forces?	Yes	More costly
Allies?	Yes: large coalition contributing money and troops	Less costly
Payment	Allies paying most incremental costs; no tax increases	Less costly
Civilian vulnerability	Targeted bombing in air campaign; no occupation plans	Less costly

financial resources to offset the United States' incremental costs for Operations Desert Shield and Desert Storm. Finally, collateral damage was not expected to generate significant costs for the United States. The bombing campaign was designed to target the regime's command-and-control facilities, and there was no plan to take the war to Baghdad or to occupy the country after the Iraqi army had been expelled from Kuwait. Thus, the costly compellence theory predicts with moderate strength that the target was likely to resist the United States' demands.

Alternative Theories

Reputation Theory

The reputation theory of compellent-threat effectiveness asserts that a threat succeeds when the threatener has a record for following through on its past threats. The data set in the second chapter demonstrates that the United States never issued an explicit threat during a Cold War crisis and subsequently failed to execute its threat when the target resisted US demands. Iraq's invasion of Kuwait coincided with the shift to unipolarity, but there would have been no reason to expect that the United States would abandon its Cold War policy of following through on compellent threats. Most recently, the United States had issued a compellent threat during the crisis with Panama in late 1989, and this crisis was resolved when the United States invaded. Thus, the logic of the reputation theory suggests that the United States' record of following through on its compellent threats would render the 1991 threat against Saddam effective.

Preponderant Power

According to the logic of preponderant power, a compellent threat succeeds when the threatener has a recognized superiority in relative power over its opponent. If we consider economic indicators, the United States clearly outclassed Iraq at the time of the 1991 threat. The World Bank estimates Iraq's GDP in 1989, the last year before the war for which data are available, at $48 billion, or roughly $2,700 per capita. The United States, on the other hand, recorded a GDP of $5.4 trillion that year. Per capita GDP for the United States in 1989 was $22,000, more than eight times that of Iraq.[75] Although the World Bank does not have a record of Iraq's military expenditures for 1990, it does report that neighbor Iran was spending 2.1 percent of its GDP on defense that year.[76] Iraq was probably spending a greater percentage of its GDP to maintain its large army and various weapon programs, but it certainly could not devote the same amount of money to defense in absolute terms as its 1991 rival. We do know, however, that the United States spent roughly $300 billion on national defense in 1990, or roughly 5.6 percent of its GDP.[77]

At the start of Operation Desert Storm, Iraq had more than 540,000 soldiers, 4,200 tanks, and 3,100 artillery pieces in the KTO. The Iraqis faced a US-led coalition of more than 540,000 troops from thirty-one countries, including seven US Army divisions, two US Marine Corps divisions, a British armored division, a French light armored division, and the equivalent of roughly four divisions from Arab states. Coalition forces were prepared to face the Iraqis with more than seventeen hundred combat aircraft, six aircraft carrier battle groups, two battleships, several submarines, and the largest amphibious landing force assembled since the Korean War.[78] At the time of the 1991 threat, Iraq had the largest air force in the Middle East, with seven hundred combat aircraft. Many of these planes were quite old, however, and their pilots were not as well trained as their US counterparts. Iraq also possessed an extensive air-defense system, an array of ballistic missiles, and robust programs for the production of chemical and biological weapons.[79]

Although Iraq mustered roughly as many troops as the coalition in 1991, US planners believed that their force enjoyed significant qualitative advantages over their Iraqi counterparts,[80] and this would prove accurate during the lightning ground offensive. The training and equipment of the Iraqi Army were both very uneven. The elite Republican Guard had the best training and equipment and constituted roughly 20 percent of Iraq's ground forces. The bulk of the ground forces were divided, however, between the regular and popular armies, the latter of which received training and equipment even worse and more uneven than the former. Most of these forces were armed with Soviet and Chinese equipment from the 1960s.[81]

It is clear that the United States vastly outclassed the Iraqis in terms of economic potential and the quality and training of its force. On the other hand, US decision makers were very worried about the number of casualties that the Iraqi force could inflict. In early 1991, Iraq commanded the world's fourth-largest military, and planners anticipated that the campaign to expel the Iraqis from Kuwait could generate ten thousand casualties. The United States enjoyed an advantage in relative power over its opponent in qualitative terms, but before Desert Storm began it believed that the Iraqis would be capable of mounting a costly defense. The United States certainly did not enjoy the kind of advantage that it would have over Libya in 2011 or even over Iraq in 2003. Thus, the preponderant power theory predicts with only moderate strength that the Iraqis were likely to concede to the United States' threat.

Expansive Demands

Finally, the expansive demands theory asserts that compellent threats fail when the threatener demands too much of the target. In the 1991 threat, the United States was demanding that Iraq evacuate territory that it had invaded and annexed six months earlier. Regardless of the claims to this piece of territory that Iraq might have made several decades before the 1990 invasion, compliance would not require Iraq to surrender a part of the territory it had held prior to August 2, 1990. Nor was Iraq being asked to surrender or degrade its military strength. If Iraqi forces evacuated Kuwait voluntarily, they would be allowed to return home unmolested. It is true that complying with the United States' demand would require a very public reversal, but that is true of compellent threats in general and not unique to this case.

The United States was not demanding regime change or the surrender of key elements of Iraqi power or critical components of Iraq's national security. The demand was not, however, so trivial that the expansive demands theory would lead us to expect concession. Because the United States' demands were neither severe nor trivial, the expansive demands theory yields no prediction about the 1991 threat against Iraq.

Four Theories, Four Predictions

The four theories yield very different predictions about Iraq's likely response in 1991. The costly compellence theory predicts resistance because the use of force would be only moderately costly for the United States. Both the reputation and preponderant power theories predict concession, but the expansive demands theory yields no prediction. Table 5.3 summarizes the four theories' predictions for the United States' 1991 threat against Iraq.

As we know, Saddam did not concede to the United States' demands, and Operation Desert Storm ultimately succeeded in expelling Iraqi forces from Kuwait. A detailed discussion of the course of the offensive is beyond the scope of this study. It is clear, however, that Saddam's resistance is consistent with the costly compellence prediction. This does not mean that the causal logic driving Saddam's decision is consistent with the theory. To evaluate whether Saddam's decision is consistent with the causal logic proposed by this or by other theories, we must evaluate primary sources on Saddam's attitudes and decision making.

Table 5.3. Predictions, Iraq 1991

Theory	Iraq's Predicted Response	Strength of Prediction
Costly compellence	Resist	Moderate
Reputation	Concede	Strong
Preponderant power	Concede	Moderate
Expansive demands	No prediction	n/a

The 1991 Threat: The View from Baghdad

The information that we have on Saddam's beliefs at the time that he invaded Kuwait suggests that the Iraqi leader was aware of the United States' military prowess and that he expected an attack. He chose to invade anyway and to resist the United States' demands for an evacuation because he doubted the United States' will to defeat him in a long and costly campaign. In a meeting with Palestinian leader Yasser Arafat in April 1990, before he had invaded Kuwait, Saddam discussed the American menace. He noted, "We know that America has larger aircraft than we do. America has more rockets than us. But I think that when the Arab people see the action of war is real, not only talk, they will do the same and fight America everywhere." He went on to explain his thinking about the course of a war with the United States: "Therefore, when the battle is on, you do not say, 'How much did you lose?' and do not have expectations, or even have some expectations for the end of the battle. It is what happened for us during the war with Iran. We had a lot of expectations for that war . . . but when the war occurred we did not have expectations about how much we were going to lose, because it was inevitable."[82] Later in the conversation, Saddam indicates his willingness to send suicide bombers to Washington in the event of a war with the United States.

This discussion suggests, first, that Saddam was well aware of the United States' superiority in raw military capability even before the Gulf War, when he was much better armed than he would be in 2003. It also suggests that Saddam was undeterred by the costs of a war with the United States—such losses were "inevitable," so dwelling on them would do the Iraqis no good. Finally, it suggests that the Iraqi leader was prepared to defeat the United States by applying the strategic logic that had succeeded in the war with Iran. Baker had urged Aziz during their meeting in January 1991 not to apply such reasoning to a war with the United States, but it seems that Saddam was already planning in these terms before the invasion.

In interviews with the Federal Bureau of Investigation (FBI) after his 2003 capture, Saddam asserted that the United States had been leading a "conspiracy" against Iraq. He claimed that the US military had been conducting exercises in Kuwait and planning to attack Iraq even before the invasion. He decided to invade Kuwait to "defend by attacking"—that is, to defend against this conspiracy ranged against him and his forces.[83] In fact, in another interview, Saddam asserted that the United States already had its forces in place in Saudi Arabia when the decision to attack was made. He seems to have been arguing that the presence of US forces made the attack on Kuwait necessary and inevitable, rather than admitting that the annexation violated international law.[84] Regardless of Saddam's efforts in 2004 to rewrite the chronology of August 1990, these interviews and the statements he made to his advisers before the war suggest that Saddam anticipated an American response to the annexation. That is, he knew that the United States had a lot of raw military capability and was likely to use it against him, but he chose to invade Kuwait anyway.

In the immediate aftermath of the invasion, Saddam told his advisers that international attention to the situation in Kuwait would wane. Saddam was unsure about the form that the United States' response would take, but he thought air strikes were likely:

I mean, what will [the Americans] do if they engage in a fight?
All they can do is bring their airplanes and start bombing: boom, boom, boom, boom, boom, boom. So what? Nothing will happen, we will give them hell. Give me one instance when an airplane has settled any situation. We are not like Panama, people to be scared by airplanes. . . . Their bombing will increase the number of refugees. The longer their aggression lasts, the more flags will be hoisted [against them].[85]

Saddam anticipated that an American intervention would take the form of air strikes, and he expected that he and his country could withstand them.

In interviews in 2004, Saddam also recalled the January 1991 meeting between Baker and Aziz. Saddam asserted that he had hoped this meeting would yield a diplomatic solution to the standoff between Iraq and the US-led coalition. According to his account, Iraq rejected proposed solutions that would have fallen outside the bounds of international law. He acknowledged that Baker had threatened to take Iraq "back to the pre-industrial age" if Iraq had not accepted the United States' demand for an evacuation of Kuwait. He objected to the format of negotiations but seems to have acknowledged the need for a settlement. The FBI's interviewer noted that Saddam believed "this matter should not have been reduced to one in which the strong side (United States) dictated to the weak side (Iraq) the terms of the agreement. Iraq sought a format which did not portray it as defeated, but rather one showing respect for the Iraqi military and for its people."[86] It is not surprising that Saddam would claim to have preferred a peaceful solution in order to place blame for the ensuing war on the United States. Nevertheless, Saddam's assessment of the meeting between Baker and Aziz suggests two things: He was aware of the United States' threat to use force in the event that its terms were not met, and he rejected the format of the negotiations. That is, he rejected the compellent framework itself, in which the United States made demands and threatened to use force so that Iraq would concede.

Regardless of whether the Baker–Aziz meeting was a genuine effort at a peaceful solution, we also know that Saddam continued to doubt the strength of the United States' commitment through the early months of 1991. As the coalition launched the ground war to evict Iraqi forces from Kuwait, Saddam maintained that media reports of Iraqi soldiers surrendering to coalition forces were fabrications intended to boost the morale of the attackers.[87] Furthermore, records of conversations from that time demonstrate that Saddam and senior Iraqi leaders believed that the Americans could be defeated as long as Iraqi forces inflicted sufficient casualties on their US counterparts. When one of Saddam's advisers noted that the Iraqi forces could succeed if they inflicted five thousand American casualties, Saddam assured him that five hundred would suffice. Saddam claimed that Iraqi forces could suffer casualties at a rate of "four for one" compared to the American forces and still prevail.[88] These discussions suggest that Saddam believed that the Iraqi military could prevail over the casualty-shy Americans by inflicting sufficient pain on US forces. That is, Saddam expected the United States would initiate military action in 1991, but he doubted that the United States was willing to pay the costs necessary to defeat Iraq.

Saddam's Assessment of the War

Saddam's assessments after the war also yield important insights into his beliefs about the United States, both in terms of how it conducted the Gulf War and how it might conduct future action against Iraq. Records from meetings in the early 1990s indicate that Saddam maintained that the Iraqis had won. In a discussion with his advisers in August 1991, Saddam asserted that "it is clear to us and clear to the whole world that [the Gulf War] is a victory for us, one way or the other." In his view, "America disclosed its weakness when it launched its military operations against us in the same way it unveiled its strength." This "weakness" was the fact that the United States had depended on the support of corporations, on the support of Arab states in the region—particularly Saudi Arabia and its wealth—and on the paralysis of the Soviet Union to conduct Operation Desert Storm.[89] He asserted that the "fighting spirit" of the Iraqi forces had urged the United States to seek a cease-fire soon after the start of hostilities.[90] In Saddam's view, "the strongest scientific, technological, and military powers and the highest financial and economic potential existing in the region and the world without any exception. They all got together against us and they did not succeed despite what happened. They did not dare attack Baghdad."[91] According to an interview Saddam gave after his capture in 2004, Iraqi forces withdrew from Kuwait "as the result of an official proclamation"—that is, as the result of a cease-fire negotiated by "the Russians." The interviewer notes that Saddam claimed "coalition attacks against Iraqi ground forces occurred while troops were retreating under official orders from the Iraqi leadership."[92]

Some of these statements may be bluster intended to downplay the coalition's routing of Iraqi forces in Kuwait and to help Saddam maintain his hold on power in the aftermath of the war. These statements also suggest that Saddam may have believed that US strength in 1991 was largely a function of the support it received from its allies. In addition, Saddam blamed George H. W. Bush's failure to secure reelection in 1992 on his "failure to achieve his goal." The American president had put himself "in the position that it's either him or Iraq."[93] In Saddam's view, the United States had failed to achieve its objective (presumably, his overthrow), and American voters had punished the president for this failure.

Saddam would also attribute much of Iraq's so-called success in the Gulf War to his possession of WMDs. Before the launch of Desert Storm in 1991, Saddam had threatened to use chemical and biological weapons against invading forces and against Israel. After the war, he concluded that these threats had deterred the coalition from advancing on Baghdad.[94] The Iraqi leader also credited WMDs with saving Iraq during its war with Iran and with enabling the regime to put down the rebellions after the 1991 war.[95] Saddam's belief in the ability of WMDs to deter an advance on Baghdad is further evidence that he believed the United States was unwilling to accept casualties in order to achieve its objectives.

The 1991 Threat against Iraq: Summary

The evidence on Saddam's decision making before the Gulf War yields several observations. First, he was aware of American military strength and expected an attack on his forces in Kuwait. He believed, however, that these attacks would be limited to air strikes and that the United States and its allies would be unwilling to withstand large numbers of casualties to secure their objectives. He also identified the support that the United States received from its allies—that is, the support that minimized the United States' costs for employing force against Iraq—as a critical component of American strength in 1991. These observations are consistent with the logic of costly compellence, which suggests that targets resist threats for which the use of force would be relatively inexpensive. Several other elements of Saddam's reasoning in the run-up to the Gulf War are also consistent with the logic of costly compellence: He did not doubt that the United States would attack, but he did doubt that the United States had the will to pursue a long and costly campaign against him. From the perspective of the United States, the war was a smashing success, as US forces evicted the Iraqis from Kuwait rapidly while suffering few casualties themselves. From the perspective of the Iraqi leader, however, the war seems to have proven that the Americans lacked the will to pursue him to Baghdad.

The reputation and preponderant power theories both suggest that the Iraqi leader would concede to the United States' demands. There is no evidence on how Saddam viewed the United States' reputation for following through on threats. We do have evidence, however, that he knew that the United States was overwhelmingly powerful, and he decided to invade Kuwait and resist US demands anyway. The demand that Iraq remove its forces from Kuwait was relatively modest on the scale of demands that one could make of a target state. For this reason, the expansive demands theory did not yield a prediction about the Iraqi leader's response in 1991.

The primary sources on Saddam's decision making demonstrate, however, that his decision to resist is not consistent with the causal mechanism proposed by the expansive demands theory. Although he claimed in interviews in 2004 that he was offended by the terms of the settlement proposed by Baker in the meeting with Aziz in early 1991, Saddam rejected the *format* of the negotiations and not the demands themselves. That is, he rejected the United States' demands because they were presented in terms of a compellent threat. It is possible that Saddam also believed the demands were too expansive, and we simply have no record of this, but that would not be consistent with his assertions that "the Russians" had negotiated a withdrawal that was rejected or ignored by the United States. The claim that Saddam resisted because the demands were too unreasonable is also inconsistent with the fact that Saddam repeatedly asserted that Iraq was offering to withdraw from Kuwait as early as August 1990— that is, he claimed that Iraq was offering the United States the same outcome as it was demanding in January, which would have been unlikely had the Iraqi leader viewed the United States' demand as deeply threatening to his state or his regime.[96] In other words, the evidence from the 1991 case does not support the argument that Saddam resisted because the demands were too extreme.

Saddam's decision to resist the United States' demand for a withdrawal from Kuwait in January 1991 is consistent with both the prediction and the causal logic proposed by the costly compellence theory. Although the campaign to expel Iraqi forces from Kuwait would involve the use of ground troops, the United States was relying on its allies to supplement its all-volunteer force and would be exploiting airpower and its advantages in technology and weaponry to protect its troops from casualties. Thus the use of force against Iraq would be only moderately costly for the United States, and hence the threat did not signal high ultimate credibility. The evidence uncovered as a result of the 2003 invasion suggests that Saddam believed as early as August 1990 that the United States would take action against him.[97] He expected, however, that the United States would attack him with air strikes in conjunction with allies helping to off-set the United States' costs and without the will to prosecute a long and costly campaign, consistent with the argument that targets resist cheap threats because they do not signal that the coercer is highly committed to achieving its objectives.

Notes

1. These sources include interviews of Iraqis detained after the 2003 invasion. Because prisoners constitute a protected class of human subjects, I submitted this research design to the Columbia University Institutional Review Board (IRB) in 2009. The IRB deemed this research exempt (protocol number IRB-AAAE7851, approved October 15, 2009, renewed October 18, 2011).

2. Gordon, "Iraq Army Invades Capital."

3. United Nations Security Council, "Resolution 660 (1990)."

4. Quoted in Apple, "Invading Iraqis Seize Kuwait."

5. Farnsworth, "Bush, in Freezing Assets."

6. Apple, "Invading Iraqis Seize Kuwait."

7. United States Department of Defense (USDOD), *Conduct of the Persian Gulf War*, 21.

8. Gordon, "Pentagon Drafts Strategy."

9. "Remarks at the Aspen Institute."

10. "Remarks and a Question-and-Answer Session."

11. "Remarks and an Exchange with Reporters."

12. Quoted in Gordon and Trainor, *Generals' War*, 49.

13. USDOD, *Conduct of the Persian Gulf War*, 31.

14. Gordon and Trainor, *Generals' War*, 48–53. In the days immediately following the invasion, there was some disagreement within the administration about the appropriate American response. Notably, Gen. Colin Powell, the chairman of the Joint Chiefs, wanted to wait for civilian policymakers to obtain support for a major operation in the Gulf before focusing on military plans. He believed that the American public would be willing to send its soldiers to protect Saudi Arabia but not to restore Kuwait's independence. Cheney wanted to focus immediately on military options. See Gordon and Trainor, *Generals' War*, 33–34.

15. UN Security Council, "Resolution 661 (1990)."

16. UN Security Council, "Resolution 662 (1990)."

17. Gordon, "Bush Orders Navy." A few days after the blockade was announced, Iraq rounded up and detained several thousand Americans and other Westerners in Iraq and Kuwait. Saddam vowed to use them as "human shields" in the event of an attack. The hostages created a major point of friction for the United States and its allies, but all the hostages were released by December 1990. See USDOD, *Conduct of the Persian Gulf War*, 28–29.

18. "Transcript of U.S. Statement about Measures against Iraq."

19. "Case 90-1: US, UN v. Iraq," in Hufbauer et al., *Economic Sanctions Reconsidered.* This case history on the supplemental CD-ROM provides a comprehensive overview of US and UN economic sanctions against Iraq before, during, and after the 1991 war.

20. USDOD, *Conduct of the Persian Gulf War*, 33.

21. Ibid., 35–36.

22. Gordon and Trainor, *Generals' War*, 60–63.

23. USDOD, *Conduct of the Persian Gulf War*, 36–37.

24. Ibid., 39.

25. Ibid., 66.

26. The plan for the strategic air campaign against Iraq was a departure from the gradual escalation that characterized the "Rolling Thunder" campaign in Vietnam. It generated considerable disagreement within the US Air Force, with the other branches, and with the civilian leadership. For more on the debate surrounding the use of airpower and the various plans for the ground campaign, see Gordon and Trainor, *Generals' War*, chapters 4–9.

27. Baker, *Politics of Diplomacy*, 303.

28. Bush, "President's News Conference on the Persian Gulf Crisis."

29. USDOD, *Conduct of the Persian Gulf War*, 70.

30. Baker, *Politics of Diplomacy*, 278.

31. "Remarks and a Question-and-Answer Session."

32. USDOD, *Conduct of the Persian Gulf War*, 21.

33. Kifner, "Confrontation in the Gulf." Only twelve of twenty-one members voted in favor of the resolution. Libya, the Palestine Liberation Organization, and Iraq voted against the resolution (and several others expressed reservations or abstained).

34. Baker, *Politics of Diplomacy*, 308–13, 320–21. Baker also secured a $4 billion line of credit from Saudi Arabia for the Soviet Union, a move that he believes was vital to keeping the Soviet Union on board with UN Resolution 678 (p. 295).

35. Baker, *Politics of Diplomacy*, 288.

36. USDOD, *Conduct of the Persian Gulf War*, 21–22.

37. Ibid., 23.

38. Ibid., 20–21.

39. Ibid., 634.

40. Ibid., 60.

41. Baker, *Politics of Diplomacy*, 305.

42. Resolutions passed by the UN Security Council in 1990 are available through the UN's website at http://www.un.org/Docs/scres/1990/scres90.htm.

43. UN Security Council, "Resolution 678 (1990)." Note that China had voted in favor of several of the earlier resolutions on Iraq.

44. Bush, "President's News Conference, 1990-11-30." See note 17 on the hostages held in Iraq and Kuwait.

45. Ibid.

46. Baker, *Politics of Diplomacy*, 352.

47. Apple, "Bush Offers to Send Baker."

48. "Iraqi Leader's Message to National Assembly."

49. Friedman, "Bush Puts Talks 'On Hold.'"

50. Friedman, "Partial Pullout by Iraq Is Feared."

51. "Statement by Press Secretary Fitzwater." Bush assured the Iraqi leader that the coalition arrayed against him could not be broken. He also urged the Iraqi leader not to assume that "diversity of opinion" in the United States indicated a lack of will to oust Iraqi forces from Kuwait.

52. "United States Department of State Memorandum of Conversation," 2.

53. Ibid., 3.

54. Ibid., 5.

55. Ibid., 7.

56. Ibid., 9.

57. Ibid., 10.

58. Ibid., 28. Interestingly, Baker continued to reassure Aziz that "I'm not threatening, I'm just stating the facts as we see them" (p. 28).

59. Ibid., 34.

60. Ibid., 38.

61. Baker, *Politics of Diplomacy*, 352, 356.

62. Authorization for Use of Military Force against Iraq Resolution.

63. USDOD, *Conduct of the Persian Gulf War*, 80.

64. "United States Department of State Memorandum of Conversation," 38–39.

65. The UN Security Council seat occupied by the Soviet Union was not transferred to the Russian Federation until December 24, 1991. See the list of UN members at http://www.un.org/en/members/index.shtml#r.

66. This does not imply that there were no risks associated with the threat and use of force against the Iraqi regime. The Bush administration was very concerned about Iraq launching Scud missiles against Israel, and the air

campaign targeted Scud launchers for this reason (see USDOD, *Conduct of the Persian Gulf War*, 166–67). In the letter to Saddam that Secretary Baker attempted to deliver to Aziz, President Bush also expressed willingness to retaliate in response to terrorist attacks or the use of biological or chemical weapons (see "Statement by Press Secretary Fitzwater"). The United States did not, however, risk a devastating war with a peer competitor when it issued its threat against Iraq in 1991.

67. Singer, "Regulation of New Warfare."

68. Gordon and Trainor, *Generals' War*, 132–33.

69. Ibid., 33–34.

70. Despite the exaltation of precision munitions and their use in the Gulf War, less than 5 percent of the bombs dropped during Desert Storm were precision-guided. See Keaney and Cohen, *Gulf War Air Power* Survey, 225–26.

71. USDOD, *Conduct of the Persian Gulf War*, 20–21.

72. Bush did, however, issue a deterrent threat promising to retaliate against "you and your country" if Saddam authorized terrorist attacks or the use of biological or chemical weapons during the war. See "Statement by Press Secretary Fitzwater."

73. Gordon and Trainor, *Generals' War*, 188. Although the targeting plans were carefully drafted, most of the bombs dropped on Iraq in 1991 were not precision-guided. See note 70.

74. After the war, the Iraqi regime suppressed rebellions in both the Shia-dominated south and the northern Kurdish region. Although the United States is not blameless for encouraging these rebellions and then failing to prevent the Iraqi government from crushing them, these civilian casualties were not highly politically costly for the Bush administration because they were inflicted by the Iraqi regime. More important, they could not have been foreseen at the time that the United States was issuing its final threat against Iraq in early 1991. On the rebellions and Schwarzkopf's decision to allow the Iraqis to use their helicopters after the war, see Gordon and Trainor, *Generals' War*, 445–50.

75. GDP figures in current US dollars, from World Bank, "GDP (current US$)." GDP per capita also reported in current US dollars, from World Bank, "GDP per capita (current US$)."

76. World Bank, "Military expenditure (% of GDP)."

77. Office of Management and Budget, "Table 3.1."

78. USDOD, *Conduct of the Persian Gulf War*, 85–86.

79. Ibid., 11–16.

80. Ibid., 86.

81. Ibid., 9–11.

82. "Saddam Meets with Yasser Arafat (aka Abu-Ammar) and a Palestinian Delegation to Discuss a Variety of Topics, including Potential Terrorist

Operations against the United States (19 April 1990)," in Woods, Palkki, and Stout, *Saddam Tapes*, 114.

83. "Interview Session 9: February 24, 2004," in Battle, *Saddam Hussein Talks to the FBI*, 5.

84. "Interview Session 10: February 27, 2004," in ibid., 1.

85. "Saddam Appraises American and International Reactions to the Invasion of Kuwait (7 August 1990)," in Woods, Palkki, and Stout, in *Saddam Tapes*, 175–76.

86. "Interview Session 12: March 5, 2004," in Battle, *Saddam Hussein Talks to the FBI*, 1.

87. "Saddam Reacts to the Onset of the Ground War (24 February 1991)," in Woods, Palkki, and Stout, *Saddam Tapes*, 191–92.

88. "Iraqi Leaders Discuss Arming the People: The Leadership Expresses the Belief That America's Casualty Aversion Can Still Allow Iraq to Win (24 February 1991)," in ibid., 195.

89. "Saddam Discusses the Role of Capitalism in America's Involvement in the Mother of All Battles (circa 19–21 August 1991)," in ibid., 39.

90. "Saddam Suggests That Iraq's 'Fighting Spirit' Led President Bush to Request a Cease-Fire (1 May 1991)," in ibid., 212. The American perspective on the timing of the cease-fire is, of course, quite different. See Gordon and Trainor, *Generals' War*, 413–29. Saddam had also tried to negotiate a withdrawal from Kuwait in February to preempt the launch of the ground campaign, with the Soviet Union acting as a mediator. Bush rejected these efforts as an attempt to stall for time and pillage Kuwait during a long withdrawal process. See Woods, Palkki, and Stout, *Saddam Tapes*, 188–94.

91. "Saddam Discusses How Iraq Won the Gulf War and Where It Should Have Engaged in Preemptive Attacks on Gathering Coalition Forces (circa March 1991)," in Woods, Palkki, and Stout, *Saddam Tapes*, 214.

92. "Interview Session 11: March 3, 2004," in Battle, *Saddam Hussein Talks to the FBI*, 3–4.

93. "Saddam and Top-Level Ba'ath Officials Discuss the Causes and Consequences of Clinton's Electoral Victory and the Potential for Improved Relations (circa 4 November 1992)," in Woods, Palkki, and Stout, *Saddam Tapes*, 42.

94. Duelfer, *Comprehensive Report of the Special Advisor to the DCI on Iraq's WMD*, vol. 1, 33. Hereafter, I refer to this source as the Duelfer Report.

95. Duelfer Report, vol. 1, 24–25.

96. On plans for a withdrawal in August 1990, see "Interview Session 11: March 3, 2004," in Battle, *Saddam Hussein Talks to the FBI*, 4. We cannot necessarily accept these assertions at face value, but it is noteworthy that Saddam was claiming to have offered the same outcome as that which the United States

had demanded. This would have been unlikely had he actually resisted because the demand to evacuate Kuwait was too outrageous.

97. In a sense, Saddam's reasoning was not disproven by the 1991 campaign. The coalition did launch extensive air strikes in anticipation of the ground assault on Iraqi forces, and it did not have to make any tough decisions about how many casualties it would be willing to take in a long march to Baghdad.

Chapter 6
The 2003 Threat against Iraq

In this chapter, I evaluate the United States' use of compellent threats against Iraq before the 2003 invasion. The case deserves our attention not only because it provides an opportunity to evaluate the United States' subsequent effort to coerce the same target as in 1990–91, but also because of the logic that the George W. Bush administration employed to justify the invasion of Iraq. It argued that preventive action ("preemptive" in the administration's terms, a point to which we will return below) was necessary because Saddam Hussein could not be contained. That is, they argued that coercion was unlikely to work against the Iraqi leader. As we will see in this chapter, however, the United States did succeed in some respects in compelling Saddam to change his behavior—notably on the issue of weapons inspections—before the final ultimatum failed in March 2003.[1] There may have been room for additional coercion had the Bush administration been willing to take "yes" for an answer. Thus, the 2003 case generates valuable insights about whether preventive war was a necessary doctrine.

The 2003 case also generates important insights about the logic of costly compellence. The 2003 threat was less costly than the threat that the United States issued against the Iraqi regime in 1991. Thus, Saddam should have been more likely to resist the United States' demands than he was before the Gulf War. The logic of the expansive demands theory suggests that resistance in 2003 was inevitable because the United States was demanding regime change. Indeed, this explanation for the failed 2003 threat emerges as the most important alternative to costly compellence for this case. Saddam's resistance in March 2003 is consistent with the prediction generated by the expansive demands theory. As we will see, however, the evidence from the primary sources on Saddam's regime is not consistent with the causal logic proposed by this theory.

I begin this chapter by examining the events leading up to the ultimatum that the Bush administration issued in March 2003 and employ this evidence to determine what the costly compellence theory predicts about the Iraqi leader's likely response. Next, I evaluate the alternative theories of compellent-threat effectiveness. I draw on observations from the previous chapter on the efforts to coerce Iraq in 1990–91 to generate relative predictions about Iraq's likely response in 2003. I also compare the 2002 threat to readmit weapons inspectors with the final ultimatum in March 2003. Finally, I draw on materials captured by or generated as a result of the 2003 invasion to evaluate Saddam's decision making. These sources suggest that Saddam resisted in 2003 not because he doubted the United States' willingness to use military force against Iraq, but because he doubted that the United States had the will to go all the way to Baghdad.

After the Gulf War: Containment and Inspections

The effort to coerce Saddam's Iraq did not end with the Gulf War. The United States clashed with Iraq several times during the following decade, mostly over the issue of weapons inspections. UN Security Council Resolution 687, which passed on April 3, 1991, formalized the terms for the cessation of hostilities and established the framework for monitoring Iraq's weapons programs after the war. The United Nations Special Commission (UNSCOM) was charged with inspecting and dismantling Iraq's programs for biological and chemical weapons and with assisting the International Atomic Energy Agency (IAEA) in the enforcement of Iraq's renunciation of nuclear weapons.[2]

During the 1990s, debate within the US policymaking community centered on two possible ways to manage Saddam's regime: rollback and containment. Rollback focused on removing Saddam and his regime from power, while the more modest goal of containment was to check Iraq's regional ambitions and complete the disarmament required by Resolution 687. Containment emerged as the default option due to constraints on the ability to overthrow the Iraqi regime. In March 1993, the Bill Clinton administration shifted away from public rhetoric demanding Saddam's removal from power, a move designed to maintain support for multinational sanctions.[3]

In the twelve years from the end of the Gulf War through the invasion of Iraq in 2003, the inspection of Iraq's facilities to verify compliance with UN resolutions on WMDs was a major point of friction between Iraq and the United States. Iraq frequently refused to cooperate with UNSCOM inspectors, blocked their access to certain sites, and refused the installation of monitoring equipment.[4] There were several major crises over UNSCOM's ability to access and inspect various locations in Iraq, some of which resulted in US air strikes.[5] Notably, Iraq announced in August 1998 that it would cease cooperation with UNSCOM and later demanded the removal of Richard Butler as UNSCOM chair and the lifting of UN sanctions in exchange for compliance. After Butler reported on December 15 that Iraq was not living up to its obligations, the United States and the United Kingdom launched air strikes that hit dozens of targets in Iraq over four days.[6]

When the air strikes ended on December 20, there was still no agreement on an inspections regime or on the means by which Iraq could suspend UN sanctions. International support for the continued use of force was lacking, however, and several states lobbied on humanitarian grounds for the lifting of economic sanctions against Iraq. In December 1999, the UN Security Council passed Resolution 1284 to replace UNSCOM with the United Nations Monitoring, Verification, and Inspection Commission (UNMOVIC).[7]

Even before the launch of Operation Desert Fox in November 1998, the United States had begun to shift policy on Iraq. On October 31, President Clinton signed the Iraq Liberation Act of 1998. The act declared that "it should be the policy of the United States to support efforts to remove the regime headed by Saddam Hussein from power in Iraq and to promote the emergence of a democratic government to replace that regime."[8] This constituted a shift away from the more restrained rhetoric that characterized Clinton's first term and suggested that the United States would no longer be satisfied with a policy of containment.

The George W. Bush Administration

President George W. Bush inherited Clinton's standing policy of regime change when he came into office. In January 2001, before the inauguration, Vice President–elect Dick Cheney asked that the incoming president be briefed on the situation in Iraq and on "different options" available for addressing Saddam.[9] President Bush did not actively focus on developing a plan to overthrow the Iraqi leader, however, until after the terrorist attacks of September 11, 2001. In their immediate aftermath, Deputy Secretary of Defense Paul Wolfowitz was the only strong advocate of launching a strike on Iraq.[10] Although Bush opted to invade Afghanistan instead, he did not rule out the possibility of going after the Iraqi regime in the future. Bush noted in an interview several years later that 9/11 had changed his thinking about how to manage Saddam. After the attacks, "keeping Saddam in a box looked less and less feasible. . . . He had used weapons of mass destruction in the past. He has created incredible instability in the neighborhood. . . . The options in Iraq were relatively limited when you are playing the containment game."[11]

On November 21, 2001, Bush asked Secretary of Defense Donald Rumsfeld to examine the Iraq war plan. Although he claimed that he was not eager to start a second war, Bush has since indicated that he knew the decision to revamp the war plan could set the United States on the path to war.[12] The plan was revised over the following month, and Gen. Tommy Franks briefed the president on the plan at his ranch on December 28. The plan constituted a new vision of war with Iraq, "one which might be executed as a preemptive strike" and would draw on "all elements of national power."[13]

In his 2002 State of the Union address one month later, Bush branded North Korea, Iran, and Iraq members of an "axis of evil." These states, which already possessed or were seeking to acquire WMDs, threatened world stability. Bush asserted that "the United States of America will not permit the world's most dangerous regimes to threaten us with the world's most destructive weapons. . . . We are protected from attack only by vigorous action abroad, and increased vigilance at home."[14] In other words, the United States would actively preempt such threats before they had the chance to materialize.

By early 2002, the question for the Bush administration was not whether Saddam would be ousted from power, but when and how. Referring to Saddam, Bush told National Security Adviser Condoleezza Rice and three senators with whom she was meeting in March 2002, "We're taking him out."[15] In early April, British prime minister Tony Blair spent a weekend with Bush at his ranch. In an interview with Britain's ITV network, Bush asserted that he had no immediate plans to attack Iraq but that he and the prime minister would be "discussing all options" for dealing with Saddam. Bush was convinced that "the worst thing that could happen would be to allow a nation like Iraq, run by Saddam Hussein, to develop weapons of mass destruction and then team up with terrorist organizations so they can blackmail the world. I'm not going to let that happen." He further asserted, "I made up my mind that Saddam needs to go. . . . The policy of my government is that Saddam Hussein not be in power." When prompted to describe how the US government would achieve this outcome, Bush responded, "Wait and see."[16]

As the military continued to revise the Iraq war plan, the Bush administration was also exploring the possibility of a covert operation to remove Saddam from power. In early 2002, the CIA officer in charge of the Iraq Operations Group informed the Bush administration that covert action would not be enough to dislodge Saddam from power. Saddam had structured his military and intelligence services in such a way that he was practically immune to a coup, and the United States had almost no human sources on the ground in Iraq. On February 16, 2002, President Bush signed a secret order directing the CIA to support the US military in overthrowing the Iraqi regime. The order came with an authorization to spend $189 million in the first year and $200 million in the second to conduct a range of operations, including sabotage, supporting opposition groups, and recruiting local allies and sources for US intelligence.[17]

There was thus a deep inconsistency in the United States' approach to the Iraqi regime by 2002. On the one hand, the United States was supporting the UN's economic sanctions in an effort to contain the Iraqi regime. On the other hand, the United States was exploring the use of covert operations to overthrow Saddam, privately telling the Jordanians and Saudis that such plans were in the works and secretly developing a war plan to physically overthrow the Iraqi leader.[18] The requirements for success in one of these tracks were different from, if not mutually exclusive of, the requirements for success in the other. The use of economic sanctions implied that the United States and the international community would be prepared to work with Saddam if he changed his behavior. The plan to overthrow Saddam through a combination of covert and direct military action implied, however, that there was no additional room for the Iraqi leader to cooperate. Furthermore, if Saddam learned or suspected that this track had been set in motion, then there was little incentive for him to comply with the sanctions or the inspections.

The War Plans Continue to Evolve

The plan for an attack on Iraq continued to evolve in early 2002. The major conflict during this period was between civilian officials, including Rumsfeld and Wolfowitz, who were pushing for a smaller, faster assault on Iraq that would bring the regime to its knees without the need for extensive ground operations, and Franks and his planners, who were more skeptical that a bombing campaign and a small ground force could do the job. Rumsfeld was pushing the concept of "shock and awe," which at this point envisioned a buildup of force and massive bombing to trigger regime change—consistent with the RMA thesis. Powell was extremely skeptical of this plan to attack Iraq with an initial force of 105,000 and of Rumsfeld's vision of "transformation."[19]

The Bush administration also stepped up its public rhetoric. At his West Point commencement speech on June 1, Bush argued that defending against the dangers posed by terrorists and by WMDs required new strategies. The United States could not afford to assume a defensive posture: "If we wait for threats to fully materialize we will have waited too long."[20] On August 27, Cheney gave a speech to the Veterans of Foreign Wars national convention. As the president had done in January's State of the Union address, Cheney asserted that there was a link between the type of terrorism that had been inflicted on the United States on September 11 and the pursuit of WMDs by states such as Iraq. The United States must understand that "wars are never won on the defensive. We must take the battle to the enemy."[21]

Cheney's speech foreshadowed the 2002 National Security Strategy, which the Bush administration unveiled three weeks later. In his introduction, President Bush asserted that "the only path to peace and security is the path of action." The strategy asserts that the threat posed by transnational terrorism is one that cannot be managed through deterrence or by responding after attacks have occurred. Citing the right in international law for a state to act preemptively to defend itself against an imminent attack, the strategy asserts that the United States has the right to eliminate threats posed by terrorists and by states seeking to acquire WMDs before these threats have had a chance to materialize. In other words, "to forestall or prevent such hostile acts by our adversaries, the United States will, if necessary, act preemptively."[22]

Turning up the Heat: Fall 2002

On September 12, 2002, President Bush addressed the UN General Assembly. He announced that "our greatest fear is that terrorists will find a shortcut to their mad ambitions when an outlaw regime supplies them with the technologies to kill on a massive scale." He then turned the focus to Iraq and argued that Saddam's regime had violated UN resolutions demanding disarmament. Bush asserted that Iraq would have had nuclear weapons by 1993 had the international community not launched the Gulf War. He listed a series of steps that Iraq needed to take in order to be at peace with the international community, including the disclosure and destruction of its WMDs. Bush asserted that the United States would work with the UN to obtain resolutions addressing Iraq's weapons programs, but "if Iraq's regime defies us again, the world must move deliberately, decisively to hold Iraq to account. . . . The security council resolutions will be enforced, the just demands of peace and security will be met or action will be unavoidable and a regime that has lost its legitimacy will also lose its power."[23]

On October 7, Bush made a nationally televised speech in which he laid out the administration's case against Iraq. He focused on Iraq's pursuit of WMDs and development of ballistic missiles in violation of various UN resolutions. Most important, he drew a direct link between the Iraqi regime and al-Qaeda, and he argued that "confronting the threat posed by Iraq is crucial to winning the war on terror." The United States could not accept the risk that Saddam would use his WMDs or would provide such weapons to terrorists.[24] Three days later, Congress passed a resolution authorizing the president to use the armed forces to defend the United States against the threat posed by Iraq and to enforce relevant UN Security Council resolutions.[25]

In the midst of this escalating rhetoric, in October 2002 the secret

US national intelligence estimate (NIE) on Iraq's WMDs was released. Most of the key judgments from this estimate have since been declassified. The October NIE asserts that "Baghdad has chemical and biological weapons as well as missiles with ranges in excess of UN restrictions; if left unchecked, it probably will have a nuclear weapon during this decade." The report also accuses Iraq of engaging in "vigorous denial and deception efforts" to conceal the scope and extent of its WMD activities. Although the report asserted that Iraq did not have sufficient nuclear material to produce a device, it concluded that Iraq was determined to acquire a nuclear weapon and had restarted its program to do so shortly after UNSCOM inspectors left Iraq at the end of 1998.[26] Notably, the State Department's Bureau of Intelligence and Research (INR) dissented from this view and asserted that "the available evidence [was] inadequate" to support the claim that Iraq was actively pursuing a nuclear weapon.[27]

The UN also stepped up its campaign against Iraq. On November 8, 2002, the Security Council passed Resolution 1441 declaring Iraq in breach of its obligations under Resolution 687, which had terminated the Gulf War and established the framework for UNSCOM. Resolution 1441 demanded that Iraq make a full disclosure of its weapons programs and stockpiles and grant immediate and unrestricted access for UNMOVIC and the IAEA to inspect, catalog, and evaluate Iraq's weapons and development facilities. UNMOVIC had not operated in Iraq since inspectors had been kicked out in 1998. Although the resolution warned that Iraq would face "serious consequences" if it continued to defy the resolutions, it did not grant member states the right to take military action (or even "all necessary means") to enforce it.[28]

Inspections Resume

On November 27, 2002, UNMOVIC and the IAEA resumed inspections inside Iraq for the first time since 1998. The inspectors met no resistance at the three sites they examined, and the Iraqis on hand were eager to emphasize their cooperation.[29] On December 7, in compliance with Resolution 1441, Iraq submitted to the UN Security Council a twelve-thousand-page document detailing its weapons programs. In a briefing to the Security Council on December 19,

UNMOVIC chairman Hans Blix assessed Iraq's December 7 declaration and described the rapid acceleration of inspections since the
end of November. Blix noted that much of the declaration contained
old information, but there was some new material on Iraq's missile
programs. Most important, Iraq maintained throughout that "there
were no weapons of mass destruction in Iraq, when inspectors left
at the end of 1998 and that none have been designed, procured,
produced or stored in the period since then." Blix then claimed that
"UNMOVIC at this point is neither in a position to confirm Iraq's
statements, nor in possession of evidence to disprove it." He noted,
however, that Iraq had deceived the international inspections regime
about its weapons activities in the past.[30]

In a statement the following day, Powell called the Iraqi disclosure "a
catalogue of recycled information and flagrant omissions. . . . These
are material omissions that, in our view, constitute another material
breach." In terms even stronger than those employed by Blix, Powell
argued that the declaration failed to provide any new information
on Iraq's materials and programs. He then asserted that the United
States would be consulting its allies on how to "compel compliance"
from Iraq, as "the world will not wait forever" for Saddam to choose
to cooperate.[31] Despite Powell's characterization of Iraq's behavior,
it is clear that Saddam was offering concessions to the United States
and the international community when he readmitted the weapons
inspectors in late November, a point to which we will return later in
this chapter.

UNMOVIC and IAEA inspections continued through early
2003. In a briefing to the Security Council on January 9, Blix denied that the inspectors had found a "smoking gun" indicating that
Iraq possessed or was seeking to produce illegal weapons. The inspections were still having an impact, but he urged Iraq to provide
"credible evidence" to back up the assertions in their December declaration.[32] On January 20, UNMOVIC and the IAEA issued a joint
statement indicating that inspectors had been granted access to all
sites requested and that the Iraqis were, in general, cooperating with
the inspectors. Some empty chemical munitions had been found at
one site, but the statement reports no other discoveries.[33]

On January 27, Blix reported that Iraq had largely cooperated
with the "process" of inspections but had yet to cooperate fully on

"substance." That is, Iraq had been granting access to various sites for inspections but was not being forthcoming in providing information about many aspects of its weapons programs. Blix noted that UNMOVIC's investigations and his examination of the December declaration suggested that Iraq possessed, or had at one time possessed, more chemical munitions and biological agents than it had disclosed. In his assessment, "Iraq appears not to have come to a genuine acceptance—not even today—of the disarmament, which was demanded of it and which it needs to carry out to win the confidence of the world and to live in peace." Most of Blix's remarks were, however, focused on the requirements for additional evidence and inspections necessary to account for discrepancies in Iraq's reporting.[34]

President Bush delivered his State of the Union address the following day. He claimed that the United States had evidence that Iraq was actively working to deceive UNMOVIC and threatening Iraqi scientists who cooperated with inspectors. He also asserted that Saddam's regime was aiding al-Qaeda and that it could give WMDs to terrorists. Speaking of the UN and the United States' allies, Bush noted that "we will consult, but let there be no misunderstanding: If Saddam Hussein does not fully disarm for the safety of our people, and for the peace of the world, we will lead a coalition to disarm him." Bush then addressed American troops deployed to the Middle East and noted that "some crucial hours may lay [sic] ahead."[35]

The Final Ultimatum Fails

In a lengthy address on February 5, 2003, Powell laid out the United States' case against Iraq. He cited Blix's assertions that Iraq's December declaration contained no new information and that Iraq had yet to accept its disarmament requirements. He claimed that "Saddam Hussein and his regime are concealing their efforts to produce more weapons of mass destruction." Powell played audiotapes in which Iraqis discussed plans to clean out empty chemical shells. He showed photographs allegedly indicating that Iraq had removed chemical weapons from storage bunkers in advance of a visit by UNMOVIC inspectors. Citing the finding from the October NIE on Iraq's efforts to acquire aluminum tubes, Powell also asserted that the Iraqi regime retained the desire to develop nuclear weapons and had direct ties to al-Qaeda. Powell argued that "this body places itself in danger of irrelevance if it allows Iraq to continue to defy its will without responding effectively and immediately." Powell urged the Security Council to force Iraq to comply with its obligations, because "Saddam Hussein and his regime will stop at nothing until something stops him."[36]

The United States and the United Kingdom submitted a draft resolution to the UN Security Council on March 7 that would have given Iraq ten days to demonstrate compliance with the disarmament obligations specified in Resolution 1441.[37] Both France and Russia promised to veto this resolution.[38] Knowing that the resolution would fail, on March 17 the United States and the United Kingdom announced that they would not be seeking a vote on the draft resolution.[39] In his address to the nation that evening, President Bush asserted that "the United Nations Security Council has not lived up to its responsibilities, so we will rise to ours." He urged foreign nationals, including inspectors, to leave Iraq, and then he issued the United States' final ultimatum to the Iraqi leader: "All the decades of deceit and cruelty have now reached an end. Saddam Hussein and his sons must leave Iraq within 48 hours. Their refusal to do so will result in military conflict, commenced at a time of our choosing."[40] Saddam and his sons did not evacuate by the appointed deadline, and the United States launched Operation Iraqi Freedom on March 19.

The Bush administration's case against Saddam's regime focused mostly on Iraq's alleged efforts to acquire WMDs. The question of why the prewar estimates about Iraq's WMD capabilities were inaccurate is complicated. The related question of whether and to what extent the Bush administration actively manipulated or distorted intelligence on Iraqi WMDs to sell the war is also complicated.[41] Both of these questions are important and deserve close examination, but they are beyond the scope of the present study. The questions at hand are what the Bush administration was communicating to the Iraqi regime and how the United States' threat of military action influenced Saddam's decision making.

The 2003 Threat: Contextual Variables

The United States' threat against Saddam on March 17 bears the classic hallmarks of a compellent ultimatum: There was a demand for a change in the status quo (Saddam and his sons must leave Iraq), a deadline for compliance (March 19), and a promise of punishment ("military conflict") in the event of noncompliance. The question at hand, then, is why Saddam chose not to comply with the United States' demands, given the obvious preparations for an attack that the United States had been making since mid-2002.

In 2003, the United States was still the world's sole superpower. Even after the economic downturn that followed the attacks of September 11, the United States retained its position as the world's economic and military leader.[42] At the end of 2002, the United States had a total of 1.4 million personnel in the active armed forces and 1.3 million reservists, all volunteers.[43] The United States had roughly 7,500 troops on the ground in Afghanistan that year.[44] In other words, the bulk of US ground forces were not tied down elsewhere as the United States prepared to attack Iraq. There were also an unknown number of private military contractors on the ground in Afghanistan at that time providing logistical support and preparing to train the new Afghan security forces.[45] These contractors would play an increasingly important role in both Afghanistan and Iraq as the United States became bogged down in these countries longer than planners had originally anticipated.

In early 2003, the United States was preparing to attack Iraq with the model of warfare that had emerged from the 1991 Gulf War and been refined over the intervening decade—a model that relies on speed, precision, and technology over mass. Rumsfeld directed planning of the 2003 campaign to focus on the United States' advantages in information technology and precision weaponry. He believed that the success of the Afghanistan campaign had demonstrated that the United States could take out the Iraqi regime with a small number of ground troops rather than the five hundred thousand for which the Gulf War–era war plans called. Rumsfeld also believed that the efforts of special operations forces could be integrated with precision bombing to maximize the impact of a small number of US ground troops.[46] When the United States launched Operation Iraqi Freedom in March 2003, the invasion force numbered 145,000, including 20,000 troops from the British First Armored Division.[47] This force was considerably smaller than the one that was assembled in 1991 to eject Iraqi forces from Kuwait.

Saddam could not have known in advance exactly what type of campaign the United States would launch against him. The course of the Afghanistan campaign and his own experience with the US military in 1991 would likely have led him to expect that the United States would again rely on a high-tech approach to attack his regime. In fact, we know from interviews with former Iraqi officials that Saddam expected any military action undertaken by the United States in late 2002 and early 2003 to take the form of air strikes, a point to which we will return later in this chapter.[48]

The American model of warfare in early 2003 suggests that issuing and executing a threat against Saddam's regime would not have been very costly for the United States. The United States was the world's sole superpower and wielded a military composed entirely of volunteers supplemented by private contractors. Furthermore, the United States commanded a military built on the RMA model: By leveraging their advantages in information technology and precision targeting, US forces could maximize the damage inflicted on the target while minimizing the risk of US casualties. These trends suggest that the Bush administration would face few political risks for the use of force against the Iraqi regime, since volunteers and contractors would be absorbing the costs. Table 6.1 summarizes the US military model in early 2003 and indicates whether the factors under consideration made the threat against Saddam more or less costly for the United States.

Threat Characteristics

The 2003 threat against Iraq would be somewhat costly for the United States to execute. Bush's ultimatum did not explicitly specify that the United States would be launching a ground operation, but the United States had been steadily deploying troops to the region

Table 6.1. Contextual Variables, Iraq 2003

Contextual Variables		Effect on US Military Action
Polarity:	Unipolar	Less costly
Conscription?	No	Less costly
Contractors?	Extensive	Less costly
RMA?	Yes	Less costly

and was, in fact, planning a combined air and ground assault on Iraq. Launching a campaign that involved ground troops would be more costly for the United States than, for example, NATO's campaign over Kosovo in 1999. By the time Bush issued his compellent threat on March 17, the coalition had more than 145,000 troops in the region. Saddam could not discount the strong possibility that they would attack. The United States had stopped short of advancing to Baghdad at the conclusion of the 1991 campaign, so it is possible that he judged the impact of a ground invasion would be limited, a point to which we will return below.

The use of ground troops would render the campaign against Iraq more costly than an air campaign alone, since these troops would be exposed to greater risk than they would be if the United States relied solely on a standoff strike to unseat the Iraqi leader. The plan for the invasion was, however, based on the idea that the attack could succeed with a relatively small number of troops. In the run-up to the war, Rumsfeld rejected several invasion plans because they called for too many ground troops. In the view of one planner involved in the process, "Rumsfeld had two goals: to demonstrate the efficacy of precision bombing and to 'do the war on the cheap.'"[49] Rumsfeld believed that "speed and agility and precision [could] take the place of mass."[50]

The United States was threatening to invade Iraq with a remarkably limited roster of allies. Unlike 1991, when the first President Bush threatened military action on behalf of a UN-sanctioned coalition of states, in 2003 George W. Bush threatened Saddam with the backing of only a few allies. Bush issued the March 17 ultimatum on the same day that the United States announced that it would not be seeking a Security Council vote on the draft resolution authorizing force against Iraq. The United Kingdom was the only one of its major allies that stood with the United States in its campaign to overthrow the Iraqi regime. The United States did secure pledges to deploy troops from several small states, including Spain, Poland, Ukraine, and Denmark, among others, but it failed to secure support from France or Germany.[51]

Even Saudi Arabia, which had made significant contributions to the Gulf War, offered only minimal support for the 2003 invasion. On his tour of Middle Eastern states in early 2002, Cheney found that the Saudis were reluctant to appear to cooperate too closely with the United States, lest they ignite fundamentalist protests in the kingdom. Eventually, Saudi Arabia did agree to permit CENTCOM to run the air campaign from the command center at Prince Sultan Air Base, but it prohibited the United States from launching bombers from Saudi territory.[52] This was in marked contrast to 1990–91, when Saudi Arabia allowed the United States to station hundreds of thousands of troops on its territory and committed billions of dollars to support the war.

On the other hand, the Bush administration was not anticipating that the attack on Iraq would be very expensive. According to Stiglitz and Bilmes, before the war, "Office of Management and Budget director Mitch Daniels and Secretary Rumsfeld estimated the costs in the range of $50–$60 billion, a portion of which they believed would be financed by other countries." Rumsfeld also expected Iraq's oil revenues would pay for postwar reconstruction.[53] The logic of costly compellence asserts that the purpose of securing support from allies is not to enhance the overall effectiveness of US military action, but rather to redistribute the costs of an operation. Although the United States failed to assemble the coalition it had in 1991, the relatively low projected cost of the operation and the anticipated remittances from oil revenues would minimize the extent to which unilateral action would prove expensive.

Furthermore, even in the absence of allied support, there were no calls in the United States for an "Iraq tax" to offset the costs of attacking the Iraqi regime. In fact, in his 2003 State of the Union address, President Bush proposed tax cuts to help stimulate the economy, despite the fact that preparations were already well under way for the operation to oust the Iraqi leader from power.[54] Instead, the Bush administration would rely on deficit spending and supplemental budget requests to fund the wars in Afghanistan and Iraq.[55] The United States' allies would not be footing the bill in 2003, but neither would the American public—at least, not immediately.

The final factor that determines the costliness of the United States' threat is the extent to which Iraqi civilians were at risk in the event of a US attack. Inflicting heavy casualties on Iraqi civilians would have entailed significant political costs for the Bush administration. In the address on March 17 in which he issued the ultimatum, Bush assured the Iraqi people that any military action that would be undertaken would be directed at the regime, not at them. He promised Iraqis that "the day of your liberation is near."[56] On the other hand, Bush also urged inspectors and foreign nationals to leave the country immediately, suggesting that there was some possibility that they would be harmed by the ensuing conflict. The bombing campaign planned for the start of Operation Iraqi Freedom was designed to minimize the harm inflicted on Iraqi civilians, but they would face some level of risk from having American troops on their soil. Table 6.2 summarizes the United States' 2003 ultimatum and indicates whether each feature made the threat more or less costly for the United States.

2003 War with Iraq: The Costly Compellence Prediction

The costly compellence theory suggests that the use of force against Iraq would be moderately costly for the United States in 2003. The United States' military manpower structure was not very expensive: The military was composed entirely of volunteers, and these volunteers were supplemented by private contractors. The plan for Operation Iraqi Freedom was explicitly designed to exploit the United States' advantages in technology and precision targeting. The use of ground troops does increase the costs of carrying out the United States' threat, compared to the use of an air campaign in isolation, but

Table 6.2. Threat Variables, Iraq 2003

Threat Variables		*Effect on US Military Action*
Ground invasion?	Small force, in conjunction with initial air attack	Moderately costly
Allies?	Few—no UN authorization; major allies absent	Moderately costly
Payment	Allies not footing the bill; tax cuts; oil revenues projected to offset costs; would employ deficit spending	Less costly
Civilian vulnerability	Targeted bombing in air campaign; occupation would put civilians at moderate risk	Moderately costly

the planned invasion force was much smaller than the one assembled to oust the Iraqis from Kuwait in 1991. The United States would be attacking Iraq without a UN resolution and with the support of very few allies, but the Bush administration anticipated that the costs of the operation would be relatively low and would be partially offset by Iraqi oil revenues. After the start of operations, the United States would turn to deficit spending rather than tax Americans to pay for the war, but these costs would have to be paid eventually.

The costly compellence argument does not generate a strong prediction about whether Saddam was likely to yield to the United States' demands in 2003. Some of the features of the US war-fighting model made the threat costly for the United States and therefore should have increased its effectiveness, while other features had the opposite effect. Overall, the relatively moderate cost of the US military model in 2002–3 suggests that Saddam was likely to resist. The prediction is not, however, a strong one. The use of force was not so obviously cheap (as it was in the 2011 intervention in Libya) that resistance was extremely likely nor so costly (as in the Cuban Missile Crisis) that Saddam was likely to concede.

If we compare the 2003 threat with the one that the United States issued in 1991, however, we can generate a relative prediction about the likely outcome. Although we cannot say that the Iraq of 2003 was identical to that of 1991, the United States was threatening the same state and the same leader in both cases. The two threats were somewhat different from the perspectives of both the United States and Iraq. The previous chapter argued that the 1991 threat was moderately costly for the United States to implement. Desert Storm did involve a significant number of US ground troops, but the United States' allies were heavily involved.

By contrast, the United States' 2003 threat was in many ways less costly than the one it issued and executed in 1991. The United States was still the unipole, and its war-fighting model was no more costly than it had been in 1991. In fact, the growing use of private military contractors had lowered to some extent the costliness of the US force structure. The RMA model had had time to develop, and Operation Iraqi Freedom was designed to exploit the features of this model. Although the United States was planning to launch a ground invasion in conjunction with a bombing campaign in 2003, the plan called for less than one third the number of troops that were assembled in Saudi Arabia in 1991.

In addition, the Bush administration projected that the 2003 war would cost $50–$60 billion. As noted in the previous chapter, the Gulf War cost about $60 billion in 1991.[57] Adjusted for inflation, this amounts to a price tag of roughly $81 billion in 2003 dollars.[58] In other words, the 2003 invasion of Iraq was projected to cost between 62 percent and 74 percent of the cost of the 1991 war. Planners had also expected that the 1991 war would generate ten thousand American casualties, while the 2003 invasion plan was driven by the theory that the United States' superior technology, training, and equipment would enable it to quickly topple the Iraqi regime while minimizing risks to US troops.

These comparisons are somewhat crude, and no state can perfectly calculate the costs of war in advance. The Bush administration was, however, selling the Iraq invasion as an operation that would be relatively quick and cheap—cheaper than the cost of expelling Iraqi forces from Kuwait in 1991. This makes sense given that the Bush administration planned to execute the war with far fewer troops. Furthermore, the fact that the administration planned to offset these costs with Iraqi oil revenues suggests that the relative lack of allies in early 2003 would make little difference in terms of the anticipated costs of the operation. Because the 2003 threat would be cheaper to execute, *costly compellence* suggests that the Iraqi regime was more likely to doubt its ultimate credibility than the 1991 threat, and thus it would be less likely to concede before the use of force.

Recall that costly compellence is a theory of coercion *before* war, not a theory of coercion *in* war. The facts that the war in Iraq became much more expensive than the Bush administration envisioned, that the United States would send tens of thousands more troops, and that it would continue combat operations for more than eight years do not bear on the prediction of costly compellence. The 2003 invasion force would be smaller, lighter, and faster than the one assembled in 1991 and would nearly pay for itself according to the Bush administration's plan. It is true that the United States would not be able to call on as many allies as it had in 1991 to share its costs, but these costs were not predicted to be large and would be offset by Iraq's oil revenues. The attack on Iraq in 2003 would still be moderately costly but less costly than the 1991 threat against Iraq. Thus, the costly compellence theory predicts that Saddam was more likely to resist in 2003 than he had been in 1991.

Alternative Theories

Reputation Theory

According to the logic of the reputation theory, Saddam should have been much more likely to concede in 2003 than in 1991. As discussed in previous chapters, the United States never issued an explicit compellent threat during the Cold War and failed to execute it in the face of the target's resistance. This trend continued during the post–Cold War period. Furthermore, the United States had demonstrated its willingness to execute threats against Iraq itself in the years following the 1991 Gulf War. The United States had also invaded Afghanistan in 2001 when the Taliban refused the compellent threat intended to convince them to hand over bin Laden. In other words, the logic of the reputation theory suggests that Saddam should have been highly likely to concede to the United States' demands in 2003.

Preponderant Power

In 2003, the United States faced an Iraq that was much weaker than it had been in 1991. After a decade of sanctions, Iraq's GDP was estimated at roughly $19 billion in 2002 ($742 per capita), compared with $48 billion in 1989. The United States recorded a GDP of roughly $10.6 trillion in 2002 ($37,000 per capita). The World Bank has no estimate of the percent of GDP that Iraq was devoting to its military in 2002, but at that time the United States was spending 3.4 percent of its GDP on military expenditures, or several times the value of Iraq's entire economy.[59]

In 1991, the United States had faced the world's fourth-largest military. As the Bush administration was planning the campaign to oust the Iraqi leader in January 2002, intelligence reports indicated that Iraq's military strength had declined significantly since 1991. The Republican Guard was down to six divisions, a loss of 15 percent, and the regular army had only seventeen divisions, 35 percent fewer than in 1991.[60] The IISS estimated that in 2002, Iraq had roughly 389,000 in the armed forces, down from roughly one million in 1985, and 650,000 in the reserves. The United States, on the other hand, had a total of 1.4 million in the active armed forces and 1.3 million reservists in 2002.[61] Furthermore, although planners worried about the possible use of chemical and biological weapons, US forces were vastly more sophisticated and better equipped than their Iraqi counterparts.[62] The regime of economic sanctions that had been in place since the Gulf War had hindered Iraq's ability to maintain and modernize its equipment. Iraq had 60 percent fewer tactical aircraft and 40 percent fewer surface-to-air missiles than it had had in 1991, and broken equipment languished for lack of spare parts.[63] Given this vast imbalance in relative power, the preponderant power theory suggests that Saddam was even more likely to concede in 2003 than he had been in 1991, when his military had been much stronger.

Expansive Demands

In the run-up to the 2003 war, the United States made a series of demands of the Iraqi leader. In the fall of 2002 and against the backdrop of military preparations that were being undertaken in the Gulf, the United States and the UN demanded that the Iraqi leader readmit weapons inspectors. He complied with this demand, although the United States consistently questioned the Iraqis' sincerity and asserted that the inspections would not be enough to prevent the spread of WMDs. On the scale of expansiveness, the demand to readmit inspectors is clearly more moderate than the final demand in March 2003 that Saddam and his sons relinquish power. It is also less expansive than the 1991 demand to evacuate Iraqi forces from Kuwait. The demand to readmit weapons inspectors was thus a moderate one. As demonstrated in the previous chapter, the expansive demands theory yields no prediction about the target's likely response in the case of moderate demands.

The 2003 ultimatum emerges, however, as a "most-likely" case for the expansive demands theory.[64] In his March 2003 ultimatum, President Bush demanded the most extreme concession that one could ask of an opponent: the elimination of the ruling regime. Thus, the expansive demands theory predicts that the Iraqi leader would be highly unlikely to concede to the March 2003 ultimatum. Although the theory yields no prediction about the 2002 threat to readmit weapons inspectors itself because the demands were moderate, we can infer that Saddam would have been more likely to resist in 2003 than in 2002 because the demand was much more extreme.

Iraq 2003: Four Predictions

For the costly compellence theory, the use of force was somewhat less costly in 2003 than in 1991 but still only modestly expensive. Thus, Saddam was more likely to resist than he had been in 1991. The reputation and preponderant power theories both predict that Saddam was more likely to concede to the 2002–3 threats than he was in 1991. They also yield identical predictions for the threat to readmit inspectors in the fall of 2002 and the 2003 ultimatum. That is, nothing changed between October 2002 and March 2003 to alter the predictions of either of these theories. Finally, the expansive demands theory predicts that Saddam was more likely to resist the 2003 threat than the one issued in the fall of 2002 and more likely to resist the 2003 ultimatum than the 1991 threat. Table 6.3 summarizes the predictions of the four theories under investigation. It also compares the predicted response for the 2003 threat (the March ultimatum) with the 1991 threat for each theory. The table also indicates whether the theories yield different predictions for the 2003 ultimatum compared to the October 2002 threat to readmit weapons inspectors.

Saddam's resistance in 2003 is thus consistent with the logic of both the costly compellence and expansive demands theories. The argument that Saddam resisted in 2003 because the demands were so overwhelming is perhaps the greatest challenge to the logic of costly compellence. The United States made the most extreme demand that it could make of another regime, and the target chose to resist. It may be the case that it is impossible to coerce a target regime into voluntarily surrendering power with the use of threats alone. Just because the target's resistance is consistent with a theory's prediction does not mean, however, that the target's decision was driven by the causal mechanism proposed by the theory. To determine why Saddam chose to resist and the extent to which his decision is consistent with the

Table 6.3. Predictions: Threats against Iraq

Theory	Iraq's Response, 2002 Threat	Iraq's Response, 2003 Ultimatum	2003 Response, Relative to 1991 Threat	2003 Response, Relative to 2002 Threat
Costly compellence	Resist	Resist	More likely	No difference
Reputation	Concede	Concede	More likely	No difference
Preponderant power	Concede	Concede	More likely	No difference
Expansive demands	Indeterminate	Resist	More likely	More likely

causal mechanisms proposed by these two theories, we must evaluate the primary sources on Saddam's beliefs and decision making.

The View from Baghdad, 2002–3

To understand how the Iraqi leader viewed the United States and its threats, we must start by examining how Saddam understood the role of WMDs. The Duelfer Report suggests that although Saddam wanted to get out from under international sanctions, during the 1990s he was more focused on deterring an attack from Iran and avoiding a revolt at home than he was worried about an attack by the United States. The report asserts that Saddam's quest to acquire WMDs was primarily motivated by his desire to balance rivals in the region.[65] Although the Duelfer Report suggests that Saddam had no real intention of complying with the UN's demands for disarmament,[66] in the fall of 2002 Saddam became sufficiently worried about a US attack that he decided to readmit inspectors. He hoped that after a series of inspections uncovered no evidence of WMD activity, he could persuade the UN to lift its sanctions.[67]

As we know, however, the United States claimed that Iraqi compliance with the UNMOVIC and IAEA inspections was less than complete. The Duelfer Report concludes that Iraq's refusal to comply fully with inspections in the run-up to the 2003 war stemmed from Saddam's desire to avoid appearing weak to regional rivals. By permitting inspections but hampering their effectiveness, Saddam could appear to comply with the UN while concealing that he was in fact weaker than he had been claiming.[68] Many Iraqi leaders were themselves confused by Saddam's contradictory claims about the regime's possession of WMDs. Although Saddam brushed aside fears about the inspections—"What can they discover, when we have nothing?"—his advisers remained worried that the United States must have had irrefutable proof that the Iraqis possessed the offending weapons to challenge them so directly.[69]

In fact, Saddam confirmed many of these conclusions in interviews with the FBI during the spring of 2004. He continued to assert that Iraq did not possess WMDs, an assertion that proved accurate once the United States surveyed Iraq's holdings after the invasion, but he acknowledged that mistakes had been made in destroying weapons without the supervision of the UN.[70] He had initially refused to allow inspectors into Iraq because of the threat from Iran, which he viewed as Iraq's greatest enemy, a point that he made in several of his interviews with the FBI. He feared that allowing the inspectors into Iraq would expose his country's weaknesses to its neighbor. Iraq could survive another strike from the United States but might not survive an attack by Iran. He finally decided to readmit inspectors in late 2002 in the hope of averting a war with the United States.[71] In other words, the United States succeeded in the fall of 2002 in using compellent threats to convince the Iraqi leader to admit inspectors.

We now know that Bush's speech at the UN in the fall of 2002 and the threat contained therein made a strong impression on the Iraqi leader. In interviews after the fall of the regime, former advisers noted that Bush's speech rattled the Iraqi dictator. Several of these advisers recalled feeling great alarm at Bush's claim that the United States would act unilaterally to strip the Iraqi regime of its WMD programs.[72] In addition to deciding to readmit inspectors, Saddam also denied requests from his son Qusay and members of the military in late 2002 and early 2003 to take preemptive action by destroying the oil infrastructure or mining the Gulf. According to the Iraqi Perspectives Project, "Saddam refused all of these requests to ensure that Iraq was not blamed for starting a war."[73] Saddam's willingness to readmit inspectors in response to pressure from the United States and his efforts to avoid actions that might provoke a US attack belie the characterization of Saddam as an irrational madman impervious to outside influence.

It became clear by early 2003, however, that the United States was not going to be satisfied with the renewal of inspections. The Bush administration had settled on the goal of regime change, and the successful use of coercion to obtain inspections in the fall of 2002 did not fulfill that goal. Saddam's interviews with the FBI from 2004 focus very little on the prelude to the 2003 invasion. They are mainly concerned with the circumstances surrounding the 1990 invasion of Kuwait and various atrocities allegedly committed by the Iraqi government.

We have been able to glean some additional information about Saddam's mindset in late 2002 and early 2003 from documents and recordings captured after the invasion and from interviews with Iraqi detainees. We know, for example, that in an address to Iraq's air defense forces in 2000, Saddam praised the superior moral fiber of the Iraqi military:

> God Almighty has given [Iraq] a strong back, a great degree of perseverance, and an extraordinary ability to endure. You have broken the morale of America, and this is much more important than warplanes and missiles. . . . We have lost some material things, true, but who remained firm in the field at the end? . . . You broke America's confidence and made people make fun of them. Despite their allegations that they are a superpower, they shamelessly say that their planes flew, bombed, and returned safely to base, as if they consider their safe return to base a gain for the superpower that considers itself the leader in technology and so forth.[74]

In other words, Saddam was unimpressed by the United States' advanced technologies, which he viewed as a cowardly means of avoiding direct engagement with his morally superior forces.

Saddam also cited the United States' fleeing Vietnam after suffering fifty-eight thousand killed—which, according to him, Iraq had nearly suffered in a single battle during the war with Iran—and the withdrawal from Somalia after the infamous "Black Hawk Down" episode as evidence of American cowardice. During the Gulf War, the United States had bombed his country before launching the ground invasion. Saddam viewed this as evidence that the Americans were afraid to attack Iraq with ground forces before they had softened up the Iraqis with their air strikes.[75] He was also unimpressed by the

United States' 2001 assault on Afghanistan: "From his perspective, he had seen America topple an enemy on the cheap, with airpower and a few Special Forces operators, and with most of the hard fighting being done by the Northern Alliance. . . . When America did have a chance to destroy its enemy at Tora Bora, it shrunk away from committing enough conventional military forces to ensure the job was done properly."[76] In other words, we can infer that Saddam's general outlook on the United States by the time of the 2003 ultimatum was that the unipole was cautious, casualty-shy, and likely to employ airpower if it chose to confront the Iraqi regime at all. The United States' threats might have had immediate credibility, but the Iraqi leader was not convinced that the United States had the will to prosecute a long and costly campaign against him.

The evidence on how Saddam assessed the likelihood of a US invasion in late 2002 and early 2003 is somewhat mixed. In a conversation with the FBI in 2004, Saddam claimed that he believed by the end of 2002 that war was inevitable.[77] His statements from the time, however, suggest otherwise. In 2002, Saddam wrote a speech in which he argued that the United States would not attack Iraq because it had already achieved its goals, presumably the readmission of weapons inspectors. He apparently made this argument again in a speech only a month before the invasion. Saddam also asserted that France and Russia would be able to prevent the United States from launching a war against Iraq. These two countries had strong economic ties to his country, and it would be in their interest to block US action.[78] In fact, they did oppose US efforts to obtain a UN mandate for the assault on Iraq, but this would not be enough to prevent the United States from carrying out its ultimatum.

In early 2003, Saddam also continued to extol the superior virtues of the Iraqi military, which fought with more "morale and faith" than the American forces: "True, we do not have the means of the Americans and the British. But our superiority in other things, which we have already mentioned, is clear and decisive."[79] Saddam had evaluated the course of American foreign policy over the preceding decade and concluded that the United States' preferred way to deal with crises—including crises with his own state—was to launch air strikes. The United States was unwilling to sustain the casualties associated with the use of any other instrument.

Saddam maintained his conviction that America was weak and lacked the will to defeat his forces through early 2003. He believed that if the invasion did come, his forces would mount "a heroic resistance and . . . inflict such enormous losses on the Americans that they would stop their advance."[80] In his view, "Iraq will not, in any way, be like Afghanistan. We will not let the war become a picnic for the American or British soldiers. No way!"[81] He continued to stress these themes throughout the early months of 2003: The United States was cowardly and would rely on its airpower, which the Iraqis could withstand. Even on March 20, as the first bombs were falling on Iraq, he asserted, "We will pursue them until they lose their nerve and until they lose hope."[82]

In fact, the evidence collected by the Iraqi Perspectives Project suggests that the Iraqi leader believed by early 2003 that an attack was likely but doubted that the United States would take the war to Baghdad. At that time, the worst-case scenario envisioned by senior Iraqi leaders was that the United States would launch air attacks, which the Iraqi regime would withstand, and then occupy southern Iraq. Saddam believed that the United States would be satisfied by an outcome short of regime change, as it had been in previous conflicts. Even as American tanks rolled into Iraq in late March, he seems to have been more worried about the threat to his regime from an internal rebellion than he was about the invading American forces.[83]

Saddam's Resistance: Assessing the Causal Logic

We will never be able to ask Saddam why he chose to resist the United States' ultimatum, but the available evidence yields several observations. First, Saddam heavily discounted the United States' military prowess. He consistently referred to the United States as weak and cowardly, citing its withdrawal from Mogadishu and its interventions in the 1990s as evidence that the United States was unable to withstand casualties. He also viewed the United States' overreliance on airpower as a manifestation of its fear and weakness. Although Saddam seems to have doubted in late 2002 that the United States would attack him, when he resigned himself to this fact in early 2003 he expected that American action would take the form of air strikes, as it had previously.

In other words, by early 2003 Saddam was convinced that the United States' threat to attack was immediately credible, but he continued to doubt the United States' commitment to the goal of regime overthrow. In fact, he perceived that the United States was threatening him with a package of force that would be relatively cheap—the use of airpower to conduct a limited strike on Iraq and at most occupying the southern part of the country. Much of this reasoning is consistent with the logic of costly compellence, which asserts that targets resist cheap threats because they are not ultimately credible. Saddam seems to have been unconvinced that the United States would make a long and costly ground invasion. That is, the Iraqi leader seems to have interpreted the United States' threat as one that would be relatively cheap to execute.

Furthermore, the focus on the 2003 ultimatum is somewhat misleading, because Saddam did concede in the face of the United States' threat in 2002.[84] Saddam's claims that the United States would not attack seem to be inconsistent with his assertion in 2004 that he decided to readmit weapons inspectors as a way to prevent the United States from invading. His behavior suggests that there was, in fact, more room to coerce the Iraqi leader short of the use of force. Had inspections been allowed to continue in 2003, they might have uncovered convincing evidence of what American forces discovered as a result of the invasion: that Iraq did not, in fact, possess WMDs.

In other words, the reasons for Saddam's resistance in 2003 are consistent with the logic of costly compellence. He resisted the United States' demands not because he doubted that the United States would launch the threatened action, but because he doubted that the United States had the motivation to incur the costs he believed would be necessary to overthrow his regime. He viewed the United States' emphasis on high-tech, low-footprint operations like the one in Afghanistan not as evidence of US strength but as evidence of US cowardice. The costly compellence theory suggests that Saddam was more likely to resist in 2003 than he was in 1991, and it is clear that Saddam viewed the action that he expected the United States to take against him as relatively cheap and thus signaling a low level of commitment.

The reputation and preponderant power theories both predict that Saddam would concede to the United States' threat before the use of force. There is no evidence to suggest that the United States' reputation for following through on threats or its advantage in relative power influenced Saddam's decision. In fact, he continually downplayed the importance of the United States' lead in military technology. Saddam's decision to resist is, however, consistent with the logic of the expansive demands theory. In terms of prediction, the theory seems to perform relatively well on this case: Saddam conceded in the fall of 2002 when the demands were more limited but resisted in 2003 when the United States demanded regime change.

The evidence on Saddam's decision making is not, however, consistent with this causal logic. Saddam readmitted inspectors in 2002 because he wanted to avoid a war with the United States. This suggests that it was the possibility of the threatened punishment, not the limited nature of the demand itself, that convinced the Iraqi leader to concede. Furthermore, we know from Saddam's testimony in 2004 that he viewed the inspections as very damaging for Iraq's security vis-à-vis Iran. He did not agree to the inspections in 2002 because he viewed the concession as trivial, as the logic of expansive demands would dictate.

It is possible that Saddam chose to resist in 2003 simply because the demand was too overwhelming and did not choose to share this belief with his associates or his interviewers. The evidence that we have suggests, however, that Saddam resisted because he thought he could withstand another limited US attack. He may have resisted for this reason and also viewed the demands as unreasonable, but the evidence from the Iraqi Perspectives Project suggests that he doubted that regime change was the United States' true objective. The demand itself seems to have been less salient than Saddam's belief that the United States would not have the will to march to Baghdad.

Coercing Saddam's Iraq: Summary

Despite successfully coercing Saddam into readmitting weapons inspectors in the fall of 2002, the United States issued an ultimatum demanding the surrender of the Iraqi regime in March 2003. When Saddam resisted, the United States launched Operation Iraqi Freedom and would eventually become bogged down in a grinding counterinsurgency that would cost hundreds of billions of dollars and thousands of lives. In Saddam's eyes (and in the eyes of civilians in the Bush administration), however, the threat in early 2003 would be only moderately expensive for the United States to execute: Saddam expected the United States to launch air strikes but did not think it had the motivation for a long and costly campaign. The logic of Saddam's resistance is consistent with costly compellence, although the theory performs less well in predicting the outcome. Nor does the available evidence indicate that the severity of the United States' demand was the determining factor in Saddam's decision to resist in 2003. Saddam chose to concede to the more moderate demand for inspections but only because he hoped to avoid a war with the United States.

The evidence that we have about the Bush administration's decision making suggests that the United States was unwilling to take yes for an answer by March 2003 and that the ultimatum was simply the prelude to an invasion. This does not seem to be the way that the Iraqi leader interpreted the conflict. He doubted that the United States was seriously committed to its stated goal of regime change and expected the casualty-shy unipole to drop a few bombs and go home, as it had over the preceding decade. That is, he judged that the threat was immediately but not ultimately credible, and thus he chose to resist in the belief that he could outlast a limited attack.

Notes

1. The data set records only the final threat issued during this crisis. This was necessary for the purposes of constructing a data set with many cases, but it is also important to evaluate the complexity of the United States' efforts to coerce Iraq in a case study such as this one.

2. UN Security Council, "Resolution 687 (1991)."

3. Litwak, *Regime Change*, 129–31. Litwak provides a thorough overview of US policy on Iraq during this period.

4. A full examination of UNSCOM's activities in Iraq is beyond the scope of this analysis. The UN provides a comprehensive chronology of UNSCOM's activities and key documents, including inspections reports, on its website at http://www.un.org/Depts/unscom/.

5. Three such crises are included in the data set presented in the second

chapter: Operation Desert Strike, UNSCOM I, and UNSCOM II / Operation Desert Fox.

6. See the case history provided by the International Crisis Behavior Project on UNSCOM II / Operation Desert Fox, at http://www.cidcm.umd.edu/icb /dataviewer/; Litwak, *Regime Change*, 135–36; and Crossette, "Baghdad Disrupts Arms Inspections."

7. UN Security Council, "Resolution 1284 (1999)."

8. Iraq Liberation Act of 1998.

9. Quoted in Woodward, *Plan of Attack*, 9.

10. Woodward's account suggests that Wolfowitz was interested in overthrowing Saddam from the start of Bush's first term but that the president himself did not become actively interested in this course of action until after 9/11. See Woodward, *Plan of Attack*, 21–27.

11. Quoted in ibid., 27.

12. Ibid., 3.

13. Ibid., 54.

14. Bush, "President's State of the Union Address."

15. Quoted in Elliott and Carney, "First Stop, Iraq."

16. "Interview with the United Kingdom's ITV Television Network, April 4, 2002," 556.

17. Woodward, *Plan of Attack*, 71, 108–9, 116–17.

18. Ibid., 72–73.

19. Ibid., 80–82.

20. "Text of Bush's Speech at West Point."

21. "Full Text of Dick Cheney's Speech."

22. National Security Council, "National Security Strategy of the United States of America," 15. Although the Bush administration would refer to this as a "preemptive" strategy, it was not preemptive in the sense that the United States was acting in the face of an imminent attack. Instead, the strategy was one of *prevention*—that is, of acting to contain a threat before it has a chance to materialize at some point in the future. The right afforded by international law for a state to take preemptive action is limited to cases in which a state anticipates that an attack by its adversary is imminent and strikes first to avoid being caught on the defensive. Action to forestall some threat that may or may not materialize at some point in the future is not covered under this right to preemptive action.

23. "George Bush's Speech to the UN General Assembly."

24. Bush, "President Bush Outlines Iraqi Threat."

25. Authorization for Use of Military Force against Iraq Resolution of 2002.

26. National Intelligence Council, *National Intelligence Estimate*, 5–6.

27. Ibid., 8–9. INR also disagreed with the estimate about Iraq's acquisition of aluminum tubes (allegedly for use in a centrifuge to produce highly enriched uranium) and disputed the claim that Iraq was seeking to acquire uranium in Africa (p. 84).

28. UN Security Council, "Resolution 1441 (2002)."

29. Burns, "Unhindered by Iraqi Officials."

30. Blix, "Briefing the Security Council, 19 December 2002."

31. "US Secretary of State Colin Powell's Statement."

32. Blix, "Briefing the Security Council, 9 January 2003."

33. "Joint Statement, Baghdad, 20 January 2003."

34. Blix, "Briefing of the Security Council, 27 January 2003." Blix would make two more briefings before the invasion, including one on the submission of the UNMOVIC quarterly report on March 7. The tone and content of these briefings were similar to those of the earlier reports: Iraq was cooperating on some fronts, but questions remained about both munitions that were unaccounted for and the lack of evidence indicating that Iraq had complied with its disarmament obligations. These briefings are available at http://www.unmovic .org/.

35. Bush, "Text of President Bush's 2003 State of the Union Address."

36. "Full Text of Colin Powell's Speech." Some of the evidence Powell cited in this briefing turned out to be untrue, including Iraq's alleged use of mobile labs for the production of biological agents. Much of the human intelligence that the Bush administration cited in the run-up to the war was provided by an individual codenamed "Curveball," who later admitted that he had fabricated claims about Iraq's biological weapons program in an effort to bring down Saddam's regime. See, for example, Chulov and Pidd, "Defector Admits to WMD Lies."

37. United Nations Security Council, "Spain, United Kingdom."

38. "France Will Use Iraq Veto."

39. "UK, US and Spain Won't Seek Vote."

40. Bush, "President Says Saddam Hussein Must Leave Iraq."

41. For explanations of the WMD intelligence failures, see Betts, *Enemies of Intelligence*; Duelfer, *Hide and Seek*; and Jervis, *Why Intelligence Fails*. Woodward's *Plan of Attack* provides a comprehensive overview of the Bush administration's planning and strategy leading up to the war.

42. See chapter 1 for a lengthy discussion of the United States' post–Cold War status.

43. International Institute for Strategic Studies (IISS), *Military Balance 2003*, 335–36.

44. IISS, *Military Balance 2002*, 127.

45. Singer, *Corporate Warriors*, 232.

46. Woodward, *Plan of Attack*, 41, 54.

47. Ricks, *Fiasco*, 117.

48. Woods et al., *Iraqi Perspectives Project*, 30–31.

49. Hersh, "Offense and Defense."

50. Quoted in Singer, *Wired for War*, 187.

51. See IISS, *Military Balance 2003*, 111, for a list of forces on the ground in and pledged to Iraq by August 2003.

52. Gordon and Trainor, *Cobra II*, 41, 174.

53. Stiglitz and Bilmes, *Three Trillion Dollar War*, 7.

54. Hacker and Pierson estimate that the 2003 tax cuts alone cost $1 trillion over ten years. See "Abandoning the Middle," 33.

55. See Stiglitz and Bilmes, *Three Trillion Dollar War*, 22–29.

56. Bush, "President Says Saddam Hussein Must Leave Iraq."

57. USDOD, *Conduct of the Persian Gulf War*, 634.

58. United States Bureau of Labor Statistics, "CPI Inflation Calculator."

59. GDP in current US dollars, from World Bank, "GDP (current US$)." Per capita figures reported in current US dollars, from World Bank, "GDP per capita (current US$)." Military expenditures as a percentage of GDP from World Bank, "Military expenditure (% of GDP)."

60. Woodward, *Plan of Attack*, 80–81.

61. IISS, *Military Balance 2003*, 335–36.

62. IISS, *Military Balance 2002*, provides a comprehensive overview of the military inventories of both the United States and Iraq in August 2002. The report notes, for example, that Iraq had 2,600 main battle tanks in 2002 but that 50 percent of Iraqi equipment lacked spare parts (p. 106). The US Army alone had more than 7,000 tanks, and the military commanded an array of sophisticated aircraft and naval assets (pp. 16–23).

63. Woodward, *Plan of Attack*, 81.

64. A most-likely case is one in which "the independent variables posited by a theory are at values that strongly posit an outcome or posit an extreme outcome." See George and Bennett, *Case Studies and Theory Development*, 121.

65. Duelfer, *Comprehensive Report of the Special Advisor to the DCI*, vol. 1, 29. Hereafter, I will cite this source as the Duelfer Report. A full discussion of the motives behind Saddam's decision to seek WMDs is beyond the scope of this study, but the Duelfer Report provides an overview of what we know about Saddam's strategic calculus. In addition, Woods, Palkki, and Stout's *Saddam Tapes* contains a chapter on Saddam's thinking about "Special Munitions."

66. Duelfer Report, vol. 1, 41.

67. Ibid., 63.

68. Ibid., 34.

69. Quoted in the Duelfer Report, vol. 1, 62.

70. "Interview Session 4: February 13, 2004," in Battle, *Saddam Hussein Talks to the FBI*, 3.

71. "Casual Conversation 3: June 11, 2004," in ibid., 2–3.

72. Duelfer Report, vol. 1, 62.

73. Woods et al., *Iraqi Perspectives Project*, 29.

74. Quoted in ibid., 15.

75. Ibid., 15–16.

76. Ibid., 16.

77. "Casual Conversation 3: June 11, 2004," in Battle, *Saddam Hussein Talks to the FBI*, 3.

78. Woods et al., *Iraqi Perspectives Project*, 28.

79. Quoted in ibid., 29.

80. Quoted in ibid., 30.

81. Quoted in ibid.

82. Quoted in ibid., 30–31.

83. Ibid., 31. The Iraqi Perspectives Project suggests that many of Iraq's senior leaders made accurate assessments of the likely outcome of a US invasion, but for reasons related to Saddam's leadership style and the compartmentalization of information in the regime, they were unable to share their calculations with him. See, for example, pp. 12–16, 25–27.

84. The decision to concede in 2002 thus presents an irregularity. Recall that the stand-alone prediction for costly compellence suggests that the threat's execution would be only moderately costly, and thus the Iraqi leader was weakly predicted to resist. There is no clear explanation from costly compellence for why the threat would have been more effective in producing concessions at this earlier stage, before the scope of the attack would have been clear.

Conclusion

The Implications of Costly Compellence for Theory and Policy

Why do leaders of weak states resist compellent military threats issued by the United States? In short: because cheap threats do not signal that the United States cares enough to do more than drop a few bombs on the target state. The costly compellence theory tells us that threats that can be issued and executed cheaply do not signal that the unipole is highly motivated to achieve its objectives. The target of a cheap threat resists not because it doubts the threat's immediate credibility but because it doubts that the United States has the motivation necessary to extract a brute-force victory from a stubbornly resistant opponent after the initial use of force fails to exact compliance.

The international distribution of power and the manner in which the United States chooses to employ force determine how costly it is to issue and to execute compellent threats and hence how effective US compellent threats are in changing target-state behavior before the use of force. The United States has been the world's sole superpower since the end of the Cold War. Because a unipole faces no peer competitor capable of restraining its behavior, it is much less risky and much less costly for a unipole to issue a compellent threat than it is for a superpower in a bipolar system. We would expect, therefore, that the United States employs compellent threats more frequently in the post–Cold War period than it did under bipolarity.

The United States has also adopted many strategies that limit its human, political, and financial costs for employing military force. Some of these policies, such as the end of conscription, date to the end of the Vietnam War, but they accelerated dramatically with the end of the Cold War. The 1991 Gulf War was the first test for a US force based on the RMA thesis. This operation, which succeeded with surprisingly few US casualties, set the bar for cost-minimizing operations in the post–Cold War period. Since then, the United

States has come to rely increasingly on private military contractors, airpower, and, most recently, UAVs to limit casualties for the AVF. Although the recent wars in Iraq and Afghanistan temporarily shifted attention toward grinding COIN operations, the 2011 Libya intervention and the Obama administration's heavy reliance on drones indicate that the United States will be reverting to this high-tech, low-footprint model in coming years. In addition, the United States has recently chosen to rely on deficit spending and contributions from its allies to fund its military operations. Finally, the general public's increasing awareness of collateral damage and the evolution of norms condemning it have pushed the United States to actively limit the pain inflicted on target states. In combination, these efforts to limit the costs of employing force make it easier for the United States to deploy its military and hence lend immediate credibility to its compellent threats, but they also undermine the effectiveness of those threats because they indicate a lack of ultimate credibility. That is, efforts to make the use of force cheap signal to a target state that the United States is not deeply invested in achieving its desired outcome and thus make it more likely that the target will resist.

A New Data Set on US Compellent Threats in Crises

This study presents a new data set on the United States' use of coercion in international crises from 1945 to 2007 to assess whether the record of US compellence is consistent with the predictions generated by costly compellence. No other data set on the use of force or study of interstate coercion contains the data necessary to assess the implications of costly compellence: that US compellent threats should be both more frequent and less effective in the post–Cold War period. The data set includes sixty-three crises in which the United States was involved, including both cases in which compellent threats were issued and cases in which they were not. This data set yields several important observations.

First, the United States does not bluff. In all cases in which the United States issued an explicit compellent threat in a crisis during the period 1945–2007 and the target resisted, the United States followed through on its threat. This deepens the puzzle of why target states would resist threats issued by the world's sole superpower. It also suggests that the United States' threats do not fail because they lack immediate credibility—that is, because targets doubt that the United States will execute the threatened punishment. Although policymakers obsess over the need to "protect the United States' reputation" in crises, this data set and the case studies demonstrate that this focus is misplaced.

Second, the data set demonstrates that the United States has issued compellent threats much more frequently in post–Cold War crises than it did under bipolarity. The United States issued a compellent threat in eleven of forty-nine Cold War crises (22.4 percent) and in eight of fourteen post–Cold war crises (57.1 percent). This is consistent with the costly compellence assertion that the unipole is freer to issue compellent threats than a bipole.

Third, and most important, the data set reveals that targets are less likely to concede to a US compellent threat in the post–Cold War period than they were before 1990. The target of the United States' compellent threat resisted US demands in five of eleven Cold War crises (45 percent) and in six of eight post–Cold War crises (75 percent). Furthermore, the target of a Cold War–era threat continued to resist after the initial application of US force in only one of four Cold War crises (25 percent) and in five of six post–Cold War crises (83 percent) in which the United States issued a compellent threat.[1] In other words, the targets of US compellent threats are more likely to resist US demands in the post–Cold War period, and they are more likely to *continue* to resist, even after the United States has launched military action against them. These results remain consistent if we date the rise of the cost-minimizing model of warfare to the end of direct US military involvement in the Vietnam War (1973) or exclude cases in which the United States demanded regime change from the target state. The record is clear: Compellent threats are less effective on average when the use of force is relatively cheap, consistent with the prediction of costly compellence.

Cases of US Threats

The four case studies of US compellence presented in this book supplement the evidence from the data set and demonstrate that costly compellence outperforms several competing theories of threat effectiveness. In the 1962 Cuban Missile Crisis, the United States' threats—both the threat conveyed by the quarantine and the final ultimatum delivered to the Soviet ambassador—were costly to issue and would have been very costly to execute. The United States was threatening the opposing bipole (the Soviet Union), and the plan to invade Cuba would have been very costly to implement. At the time, the United States relied on conscription and did not employ private contractors, had not yet adopted a technology-heavy force structure consistent with the RMA thesis, and was threatening an invasion with ground troops supported by air strikes. The United States was not soliciting contributions from its allies to conduct the invasion. Furthermore, US and Soviet civilians would have been at great risk had the conflict escalated to a nuclear exchange. All of these factors suggest that issuing and executing the threat against the Soviet Union in October 1962 would be very costly for the United States and consequently that the threat would be effective. Khrushchev did agree to remove the missiles from Cuba. There is evidence that it was the willingness of the United States to run such a high risk of escalation that convinced the premier to concede, consistent with the logic of costly compellence.

By contrast, the United States' threat against Libya in 2011 and the ensuing no-fly zone is a perfect example of the cost-minimizing model of warfare that has evolved since the end of the Cold War, and it is a clear case of compellent threat failure. In March 2011, the United States threatened and then deployed airpower in conjunction with its allies, ostensibly to halt attacks on Libyan civilians. From the start of Operation Odyssey Dawn, the United States ruled out the use of ground troops, and it passed control of operations to its allies as quickly as possible. Because it was not costly for the United States to issue or to execute such a threat, the costly compellence theory predicts that the threat would fail to convince Qaddafi to concede to US demands before the application of force. That is indeed what happened in the spring of 2011: Qaddafi resisted the demands of the United States and the international community for a cease-fire, and he continued to resist after the fall of Tripoli. The campaign may have "succeeded" in overthrowing Qaddafi, but as an act of coercion it was a total failure. The target was not persuaded to back down before (or even after) the use of force.

The United States' threats against Iraq in 1991 and 2003 both failed to convince Saddam to concede before the use of force. The 1991 threat was moderately costly for the United States: The threat was issued at the dawn of unipolarity, at a time when the United States employed an all-volunteer military with minimal use of private contractors. Furthermore, the United States threatened action on behalf of a large coalition of states and with the backing of the UN. Although US planners expected that the use of such a large contingent of ground troops could be very costly in human terms, the ground campaign would be preceded by a lengthy air campaign against Iraqi targets. Costly compellence weakly predicts that the United States' compellent threat would fail, and thus Saddam's refusal to evacuate Kuwait voluntarily is consistent with the theory.

The 2003 threat was, however, somewhat less costly for the United States than the 1991 ultimatum, and thus Saddam should have been more likely to resist than he had been in 1991. The United States was still a unipole with an all-volunteer military now heavily supplemented by private contractors and structured according to the RMA thesis. The planned operation would rely on a much smaller contingent of ground forces than the Gulf War, and the Bush administration sold the invasion as one that would nearly pay for itself. The United States was acting with fewer allies in 2003 than it had in 1991, but given that the attack was supposed to be relatively cheap, this did not dramatically increase the costs of the operation. The war would ultimately prove to be a much longer and more costly operation than anticipated, but this does not affect our assessment of how costly the compellent threat was in 2003 and therefore how the Iraqi regime would have assessed that United States' ultimate credibility at that time.

In fact, Saddam did concede to the United States' demand to readmit weapons inspectors in the fall of 2002. The United States was not satisfied, however, by this concession and so demanded the surrender of the Iraqi regime in its March 2003 ultimatum. The evidence from the primary sources generated as a result of the 2003 invasion suggests that the Iraqi leader doubted the United States' willingness to attack him as late as December 2002. When Saddam did become convinced that an attack was looming in early 2003, he believed that the United States would limit its response to air strikes or would occupy the southern part of his country but would not have the will to march all the way to Baghdad. Indeed, even as the bombs began to fall on Iraq, Saddam remained convinced that he could outlast a casualty-shy unipole that hid behind its superior technology. In other words, Saddam's decision to resist in 2003 is largely consistent with the logic of the costly compellence theory: He believed that the United States would attack him, but he doubted that the unipole had the motivation to pursue a long and costly campaign to prevail.

The alternative theories under investigation in this study performed poorly on these cases relative to costly compellence. Neither the reputation theory nor the preponderant power theory correctly predicted the outcome of any of the four cases examined. Nor does the process-tracing evidence suggest that the causal mechanisms proposed by these two theories were at work. Those who argue that the United States must act to maintain its "reputation" in order to prevail in future crises can and should relax. The logic of this argument is not supported by any of the cases under investigation in this study.

The expansive demands theory correctly predicts the outcome of only two of the four cases: the 2011 Libya crisis and the 2003 threat against Iraq. The theory yielded no prediction for the other two cases because the United States' demands were relatively moderate. The process-tracing evidence on the target's decision making is, however, more consistent with the logic of costly compellence than with this theory, even in the case of the 2003 threat against Iraq. Interviews after the invasion and captured documents demonstrate that Saddam resisted in 2003 in the belief that the United States would inflict a limited amount of damage on his country and give up before reaching Baghdad, not because the demands were too great. The 1991 case also falls apart under closer observation: Saddam claimed in interviews after his capture that he had offered several times to negotiate a withdrawal from Kuwait, which seems unlikely had he felt that the United States' demands in 1991 were too extreme. The expansive demands theory may be useful in understanding compellent threats at the extremes, where the demands are very minor or very severe, but it is not useful for understanding cases of moderate demands or for explaining why a target chooses to resist a demand that is not extreme.

Given the limited nature of the data that we have on these targets, it is impossible to definitively rule out the applicability of these alternatives. We can say, however, that the data we would need to confirm or deny each of these theories—including costly compellence—is the same: firsthand testimony from target-state leaders about their decision-making process, the supply of which is very limited. The fact that much of the evidence we do have conforms to the causal logic proposed by costly compellence suggests that the theory can be very useful for predicting and understanding the behavior of target states facing a compellent threat issued by the world's sole superpower.

Implications of Costly Compellence

Theories of Unipolar Politics

The costly compellence theory suggests that a unipole issues compellent threats more frequently than a bipole because there is no peer competitor to rein in its behavior. This argument draws on structural realist logic, which suggests that superpowers in a bipolar system restrain their behavior because of the fear of angering their opponent. The logic of costly compellence suggests, therefore, that there is no reason to assume that unipolarity will be peaceful as far as smaller, weaker powers are concerned. A unipole is likely to employ compellent threats frequently because it can do so at relatively low risk to itself. This willingness to issue compellent threats will not, however, convince target states that the unipole is highly motivated to defeat them.

The unipole's tendencies to issue and to execute compellent threats frequently may backfire, however, if they encourage weak states to pursue the means necessary to deter the unipole from threatening and attacking them. That is, the fact that the United States is likely to continue to employ compellent threats may propel weak states to seek the very weapons that the unipole has often hoped to eliminate through the use of such threats. The United States has so far refrained from explicitly threatening or attacking nuclear-armed North Korea, but it did threaten and helped to overthrow Qaddafi after he surrendered his WMDs. This lesson is not likely to be lost on states that fear they may become the United States' next target.

On the other hand, the costly compellence theory suggests that the unipole will be no less restrained in its dealings with powerful states than a bipole. In some situations, the unipole may find that it is very risky to issue a compellent threat. We would expect that the United States would be more likely to employ diplomacy and other nonviolent instruments to coerce states that have the potential to disrupt a critical region or to damage an important ally. It seems unlikely that the United States would resort to explicit compellent threats to coerce North Korea, both because it is armed with nuclear weapons and because it can damage its neighbor to the south even without those weapons. We would also expect the United States to be restrained in its use of coercive diplomacy with a state such as China, which is relatively powerful in its region and capable of damaging the United States' local allies. In other words, unipolarity is likely to be peaceful for powerful states or those that possess WMDs, but weak states may frequently find themselves the targets of compellent threats when their behavior displeases the unipole.

Furthermore, the logic of costly compellence suggests that it may simply be very difficult for a unipole to accurately signal its interests in a crisis. The relative ease with which the unipole will be able to sustain costs—even costs many times greater in absolute terms than those that a weaker target could sustain—will make it difficult for the unipole to accurately signal a high level of motivation. This suggests that it may be uniquely challenging to resolve crises involving two states with vast power and resource discrepancies because the more powerful state cannot communicate with the weaker how motivated it is to secure its preferred outcome. The United States has deliberately adopted a model of warfare that limits its costs for employing force, but even if this were not the case, it might be very difficult for the United States to use its power in a way that is deeply costly to itself.

Deterrence

The costly compellence theory is designed for situations in which a unipole employs a military threat to compel a change in the behavior of a target state. Deterrent threats were explicitly excluded from this analysis, but many of the arguments about compellent threats should also apply to cases in which a unipole is threatening a small state to prevent it from taking some future action. For example, it seems likely that the two stages of compellent threat effectiveness—immediate versus ultimate credibility—would also apply to a deterrent threat issued against a weak state. That is, the target of a deterrent threat from the United States may be as likely as the target of a compellent threat to consider both whether it believes the United States would follow through on the threatened punishment and whether it believes the United States would then apply additional violence if the target continues its course of action. If the United States is threatening to employ a cheap instrument—for example, airpower—to deter a target from undertaking some future action, then the logic of costly compellence suggests that the threat would fail if the target believes it can withstand this limited strike and expects that the United States would then lose interest. Costly compellence suggests that deterrent threats that depend on the use of cheap force by the United States are unlikely to succeed in coercing weak states.

On the other hand, the theory gives us no reason to believe that deterrence would fail in cases where the United States' vital interests are engaged and it is prepared to make serious sacrifices for them or in contests with regional powers. The fact that the United States is so much more powerful than all the other states in the system suggests that it may be hardest to deter small, weak states that can be punished at very low cost to the United States. It will be easiest for the United States to deter powerful states, or those armed with nuclear weapons, because the choice to attack powerful opponents would be much more costly for the unipole. Although the logic of costly compellence suggests that unipolarity may be dangerous for small and weak states, we should expect stability in the United States' crises with more powerful opponents.

The logic of costly compellence also suggests that threats must be costly enough that they have ultimate credibility but not so costly that the target doubts the unipole's willingness to follow through on the threatened action. In other words, threats that are too costly for the unipole to execute may not be viewed as immediately credible by target states. This study did not include cases where the threatened action is so costly for the unipole that the target doubts the threat's immediate credibility, but this is an important consideration in the study of nuclear deterrence. As I argued above, it is likely to be very difficult for the unipole to threaten and undertake actions that will be highly costly to itself, with the exception of a threat that might risk an attack with nuclear weapons.

Making Compellent Threats More Effective

Given that cheap threats fail to compel target states to change their behavior, are there any strategies that the United States could pursue to make its compellent threats more effective? First, the United States could reinstate the draft. It would still have to maintain a volunteer officer corps to develop and retain skills over the long term, but reintroducing conscription would expose a cross section of American society to the human costs of war. This would dramatically increase the political costs of sending American troops into harm's way and would therefore make US compellent threats more effective.

If conscription were off the table, then policymakers could expand the size of the active-duty force to eliminate the need for private military contractors. Employing the AVF exclusively would be less politically costly than reinstating a draft, but it would be more politically costly than hiring contractors to perform functions for which there are not enough uniformed personnel. Such a policy would likely be very expensive in dollar terms, however, if the wars in Iraq and Afghanistan are any indication. Furthermore, the main appeal of contractors is that they can be hired as needed, on a short-term basis. It would be difficult in practice to recruit and train an additional hundred thousand volunteers to conduct a specific operation, but it could be done if the United States had the will to do so and were willing to foot the bill.

Another way to make US compellent threats more effective would be to pass a law requiring the United States to pay for operations with current revenues. To execute military action against a small state, the administration would be required to increase taxes or tap an outstanding budget surplus. By making Americans pay the direct financial costs of fighting, policymakers could better convince the target of a US compellent threat that the United States is highly motivated to defeat it. Or the United States could pass a law requiring it to incorporate the use of a significant number of ground troops in any offensive military operation. This would prevent policymakers from threatening and executing strategies that rely solely on standoff strikes and would more effectively compel US targets.

If these scenarios seem unlikely and perhaps even fantastical, that is because they are. It is almost unthinkable that in the current political climate the United States would reinstate conscription, abandon private contractors, or mandate the use of costly ground troops when drones and airpower are so alluring. That is precisely the point and precisely why the United States will continue to struggle to make its compellent threats effective: The United States developed the military model that it has today because it wants to minimize the costs of war as much as possible. The relative cheapness of US compellent threats is partly a function of the United States' status as unipole, but it is mainly a function of a military model rooted in a deep ambivalence about the use of force that permeates US society. Americans want to play an active role in managing world affairs without actually paying for that role. There are steps that the United States could take to make its compellent threats more effective, but the evidence suggests that it is not going to take these steps in the foreseeable future.

Looking to the Future: The Paradox of Cheap American Force

The Department of Defense released new strategic guidance in January 2012. The 2012 guidance asserts that the United States will, in the coming decade, "strik[e] the most dangerous [terrorist] groups and individuals when necessary,"[2] which suggests that the drone campaign against al-Qaeda leaders in Pakistan, Afghanistan, Yemen, and elsewhere is likely to continue. Importantly, "*U.S. forces will no longer be sized to conduct large-scale, prolonged stability operations.*"[3] In other words, the military will not be maintaining the capability to conduct long-term counterinsurgency operations like those it undertook in Iraq and Afghanistan.

The 2014 Quadrennial Defense Review (QDR) builds on the 2012 guidance and focuses on "rebalancing our defense efforts in a period of increasing fiscal constraint."[4] Consistent with the 2012 guidance, the QDR asserts that the US military will focus on preparing for a "full spectrum of possible operations" and that it will not be designed for long-term stability operations.[5] The QDR describes plans to reduce the size of the army, including cuts to both active forces and reserves, and preparations by the air force and navy to retire equipment if sequestration is not lifted. The plan does call, however, for increases in special operations forces to fulfill counterterrorism missions.[6] Interestingly, a photograph of an MQ-9 Reaper drone appears on the first page of the section of the report describing the future security environment.[7] It would seem that the UAVs are here to stay. In other words, both the strategic guidance released in 2012 and the 2014 QDR indicate that a leaner US military will be increasingly invested in specialized, low-footprint operations that maximize American advantages in technology and limit risks and costs for US soldiers.

Despite its failure as a coercive campaign, the 2011 Libya intervention does reveal important information about the way President Obama views the use of limited American force. A major controversy arose over the constitutionality of his use of force against Qaddafi, both at the outset of Operation Odyssey Dawn and after the deadline mandated by the War Powers Resolution for congressional authorization of deployments had passed.[8] The White House Office of Legal Counsel released a memo asserting that Obama did not require congressional authorization for US participation in Operation Odyssey Dawn. In its view, the operation over Libya did not qualify as a "war" because such military operations are "limited in their nature, scope, and duration."[9] This memo asserts that the president can use force without congressional authorization, so long as the force employed is limited. In other words, it suggests that the president faces no political barriers to the use of limited force.[10]

The Obama administration's declaration that its participation in Odyssey Dawn did not "count" as a war will likely pave the way for future presidents to claim similar rights to use limited force without congressional approval. The prominent role played by UAVs in the operation—which was initially hailed as a smashing success—as well as the continued use of drones to attack targets in Pakistan, Yemen, and elsewhere suggest that the reliance on high-tech, low-footprint operations is likely to persist. The costly compellence theory suggests, however, that reliance on these cheap instruments will not enhance the United States' ability to wield force effectively in international politics. Instead, these strategies for minimizing the costs of force will continue to undermine the effectiveness of US compellent threats and thus make it more difficult to coerce target states.

The costly compellence theory thus reveals a paradox: Efforts to make the use of force easier and more efficient erode the utility of force as a coercive instrument before war. By making the use of force cheaper and thus making threats more likely to fail, these strategies also make it more likely that force will be used. That is, the United States' efforts to minimize the human costs of war—both for its own soldiers and for target-state civilians—may actually make the loss of human life more likely because they encourage target states to resist in the face of a cheap compellent threat.

The Way Forward

The purpose of this study is not to suggest that the United States should conscript all young people from the ages of eighteen to twenty-five, abandon the use of drones, and begin to bomb target states indiscriminately. As discussed above, it is extremely unlikely that the American public would accept the reinstatement of conscription, that the US military would relinquish its programs to develop increasingly sophisticated and unmanned technologies, or that Congress would pass a law mandating tax increases to pay for military operations. Given these constraints, however, the United States should acknowledge limits on its ability to employ cheap force as an effective tool of compellence against weak states.

US policymakers should acknowledge that it will be very difficult to compel a target to change its behavior with the threat of an air attack, a drone campaign, or another type of limited intervention because these actions telegraph that the United States is not sufficiently invested in the outcome to place itself or its soldiers at any real risk. If we accept that the "easy" option of coercing with cheap threats of force is likely to fail, then perhaps the United States can reason more clearly about the limited benefits and dramatic consequences of using force against weak states that pose a marginal threat to US interests.

For example, costly compellence suggests that threatening the Syrian regime with air strikes to compel an end to the violence in that country is unlikely to be effective. Such a threat will not convince Syrian leadership that the United States has the will to make costly sacrifices to enforce a cease-fire. Similarly, we should not expect the threat of air strikes or a drone campaign to compel insurgent groups such as the Islamic State to abandon their violent behavior in Iraq and elsewhere.

Or consider a different type of challenge: Iran's alleged pursuit of a nuclear weapon. So far, the United States has avoided the use of compellent threats to try to persuade the Iranian regime to forego nuclear weapons and to reach an agreement about its nuclear activities. This is prudent, as attempts to threaten the regime with air strikes, a limited invasion like the one planned for Iraq in 2003, or some sort of drone campaign to attack nuclear installations or even nuclear scientists would fail to compel the Iranian regime to change its behavior. Do Americans have the willingness to send five million troops to Iran to forcibly control all of the nuclear facilities in that country and to occupy it for the next fifty years to prevent the program from restarting itself? No, they do not. Given that that may be the only guaranteed *military* solution to the long-term challenge of Iranian nuclear proliferation, US policymakers would be wise to continue the slow, painstaking, and unglamorous route of diplomatic negotiations. They would also be wise to remember that all the currently acknowledged nuclear states have managed their weapons responsibly and that there is no particular reason (other than ethnocentric racism) to expect that Iran could not behave in a similar manner. Similarly, they should take responsibility for the fact that the United States' practice of invading countries for the purpose of disarming them encourages rational observers to seek the means of deterring such invasions.

The fact that cheap compellent threats would be inappropriate for addressing the aforementioned situations does not mean that the American military has no role to play in international politics. One of the challenges in measuring the utility of force is the fact that it can influence the course of international politics without being actively threatened or employed. The United States' arsenal of conventional military power likely deters many states from taking action that they would otherwise take in its absence. US military power may also influence the types of events that escalate to the crisis stage. That is, fear of the US military instrument likely prevents many weak states from acting in ways that would put them on the radars of US policymakers. It is difficult to measure the impact of force in such situations because when deterrent force works effectively, the target responds with inaction. The costly compellence theory does not suggest that deterrence will fail in situations where the United States' interests are truly at stake or in conflicts with more powerful states such as China. In fact, it suggests that coercion is most likely to be effective in situations where the United States' interests are most at risk.

The United States should, therefore, retain the ability to conduct major military operations in the event that it faces a vital threat to its national interest, and it can expect that the threat of US force will be most effective in those situations. The United States would gain nothing by allowing its military to slip from its position atop the global hierarchy of capability and competency. To deter and to meet future threats, the United States should maintain a robust military, but it must also accept the fact that threatening to launch high-tech, low-risk operations will not scare weak target states into doing the United States' bidding.

More specifically, the logic of costly compellence suggests that the United States should maintain the ability to conduct large-scale ground operations if it hopes to coerce target states, even as it continues to develop unmanned capabilities and precision weapons. It is precisely the fact that the use of ground troops is so costly that the threat to do so will be more effective in coercing target states. Drone campaigns and night raids by special operations forces may be useful for killing and capturing terrorists, but they will not be useful for coercing target states because they do not signal that the United States is highly motivated to achieve its objectives. Similarly, strategic bombing campaigns may eliminate infrastructure in target states with growing precision, but the threat to launch air strikes alone will not be enough to convince target states to change their behavior because such raids are so cheap for the United States to implement.

In sum, costly compellence asserts that the ease with which the United States can employ military force undermines its ability to coerce weak states with compellent military threats. The ambivalence of the American public about the use of force and their insulation from the costs of war suggest that the trend toward relatively low-cost military operations is likely to continue for the foreseeable future. US policymakers should recognize that cheap compellent threats are unlikely to convince weak target states to modify their behavior. Knowing this, policymakers should carefully consider the risks and rewards of employing force against marginally threatening states. The United States remains remarkably secure relative to most states today and throughout history, and it should reserve its strength for those situations in which its interests are truly threatened.

Notes

1. The target resisted US demands in five Cold War crises, but the United States executed its threat in only four of these cases. In the fifth case (North Korea's seizure of the *Pueblo*), the United States issued a passive implicit threat but did not apply force when North Korea refused to release the ship.

2. United States Department of Defense (USDOD), *Sustaining U.S. Global Leadership*, 1.

3. Ibid., 6, emphasis in original.

4. USDOD, *Quadrennial Defense Review 2014*, iv.

5. Ibid., vii.

6. Ibid., ix–xi.

7. Ibid., 3.

8. For a review of this controversy, see Chesney, "Primer on the Libya / War Powers Resolution Compliance Debate."

9. Krass, "Authority to Use Military Force in Libya."

10. The memo also lists the "exposure of U.S. military personnel to significant risk over a substantial period" as a key identifying characteristic of a "war." Operations that do not involve the use of ground troops do not, according to this memo, expose US military personnel to significant risks and thus do not require congressional approval. See pp. 8–9.

Appendix

How the Data Set Was Constructed

This appendix explains how the data set on US compellent threats was constructed, how each variable in the data set was coded, and how the tables presented in chapter 2 were created. As that chapter explains, the data set was derived from the list of crises generated by the International Crisis Behavior (ICB) Project.

Background on the ICB Project Data

The original investigators employed the following criteria to determine whether an event should be included in the ICB data set: "There are two defining conditions of an *international crisis*: (1) a change in type and/or an increase in intensity of *disruptive*, that is, hostile verbal or physical, *interactions* between two or more states, with a heightened probability of *military hostilities*; that, in turn, (2) destabilizes their relationship and *challenges* the *structure* of an international system—global, dominant, or subsystem."[1]

The ICB investigators used these criteria to assemble a list of potential crises from news archives. This list of candidates was then narrowed by additional criteria to determine the final roster of crises to include in the data set, and it has been updated during the five phases of the project. A crisis begins with "a disruptive act or event, a *breakpoint (trigger)*" and ends "with an act or event that denotes a qualitative reduction in conflictual activity."[2] I adopt the ICB Project's definition of "crisis" for the sake of consistency in constructing the data set, but the definition does not affect the logic of costly compellence or the findings.

The ICB Project identifies the "crisis actors" for each case. To be recorded in the data set, a crisis actor must be a sovereign state or a coalition of sovereign states. Consequently, crises that involve only terrorist or nationalist groups were not included in the data set.[3] In addition, to be counted as a crisis actor for a particular case, a state must believe that it is experiencing a foreign policy crisis. According to the terms employed by the ICB Project, a state experiences a foreign policy crisis when "the highest level decision makers of the state" perceive the following: "a *threat to one or more basic values*, along with an awareness of *finite time for response* to the value threat, and a *heightened probability of involvement in military hostilities*."[4] If a state's top decision makers do not hold these beliefs, then the ICB Project does not record the state as a crisis actor.

To compile the data set on US compellent threats, I started by identifying all crises from 1945 to 2007, excluding crises that occurred before the end of World War II.[5] This yielded a total of 349 international crises from 1945 to 2007.[6] From this list, I isolated the crises for which the United States was identified as a crisis actor.[7] This yielded a total of sixty-three crises. I then examined each crisis in detail. First, I identified the United States' opponent in the crisis. This state may have been identified by the ICB Project as a crisis actor—that is, as a state also experiencing a foreign policy crisis. Or the state may not have been a crisis actor but was still the object of the United States' focus. For example, I identified the Soviet Union as the opponent in the Turkish Straits Crisis (case 111) because the United States' objective was to influence Soviet behavior. The ICB Project does not identify the Soviet Union as a crisis actor in this case, however, because it did not meet the criteria for a state experiencing a foreign policy crisis. In some cases, the United States faced more than one opponent. For example, I identified both Syria and the Soviet Union as the United States' opponents in the Black September Crisis (case 238) because the United States was attempting to influence the behavior of both states.

Coding Compellent Threats

I then consulted the ICB case summaries and coding of threat-related variables and additional primary and secondary sources to determine whether the United States issued a compellent threat against the opponent(s). In cases where the United States did issue a threat, the threat was classified according to five different types that will be described in greater detail below. I recorded that the United States issued a compellent threat against the opponent if the United States undertook limited military action (for example, the movement of forces) or made explicit statements, either publicly or in private communication, demanding that the target change its behavior or face military action by the United States. That is, a compellent threat has two necessary components: a demand that the target change its behavior and the promise that the target will suffer a military attack if it does not.

A compellent threat seeks a change in the target's behavior and promises or implies that the target will suffer future military action for noncompliance. A threat that was intended solely to prevent future action by the target—that is, a deterrent threat—was not counted as a threat in this data set. In some cases, I determined that a single threat was intended both to compel a change in current behavior and to deter future action. I counted such a threat as a compellent threat for the purposes of this data set. For example, during the Pathet Lao Crisis (case 180), the United States issued a threat to compel a cease-fire from the Pathet Lao. I determined that the threat was also intended to deter the Soviet Union from intervening in the crisis. Because one of the threat's objectives was to compel a change of behavior by the Pathet Lao, I recorded this as a compellent threat.

In addition, to be counted as a compellent threat, the punishment threatened (or undertaken in limited form) must be intended to achieve a change in the target's behavior through coercion and not through brute force. That is, any action that the United States threatens or undertakes must be designed to convince the target to yield by the threat of future pain, not by bludgeoning it until it can no longer resist. Military action undertaken to deny the opponent the ability to pursue its preferred strategy is not coercion but a brute-force method of extracting compliance. It can be somewhat difficult to distinguish between coercion and brute force in cases where the threat is conveyed by the movement of military assets or the limited application of force. Limited military action intended to convince the opponent to yield by raising the specter of future pain would be considered compellence (threat type 2, specified in greater detail below). An operation that makes it impossible for the opponent to execute its own operations or to continue with its current plan of action would not be considered compellence.

For example, during the Congo II Crisis in 1964 (case 211), the

United States dispatched troops to rescue hostages held by rebel forces in Stanleyville. I uncovered no evidence that the dispatch of troops was intended to accomplish anything other than the physical rescue of the hostages. In other words, the United States intended to retrieve the hostages through brute force, not by coercing the rebels into releasing them. For this reason, I did not record US action in this crisis as compellence. Had the US troops remained in place at the border for several weeks during negotiations to release the hostages, then the positioning of forces would have been coded as a compellent threat (of type 1). Similarly, the secret bombing of Cambodia in 1969 prompted by the Vietnam Spring Offensive (case 230) was a denial mission aimed at eroding North Vietnamese military capability. US action was intended to deprive the opponent of the ability to continue with its course of action, not to persuade the opponent to yield with the specter of future violence. For this reason, I did not record US action in this case as compellence.

In some cases, the United States issued more than one compellent threat against the target. To avoid overcounting threats (and undercounting nonthreats), I did not split the crises into separate events. Instead, I employed the last threat issued or implied by the United States during the crisis to classify the threat type.

Threat Type

After determining whether the United States issued a compellent threat, I placed each compellent threat issued by the United States into one of five categories, according to the following criteria:

- An *ultimatum* (type 5) is a compellent threat conveyed by a public statement or private communication with specific demands of the target, a specific punishment for noncompliance, and a deadline for compliance.
- An *open-ended* (type 4) threat is conveyed by a public statement or private communication in which demands and punishment are specified but the timeline for compliance is not indicated. An open-ended threat is similar to an ultimatum except for the lack of deadline.
- A *vague* (type 3) threat is conveyed by public statement or

private communication but lacks specificity in demands and/ or punishment. The demands of the target are not clearly specified and/or the action to be taken against the target in the event of noncompliance is vague or unspecified (e.g., "all options are on the table"). A vague threat also lacks the time pressure of an ultimatum.

- An *active implicit* (type 2) threat is communicated by the application of limited force against the target. An active implicit threat is intended to generate target compliance by raising the fear of future pain. The threatener does not explicitly articulate its demands or a timeline for compliance.

- A *passive implicit* (type 1) threat is communicated to the target by the movement of military assets. No force is actually applied to the target to generate fear of future violence. The threatener does not explicitly articulate its demands to the target or the punishment for noncompliance.

Threats of types 3, 4, and 5 are communicated explicitly to the target by the United States ("explicit threats,"), while types 1 and 2 ("implicit threats") are communicated solely by the movement or limited application of military force.

Threat Effectiveness

After classifying the threat type, I evaluated how both the target and the United States responded. If the United States issued the threat with or on behalf of at least one other state or a coalition of states, then I coded the "threat by coalition" variable in the affirmative. I then determined the target's initial reaction to the United States' threat.[8] I coded the target's initial "response to threat" as *resist* if the target did not agree to the United States' demands after a threat was issued and before the threat was executed. I coded the target's response as *concede* if the target modified its behavior in accordance with the United States' demands, stated or implied, after the threat was issued and before the threat was executed. If the United States executed the threatened action, then I coded the "threat executed" variable in the affirmative. In the case of active implicit threats—that is, those communicated through a limited application of force—I coded this variable in the affirmative unless the United States made one discrete application of force (e.g., one bombing raid) and stopped before administering any additional violence.[9]

Finally, I considered how the target responded to the threat's execution. If the United States executed its compellent threat and the target offered concessions shortly after the launch of military action, then I coded the target's reaction as *capitulation*. If, on the other hand, the United States issued and executed a threat and the target did not offer concessions shortly after the initiation of military action, then I coded the target's reaction as *continued resistance*. In keeping with the definition of a compellent threat, if the United States achieved its objectives only after overrunning the target or defeating it on the battlefield—that is, through brute force—then I coded the target's reaction at this stage as *continued resistance*. Coercion failed in such cases even though the United States may have been able to seize its objectives with force.

Sample Case: Haiti Regime Crisis

To better illustrate the process by which I coded the variables in this data set, I will explain how I investigated the case of the 1994 Haiti Regime Crisis (ICB case 411). First, I consulted the extensive summary of the crisis available in the ICB data viewer.[10] The crisis began for the United States in mid-July when a flood of refugees fleeing the repressive Raoul Cédras regime threatened US domestic stability. The ICB crisis summary indicates that President Clinton threatened on September 15 to intervene in Haiti, with the goal of ousting the sitting regime. I consulted additional sources, including a firsthand account of the mediation efforts and newspapers from the period, to confirm that Clinton's statements met the definition of a compellent threat. These sources also confirmed that the United States and Haiti were the only two actors involved in the crisis. Although the UN Security Council passed a resolution (940) at the end of July authorizing member states to take "all necessary means" to facilitate the departure of the Cédras regime, and President Clinton pledged to lead a coalition to enforce the will of the United Nations, I determined that the United States and Haiti were the only states actively involved in the crisis.[11]

I consulted the text of President Clinton's speech of September 15, 1994, to decide how to classify the threat. I determined that the United States' demands and the threatened punishment were explicit. After describing the preparations he had ordered for an invasion of the island nation, Clinton asserted, "The message of the United States to the Haitian dictators is clear: Your time is up. Leave now or we will force you from power."[12] He did not, however, specify a deadline for compliance or the date at which the threatened invasion would commence. For this reason, I determined that the threat met the terms of an open-ended threat (type 4), not an ultimatum. Clinton also promised to lead a multinational coalition to "carry out the will of the United Nations" in Haiti. For this reason, I determined that the United States acted on behalf of a coalition in this case.

Determining the target's reaction to the United States' threat was less straightforward. The ICB Project lists "negotiation" as the primary crisis-management technique.[13] There was a diplomatic mission led by former president Jimmy Carter to try to manage a power transition. An agreement was only reached, however, after the launch of the threatened military action: US troops were in the air and preparing to land on the island on the 19th when the crisis was finally defused.[14] I determined, therefore, that the target initially responded with resistance, that the United States executed its threat, and that the target capitulated after the threat was executed.

Constructing the Data Tables

Table 2.1 in chapter 2 presents basic information about each crisis and indicates whether the United States issued a compellent threat. The crisis number, name, and dates were taken directly from the ICB data. The "opponent" variable was coded as described above. I employed the ICB crisis summaries to identify the "other actors" for each crisis, which include both adversaries and allies of the United States. The "gravity of crisis" variable for both the United States and the opponent was taken from the actor-level data of ICB version 10 (variable "GRAVTY"). This variable records "the object of greatest threat at any time during the crisis, as perceived by the principal decision makers of the crisis actor." The variable can take on the following values, in ascending order: economic threat, limited military threat, political threat, territorial threat, threat to influence in the international system or regional subsystem, threat of grave damage, and threat to existence.[15] The ICB authors note that this is not a perfect ascending scale. For example, the severity of a territorial threat can vary greatly, and a political threat could be similar to a threat to existence for a leader facing overthrow. It is a useful scale, however, for evaluating how the stakes may differ for the actors involved in a crisis.

Table 2.2 presents information on the crises in which the United States issued compellent threats. The case number and name were taken from the ICB data. I determined the United States' demands by consulting primary and secondary sources for each crisis, as described above. The "power discrepancy" variable was taken from the actor-level ICB data. The researchers calculated this variable ("POWDIS") by adding measures of "population, GNP, territorial size, alliance capability, military expenditure, and nuclear capability" for the United States and comparing its score with that of its "principal adversary" in the crisis. A larger positive value indicates that the United States (and its allies, where applicable) enjoyed a larger advantage in relative power over the adversary (and its allies). A negative value indicates that the opponent(s) had an advantage over the United States.[16] This variable is not a perfect measure of relative power, but it is calculated consistently across the data set and it allows us to examine the United States' advantage in relative power across different crises.

Table 2.3 highlights the United States' demands in cases where a compellent threat was issued. These demands were coded as described above. Table 2.4 presents a more detailed description of the crises in which a threat was issued. I consulted the case descriptions available in the ICB data viewer,[17] along with additional sources included in the bibliography, to construct these descriptions.

Logit Model: Threat Frequency

I ran a simple logit model to evaluate whether the difference in threat frequency in the Cold War and post–Cold War periods is significant. The dependent variable in the model is a dummy variable indicating

Table A.1. Logit Model Results: Threat Frequency

	Estimate	Std. Error	z Value	Pr(> |z|)
(Intercept)	–1.26515 *	0.53139	–2.381	0.0173 *
Post.Cold.War	1.52511 *	0.64038	2.382	0.0172 *
Prev.Threat	0.03885	0.61767	0.063	0.9499

N = 63.
Null deviance: 77.138 on 62 degrees of freedom.
Residual deviance: 71.306 on 60 degrees of freedom.
AIC: 77.306.
* = significant at 0.05 level.

whether the United States issued a compellent threat in a crisis. The "Post.Cold.War" variable is a dummy indicating whether the crisis occurred during the post–Cold War period, and "Prev.Threat" is a dummy variable indicating whether the United States had issued a compellent threat in a crisis against the same target at some point after 1945.

Table A.1 presents the results of the model. The coefficient on Post. Cold.War is positive and significant at the 0.05 level. The dummy that captures whether the United States had issued a previous threat against the target (Prev.Threat) is not significant. The odds ratio suggests that, if the crisis occurs in the post–Cold War period, the odds are more than 4.5 times higher that the United States will issue a compellent threat.[18] In other words, the data suggest that the United States is significantly more likely to issue a threat in a post–Cold War crisis, consistent with the logic of costly compellence.

Notes

1. Brecher and Wilkenfeld, *Study of Crisis*, 4–5, emphasis in original.

2. Ibid., 5, emphasis in original.

3. Ibid., 41. For a more complete description of ICB data collection procedures and selection criteria, see "Part II: Methodology," 39–64.

4. Ibid., 3, emphasis in original.

5. The raw data were downloaded from Center for International Development and Conflict Management, International Crisis Behavior Project (hereafter cited as CIDCM, ICB Project), http://www.cidcm.umd.edu/icb/data/, on June 8, 2011.

6. Case 106, the Kars-Ardahan Crisis (June 1945), was included in this total because it broke out after the end of World War II in Europe. Case 107 was the dropping of the atomic bombs on Japan to end World War II in the Pacific and was therefore excluded. Case 108, the Azerbaijan Crisis (August 1945), and all subsequent crises were included in this total of international crises from 1945 to 2007.

7. Although a state can have an impact on a crisis without qualifying as a crisis actor in these terms, I included only cases in which the United States was identified as a crisis actor.

8. Recall that in some cases the United States issued more than one threat. I coded the target's response to the last threat issued by the United States during the crisis.

9. In cases like these (active implicit threats) in which the target conceded to US demands, the target's reaction to the threat's execution was coded as *capitulation*.

10. Available at CIDCM, ICB Project, http://www.cidcm.umd.edu/icb /dataviewer/. Description of the crisis based on the information available in the summary of case 411, Haiti Military Regime Crisis, unless otherwise noted.

11. Pastor, "Delicate Balance," various articles from the *New York Times* from September 1994, and the text of Clinton's speech in "Showdown in Haiti."

12. "Showdown in Haiti."

13. Summary of case 411, Haiti Military Regime Crisis, available through the ICB Data Viewer: http://www.cidcm.umd.edu/icb/dataviewer/.

14. Pastor, "Delicate Balance," 136. Pastor was part of the diplomatic delegation headed by Carter, and he reports that the announcement on the 18th that US troops were preparing for departure had secured a provisional agreement. The invasion was postponed until the following morning, but Cédras finally agreed to the United States' terms only when US troops were preparing to land on the 19th (pp. 135–36).

15. From the description of variable 67 (GRAVTY) in Wilkenfeld and Brecher, "Codebook for ICB2." Data for the variable GRAVTY were taken from the actor-level data set available at CIDCM, ICB Project, http://www .cidcm.umd.edu/icb/data/. Note that the term "threat" is not used here to indicate that a state has issued a demand and backed it with a promise of military force for noncompliance. The ICB uses "threat" to refer to something potentially damaging to a state's interests.

16. The ICB identified the Soviet Union as the primary adversary in cases 140 and 213 and North Vietnam in case 180. I dropped the power-discrepancy scores from these cases (scored "n/a") because they were not calculated in reference to the state that I identified as the United States' crisis opponent. The

description of POWDIS (variable 54) is from Wilkenfeld and Brecher, "Code-book for ICB2."

17. Available at CIDCM, ICB Project, http://www.cidcm.umd.edu/icb/dataviewer/.

18. The odds ratio is computed as follows: "For a unit change in x_k, the odds are expected to change by a factor of $\exp(\beta_k)$, holding all other variables constant." From Long, *Regression Models*, 80. Thus, to compute the odds ratio for Post.Cold.War, we calculate $\exp(1.52511)$.

Bibliography

Allen, Michael A., and Benjamin O. Fordham. "From Melos to Baghdad: Explaining Resistance to Militarized Challenges from More Powerful States." *International Studies Quarterly* 55, no. 4 (2011): 1025–45. http://dx.doi .org/10.1111/j.1468-2478.2011.00680.x.

Allison, Graham, and Philip Zelikow. *Essence of Decision: Explaining the Cuban Missile Crisis.* 2nd ed. New York: Longman, 1999.

Alterman, Jon B. "Coercive Diplomacy against Iraq, 1990–98." In Art and Cronin, *The United States and Coercive Diplomacy,* 275–303.

Anderson, Jon Lee. "King of Kings: The Last Days of Muammar Qaddafi." *New Yorker,* November 7, 2011, 44–57.

"Anti-Militia Protest Turns Deadly in Libya." Al Jazeera. November 15, 2013. http://america.aljazeera.com/articles/2013/11/15/anti-militia-proteststurn deadlyinlibya.html.

Apple, R. W., Jr. "Bush Offers to Send Baker on a Peace Mission to Iraq, but Vows Resolve in a War; Surprise Overture." *New York Times,* November 30, 1990. http://www.nytimes.com/1990/12/01/world/mideast-tensions-bush -offers-send-baker-peace-mission-iraq-but-vows-resolve-war.html?scp=8&sq =iraq%20baker&st=nyt&pagewanted=1.

———. "Invading Iraqis Seize Kuwait and Its Oil; U.S. Condemns Attack, Urges United Action." *New York Times,* August 3, 1990. http://www.nytimes .com/1990/08/03/world/iraqi-invasion-invading-iraqis-seize-kuwait-its-oil -us-condemns-attack-urges.html?scp=18&sq=iraq&st=nyt&pagewanted=1.

Art, Robert J. "American Foreign Policy and the Fungibility of Force." *Security Studies* 5, no. 4 (1996): 7–42. http://dx.doi.org/10.1080/09636419608 429287.

———, and Patrick M. Cronin, eds. *The United States and Coercive Diplomacy.* Washington, DC: United States Institute of Peace Press, 2003.

Aspin, Les, and William Dickinson. *Defense for a New Era: Lessons of the Persian Gulf War.* Washington, DC: Brassey's (US), Inc., 1992.

Authorization for Use of Military Force against Iraq Resolution, Pub. L. No. 102–1, 105 Stat. 3–4 (1991).

Authorization for Use of Military Force against Iraq Resolution of 2002, Pub. L. No. 107–243, 116 Stat. 1498–1502 (2002).

Baker, James A., III, with Thomas M. DeFrank. *The Politics of Diplomacy: Revolution, War and Peace 1989–1992.* New York: G. P. Putnam's Sons, 1995.

Battle, Joyce, ed. *Saddam Hussein Talks to the FBI: Twenty Interviews and Five Conversations with "High Value Detainee #1" in 2004.* National Security Archives, July 1, 2009. http://www.gwu.edu/~nsarchiv/NSAEBB/NSAEBB279.

"Battle for Libya: Key Moments." Al Jazeera. November 19, 2011. http://www
.aljazeera.com/indepth/spotlight/libya/2011/10/20111020104244706760
.html.

Becker, Elizabeth. "Deadline in the Balkans: The Overview; No 'Stonewalling'
on Kosovo Peace, Milosevic Is Told." *New York Times*, February 19, 1999.
http://www.nytimes.com/1999/02/20/world/deadline-balkans-overview-no
-stonewalling-kosovo-peace-milosevic-told.html?scp=1&sq=nato+threatens
+serbia&st=nyt.

Beckley, Michael. "China's Century? Why America's Edge Will Endure." *International Security* 36, no. 3 (Winter 2011–12): 41–78. http://dx.doi.org/10.1162
/ISEC_a_00066.

"Benghazi Attack under Microscope." *Washington Times*, accessed June 10, 2014.
http://www.washingtontimes.com/specials/benghazi-attack-and-scandal/.

Betts, Richard K. "Comment on Mueller: Interests, Burdens, and Persistence:
Asymmetries between Washington and Hanoi." *International Studies Quarterly*
24, no. 4 (1980): 520–24. http://dx.doi.org/10.2307/2600288.

———. *Enemies of Intelligence: Knowledge and Power in American National Security*. New York: Columbia University Press, 2009.

———. *Nuclear Blackmail and Nuclear Balance*. Washington, DC: Brookings
Institution, 1987.

Bianco, William T., and Jamie Markham. "Vanishing Veterans: The Decline of
Military Experience in the U.S. Congress." In Feaver and Kohn, *Soldiers and
Civilians*, 275–87.

Biddle, Stephen. *Military Power: Explaining Victory and Defeat in Modern Battle*.
Princeton, NJ: Princeton University Press, 2004.

Biddle, Tami Davis. *Rhetoric and Reality in Air Warfare: The Evolution of British and American Ideas about Strategic Bombing, 1914–1945*. Princeton, NJ:
Princeton University Press, 2002.

Bin Laden, Osama. "Declaration of War against the Americans Occupying the
Land of the Two Holy Places." August 1996. http://www.pbs.org/newshour
/updates/military-july-dec96-fatwa_1996/.

"Bin Laden Praises God for Terrorism." *Michigan Daily*, October 8, 2001.
http://www.michigandaily.com/content/bin-laden-praises-god-terrorism.

Blainey, Geoffrey. *The Causes of War*. 3rd ed. New York: Free Press, 1988.

Blasko, Dennis J., Chas W. Freeman, Jr., Stanley A. Horowitz, et al. *Defense-
Related Spending in China: A Preliminary Analysis and Comparison with American Equivalents*. United States–China Policy Foundation, 2007.
http://www.uscpf.org/v2/pdf/defensereport.pdf.

Blechman, Barry M., and Stephen S. Kaplan. *Force without War*. Washington,
DC: Brookings Institution, 1978.

———, and Tamara Cofman Wittes. "Defining Moment: The Threat and Use
of Force in American Foreign Policy." *Political Science Quarterly* 114, no. 1
(1999): 1–30. http://dx.doi.org/10.2307/2657989.

Blix, Hans. "Briefing the Security Council, 19 December 2002: Inspections in
Iraq and a Preliminary Assessment of Iraq's Weapons Declaration."

UNMOVIC: Selected Security Council Briefings. December 19, 2002. http://www.un.org/depts/unmovic/new/pages/security_council_briefings.asp#2Q1.

————. "Briefing the Security Council, 9 January 2003: Inspections in Iraq and a Further Assessment of Iraq's Weapons Declaration." UNMOVIC: Selected Security Council Briefings. January 9, 2003. http://www.unmovic.org/.

————. "Briefing of the Security Council, 27 January 2003: An Update on Inspections." UNMOVIC: Selected Security Council Briefings. January 27, 2003. http://www.unmovic.org/.

Bowman, Tom. "War Casualties Could Test Public's Resolve." *Baltimore Sun*, November 18, 2001.

Brecher, Michael, and Jonathan Wilkenfeld. *A Study of Crisis*. Ann Arbor: University of Michigan Press, 1997.

Broder, John M. "Clinton Says Iraq Can Avert Attack by Giving in to the UN." *New York Times*, November 14, 1997. http://www.nytimes.com/1998/11/14/world/clinton-says-iraq-can-avert-attack-by-giving-in-to-un.html?scp=3&sq=iraq%20november%2014%201998&st=cse.

Brooks, Stephen G., and William C. Wohlforth. *World out of Balance: International Relations and the Challenge of American Primacy*. Princeton, NJ: Princeton University Press, 2008. http://dx.doi.org/10.1515/9781400837601.

Bumiller, Elisabeth, and David D. Kirkpatrick. "Obama Warns Libya, but Attacks Go On." *New York Times*, March 18, 2011. http://www.nytimes.com/2011/03/19/world/africa/19libya.html.

Bundy, McGeorge. *Danger and Survival: Choices about the Bomb in the First Fifty Years*. New York: Random House, 1988.

Bureau of Economic Analysis. "Per Capita Personal Income." Regional Economic Accounts. September 2010. http://www.bea.gov/regional/spi/ drill.cfm?sel Table=SA30&selLineCode=110&selYears=2009,2008&rformat=Display.

Burg, Steven L. "Coercive Diplomacy in the Balkans: The U.S. Use of Force in Bosnia and Kosovo." In Art and Cronin, *The United States and Coercive Diplomacy*, 57–118.

Burns, John F. "Unhindered by Iraqi Officials, Arms Inspectors Visit 3 Sites." *New York Times*, November 28, 2002. http://www.nytimes.com/2002/11/28/world/threats-responses-hunt-for-weapons-unhindered-iraqi-officials-arms-inspectors.html?scp=2&sq=iraq+inspections&st=nyt.

Bush, George H. W. "The President's News Conference on the Persian Gulf Crisis." George Bush Presidential Library and Museum: Public Papers. November 8, 1990. http://bush41library.tamu.edu/archives/public-papers/2416.

————. "The President's News Conference, 1990-11-30." George Bush Presidential Library and Museum: Public Papers. November 30, 1990. http://bush41library.tamu.edu/archives/public-papers/2516.

Bush, George W. "President Bush Outlines Iraqi Threat: Remarks by the President on Iraq, Cincinnati Museum Center–Cincinnati Union Terminal." White House Archives. October 7, 2002. http://georgewbush-whitehouse.archives.gov/news/releases/2002/10/20021007-8.html.

————. "President Says Saddam Hussein Must Leave Iraq within 48 Hours:

Remarks by the President in Address to the Nation." White House Archives. March 17, 2003. http://georgewbush-whitehouse.archives.gov/news/releases /2003/03/20030317-7.html.

———. "The President's State of the Union Address." White House Archives. January 29, 2002. http://georgewbush-whitehouse.archives.gov/news/releases /2002/01/20020129-11.html.

———. "Text of President Bush's 2003 State of the Union Address." *Washington Post*, January 28, 2003. http://www.washingtonpost.com/wp-srv/onpolitics /transcripts/bushtext_012803.html.

———. "Text: President Bush Addresses the Nation." *Washington Post*, September 20, 2001. http://www.washingtonpost.com/wp-srv/nation/specials /attacked/transcripts/bushaddress_092001.html.

Byman, Daniel L., and Matthew C. Waxman. "Kosovo and the Great Air Power Debate." *International Security* 24, no. 4 (2000): 5–38. http://dx.doi.org /10.1162/016228800560291.

Carter, Jimmy. "Oil Imports from Iran Remarks Announcing Discontinuance of United States Imports: November 12, 1979." The American Presidency Project. Edited by John T. Woolley and Gerhard Peters. http://www.presidency .ucsb.edu/ws/index.php?pid=31674&st=iran&st1=hostage#axzz1UShuxQJ4.

———. "Soviet Invasion of Afghanistan Address to the Nation: January 4, 1980." The American Presidency Project. Edited by John T. Woolley and Gerhard Peters. http://www.presidency.ucsb.edu/ws/index.php?pid=32911#ax zz1UShuxQJ4.

———. "White House Statement on American Hostages in Iran: November 9, 1979." The American Presidency Project. Edited by John T. Woolley and Gerhard Peters. http://www.presidency.ucsb.edu/ws/index.php?pid=31666&st =iran&st1=hostage#axzz1UShuxQJ4.

Center for International Development and Conflict Management (CIDCM). International Crisis Behavior Project. 2010. http://www.cidcm.umd.edu/icb /info/project_information.aspx.

Chang, Gordon H. "To the Nuclear Brink: Eisenhower, Dulles, and the Quemoy–Matsu Crisis." *International Security* 12, no. 4 (1988): 96–123. http://dx.doi .org/10.2307/2538996.

———, and He Di. "The Absence of War in the U.S.–China Confrontation over Quemoy and Matsu in 1954–1955: Contingency, Luck, Deterrence." *American Historical Review* 98, no. 5 (1993): 1500–1524. http://dx.doi.org/10 .2307/2167064.

Chesney, Robert M. "A Primer on the Libya / War Powers Resolution Compliance Debate." Brookings. June 17, 2011. http://www.brookings.edu/opinions /2011/ 0617_war_powers_chesney.aspx.

Chulov, Martin, and Helen Pidd. "Defector Admits to WMD Lies That Triggered Iraq War." *Guardian*, February 15, 2011. http://www.guardian.co.uk/world /2011/feb/15/defector-admits-wmd-lies-iraq-war.

Clark, Wesley K. *Waging Modern War.* New York: PublicAffairs, 2001.

Clausewitz, Carl von. *On War*. Edited and translated by Michael Howard and Peter Paret. Princeton, NJ: Princeton University Press, 1976.

"Clinton Voices Anger and Compassion at Serbian Intransigence on Kosovo." *New York Times*, March 19, 1999. http://www.nytimes.com/1999/03/20 /world/clinton-voices-anger-and-compassion-at-serbian-intransigence-on -kosovo.html?scp=2&sq=nato+threatens+serbia&st=nyt.

Clodfelter, Mark. *The Limits of Air Power: The American Bombing of North Vietnam*. New York: Free Press, 1989.

Clodfelter, Micheal. *Warfare and Armed Conflicts: A Statistical Reference to Casualty and Other Figures, 1500–2000*. 2nd ed. Jefferson, NC: McFarland, 2002.

Cohen, Eliot A. *Citizens and Soldiers: The Dilemmas of Military Service*. Ithaca, NY: Cornell University Press, 1985.

———. "The Mystique of U.S. Air Power." *Foreign Affairs* 73, no. 1 (1994): 109–24. http://dx.doi.org/10.2307/20045895.

Conway-Lanz, Sahr. *Collateral Damage*. New York: Routledge, 2006.

Correlates of War Project. "Chronological List of All Wars." COW War Data, 1816–2007 (v4.0). 2010. http://www.correlatesofwar.org/data-sets/COW -war/cow-war-list.

Crane, Conrad C. "Sky High: Illusions of Air Power." *National Interest* no. 65 (Fall 2001): 116–22.

Crenshaw, Martha. "Coercive Diplomacy and the Response to Terrorism." In Art and Cronin, *The United States and Coercive Diplomacy*, 305–57.

Crossette, Barbara. "Baghdad Disrupts Arms Inspections." *New York Times*, November 21, 1998. http://www.nytimes.com/1998/11/21/world/baghdad -disrupts-arms-inspections.html?scp=27&sq=iraq&st=nyt.

———. "Unanimous Security Council Tightens the Vise on Iraq." *New York Times*, November 13, 1997. http://www.nytimes.com/1997/11/13/world /unanimous-security-council-tightens-the-vise-on-iraq.html?scp=29&sq =iraq&st=nyt.

"Documentation: White House Tapes and Minutes of the Cuban Missile Crisis." *International Security* 10, no. 1 (1985): 164–203. http://dx.doi.org /10.2307/2538794.

Downes, Alexander B. *Targeting Civilians in War*. Ithaca, NY: Cornell University Press, 2008.

Drennan, William M. "Nuclear Weapons and North Korea: Who's Coercing Whom?" In Art and Cronin, *The United States and Coercive Diplomacy*, 157–223.

Duelfer, Charles. *Comprehensive Report of the Special Advisor to the DCI on Iraq's WMD* (Duelfer Report). 3 vols. Washington, DC: Government Printing Office, 2004.

———. *Hide and Seek: The Search for Truth in Iraq*. New York: PublicAffairs, 2009.

Eichenberg, Richard C. "Victory Has Many Friends: U.S. Public Opinion and the Use of Military Force, 1981–2005." *International Security* 30, no. 1 (2005): 140–77. http://dx.doi.org/10.1162/0162288054894616.

Elliott, Michael, and James Carney. "First Stop, Iraq." *Time*, March 31, 2003. http://content.time.com/time/magazine/article/0,9171,1004567,00.html.

Ellis, John. *World War II: A Statistical Survey*. New York: Facts on File, 1993.

———, and Michael Cox. *The World War I Databook: The Essential Facts and Figures for All the Combatants*. London: Aurum Press, 2001.

Etzioni, Amitai. "The Coming Test of U.S. Credibility." *Military Review* 91, no. 2 (March–April 2011): 2–11.

"Excerpts from Pentagon Briefing on Libyan Jets." *New York Times*, January 5, 1989. http://www.nytimes.com/1989/01/05/world/excerpts-from-pentagon -briefing-on-libyan-jets.html?scp=8&sq=libya+jets&st=nyt.

Fahim, Kareem. "In His Last Days, Qaddafi Wearied of Fugitive's Life." *New York Times*, October 22, 2011. http://www.nytimes.com/2011/10/23/world/africa /in-his-last-days-qaddafi-wearied-of-fugitives-life.html.

———, and David D. Kirkpatrick. "Heavy Fighting Reported in Tripoli; Rebels Encircle City." *New York Times*, August 20, 2011. http://www.nytimes.com /2011/08/21/world/africa/21libya.html.

———. "Jubilant Rebels Control Much of Tripoli." *New York Times*, August 21, 2011. http://www.nytimes.com/2011/08/22/world/africa/22libya.html.

———, Anthony Shadid, and Rick Gladstone. "Violent End to an Era as Qaddafi Dies in Libya." *New York Times*, October 20, 2011. http://www.ny times.com/2011/10/21/world/africa/qaddafi-is-killed-as-libyan-forces-take -surt.html?pagewanted=1&sq=libya&st=nyt&scp=6.

Farnsworth, Clyde H. "Bush, in Freezing Assets, Bars $30 Billion to Hussein." *New York Times*, August 3, 1990. http://www.nytimes.com/1990/08/03/world /the-iraqi-invasion-bush-in-freezing-assets-bars-30-billion-to-hussein.html.

Fearon, James D. "Domestic Political Audiences and the Escalation of Interna- tional Disputes." *American Political Science Review* 88, no. 3 (1994): 577–92. http://dx.doi.org/10.2307/2944796.

———. "Signaling Foreign Policy Interests: Tying Hands versus Sinking Costs." *Journal of Conflict Resolution* 41, no. 1 (1997): 68–90. http://dx.doi.org/10.11 77/0022002797041001004.

Feaver, Peter D., and Richard H. Kohn, eds. *Soldiers and Civilians: The Civil– Military Gap and American National Security*. Cambridge, MA: MIT Press, 2001.

Filkins, Dexter. "U.S. Tightens Airstrike Policy in Afghanistan." *New York Times*, June 22, 2009. http://www.nytimes.com/2009/06/22/world/asia/22airstrikes .html.

Flynn, George Q. "Conscription and Equity in Western Democracies, 1940–75." *Journal of Contemporary History* 33, no. 1 (1998): 5–20.

Foot, Rosemary J. "Nuclear Coercion and the Ending of the Korean Conflict." *International Security* 13, no. 3 (Winter 1988–89): 92–112. http://dx.doi.org /10.2307/2538737.

"France Will Use Iraq Veto." BBC News, March 10, 2003. http://news.bbc.co .uk/2/hi/middle_east/2838269.stm.

Freedman, Lawrence. *The Evolution of Nuclear Strategy*. 3rd ed. Houndsmills, UK: Palgrave Macmillan, 2003. http://dx.doi.org/10.1057/9780230379435.

———. "Strategic Coercion." In *Strategic Coercion: Concepts and Cases*, edited by Lawrence Freedman, 15–36. Oxford: Oxford University Press, 1998.

Friedman, Thomas L. "Bush Puts Talks 'on Hold' till Iraq Accepts His Dates." *New York Times*, December 14, 1990. http://www.nytimes.com/1990/12/15 /world/standoff-in-the-gulf-bush-puts-talks-on-hold-till-iraq-accepts-his-dates .html?scp=20&sq=iraq%20baker&st=nyt&pagewanted=1.

———. "Confrontation in the Gulf; Iraqi, in Geneva, Says Pressure Won't Work." *New York Times*, January 8, 1991. http://www.nytimes.com/1991 /01/09/world/confrontation-in-the-gulf-iraqi-in-geneva-says-pressure-won-t -work.html?scp=31&sq=iraq&st=nyt.

———. "Panama Shooting Condemned by U.S." *New York Times*, December 17, 1989. http://www.nytimes.com/1989/12/18/world/panama-shooting -condemned-by-us.html?scp=15&sq=panama&st=nyt.

———. "A Partial Pullout by Iraq Is Feared as Deadline 'Ploy.'" *New York Times*, December 17, 1990. http://www.nytimes.com/1990/12/18/world/standoff-in -the-gulf-a-partial-pullout-by-iraq-is-feared-as-deadline-ploy.html?scp=35&sq =iraq+baker&st=nyt.

"Full Text of Colin Powell's Speech: US Secretary of State's Address to the United Nations Security Council." *Guardian*, February 5, 2003. http://www.the guardian.com/world/2003/feb/05/iraq.

"Full Text of Dick Cheney's Speech." *Guardian*, August 27, 2002. http://www .theguardian.com/world/2002/aug/27/usa.iraq.

Fursenko, Aleksandr, and Timothy Naftali. *Khrushchev's Cold War*. New York: W. W. Norton, 2006.

———. *"One Hell of a Gamble": Khrushchev, Castro, and Kennedy, 1958–1964*. New York: W. W. Norton, 1997.

"Gaddafi Statement: Response to Coalition." *Financial Times*, March 29, 2011. http://www.ft.com/intl/cms/s/0/b77bc90e-5a36-11e0-86d3-00144feab49a .html#axzz3jl4BXQ8s.

"Gaddafi Warns West against Military Action in Libya." Reuters. March 19, 2011. http://in.reuters.com/article/2011/03/19/idINIndia-5571402011 0319.

Garamone, Jim. "NATO Assumes Command of Libya Operations." United States Department of Defense, American Forces Press Service, March 31, 2011. http://www.defense.gov/news/newsarticle.aspx?id=63384 accessed 12/6/11.

Garthoff, Raymond L. "Berlin 1961: The Record Corrected." *Foreign Policy* 84 (Autumn 1991): 142–56.

———. "Handling the Cienfuegos Crisis." *International Security* 8, no. 1 (1983): 46–66. http://dx.doi.org/10.2307/2538485.

———. *Intelligence Assessment and Policymaking: A Decision Point in the Kennedy Administration*. Washington, DC: Brookings Institution, 1984.

Gartner, Scott Sigmund, Gary M. Segura, and Bethany A. Barratt. "War Casualties, Policy Positions, and the Fate of Legislators." *Political Research Quarterly* 57, no. 3 (2004): 467–77. http://dx.doi.org/10.1177/106591290405700311.

Gartzke, Erik. "Democracy and the Preparation for War: Does Regime Type Affect States' Anticipation of Casualties?" *International Studies Quarterly* 45, no. 3 (2001): 467–84. http://dx.doi.org/10.1111/0020-8833.00210.

Gelpi, Christopher, Peter D. Feaver, and Jason Reifler. *Paying the Human Costs of War: American Public Opinion and Casualties in Military Conflict.* Princeton, NJ: Princeton University Press, 2009. http://dx.doi.org/10.1515/97814008 30091.

George, Alexander L. "The Cuban Missile Crisis: Peaceful Resolution through Coercive Diplomacy." In George and Simons, *Limits of Coercive Diplomacy*, 2nd ed., 111–32.

———, and Andrew Bennett. *Case Studies and Theory Development in the Social Sciences.* Cambridge, MA: MIT Press, 2005.

———, David K. Hall, and William E. Simons. *The Limits of Coercive Diplomacy: Laos, Cuba, Vietnam.* Boston: Little, Brown, 1971.

———, and William E. Simons, eds. *The Limits of Coercive Diplomacy.* 2nd ed. Boulder, CO: Westview, 1994.

"George Bush's Speech to the UN General Assembly." *Guardian*, September 12, 2002. http://www.theguardian.com/world/2002/sep/12/iraq.usa3.

Gertler, Jeremiah. *U.S. Unmanned Aerial Systems: Congressional Research Service Report R42136.* January 3, 2012. http://www.fas.org/sgp/crs/natsec/R42136 .pdf.

———, Christopher M. Blanchard, Stephen Daggett, Catherine Dale, Jennifer K. Elsea, and Richard F. Grimmett. *No-Fly Zones: Strategic, Operational, and Legal Considerations for Congress.* Congressional Research Service, March 18 2011.

Gilpin, Robert. *War and Change in World Politics.* Cambridge, UK: Cambridge University Press, 1981. http://dx.doi.org/10.1017/CBO9780511664267.

Gordon, Michael R. "Bush Orders Navy to Halt All Shipments of Iraq's Oil and Almost All Imports." *New York Times*, August 13, 1990. http://www.nytimes .com/1990/08/13/world/confrontation-gulf-bush-orders-navy-halt-all-ship ments-iraq-s-oil-almost-all-its.html?scp=2&sq=iraq&st=nyt.

———. "Iraq Army Invades Capital of Kuwait in Fierce Fighting." *New York Times*, August 2, 1990. http://www.nytimes.com/1990/08/02/world/iraq -army-invades-capital-of-kuwait-in-fierce-fighting.html?scp=6&sq=iraq&st =nyt&pagewanted=1.

———. "Pentagon Drafts Strategy for Post–Cold War World." *New York Times*, August 1, 1990. http://www.nytimes.com/1990/08/02/us/pentagon-drafts -strategy-for-post-cold-war-world.html?scp=5&sq=iraq&st=nyt&pagewan ted=1.

———. "U.S. Troops Move in Panama in Effort to Seize Noriega; Gunfire Is Heard in Capital." *New York Times*, December 20, 1989. http://www.nytimes

.com/1989/12/20/world/us-troops-move-in-panama-in-effort-to-seize-noriega
-gunfire-is-heard-in-capital.html?scp=1&sq=panama&st=nyt&pagewanted=1.

———, and Bernard E. Trainor. *Cobra II: The Inside Story of the Invasion and Occupation of Iraq*. New York: Pantheon, 2006.

———. *The Generals' War: The Inside Story of the Conflict in the Gulf*. Boston: Little, Brown, 1995.

Graff, Peter. "Gaddafi Defiant as NATO Intensifies Tripoli Strikes." Reuters. June 7, 2011. http://www.reuters.com/article/2011/06/07/us-libya-idUSTRE 7270JP20110607.

Greenberg Research. "The People on War Report: ICRC Worldwide Consultation on the Rules of War." 2000. https://www.icrc.org/eng/resources/documents /publication/p0758.htm.

"Gunmen Assassinate Libya's Deputy Industry Minister." Al Jazeera. January 12, 2014. http://america.aljazeera.com/articles/2014/1/12/gunmen-assassinatelib yasdeputyindustryminister.html.

Hacker, Jacob S., and Paul Pierson. "Abandoning the Middle: The Bush Tax Cuts and the Limits of Democratic Control." *Perspectives on Politics* 3, no. 1 (2005): 33–53. http://dx.doi.org/10.1017/S1537592705050048.

Hall, David K. "The Laos Crisis, 1960–1961." In George, Hall, and Simons, *The Limits of Coercive Diplomacy: Laos, Cuba, Vietnam*, 36–85.

Hamm, Michael J. "The *Pueblo* and *Mayaguez* Incidents: A Study of Flexible Response and Decision-Making." *Asian Survey* 17, no. 6 (1977): 545–55. http://dx.doi.org/10.2307/2643155.

Hersh, Seymour M. "Offense and Defense: The Battle between Donald Rumsfeld and the Pentagon." *New Yorker*, April 7, 2003, 43–45 http://www.newyorker .com/magazine/2003/04/07/offense-and-defense Q2.

Howard, Michael. *War in European History*. Updated ed. Oxford, UK: Oxford University Press, 2009.

Hufbauer, Gary Clyde, Jeffrey J. Schott, Kimberly Ann Elliott, et al. *Economic Sanctions Reconsidered*. 3rd ed. Washington, DC: Peter G. Peterson Institute for International Economics, 2007.

Huntington, Samuel P. *The Soldier and the State: The Theory and Politics of Civil–Military Relations*. Cambridge, MA: Harvard University Press, 1957.

Institute for Strategic Studies (ISS). *The Communist Bloc and the Western Alliances: The Military Balance 1962–1963*. London: Institute for Strategic Studies, 1962.

International Institute for Strategic Studies (IISS). *The Military Balance 2002*. London: Routledge, 2003.

———. *The Military Balance 2003*. London: Routledge, 2004.

———. *The Military Balance 2011*. London: Routledge, 2011.

———. *The Military Balance 2012*. London: Routledge, 2012.

———. *The Military Balance 2013*. London: Routledge, 2013.

———. *The Military Balance 2015*. London: Routledge, 2015.

"Interview with the United Kingdom's ITV Television Network, April 4, 2002."

In *Public Papers of the Presidents of the United States: George W. Bush; Book 1, January 1–June 30 2002*, 553–59. Washington, DC: National Archives and Records Administration, Office of the Federal Registrar, 2004.

"Iraqi Leader's Message to National Assembly." *New York Times*, December 7, 1990. http://www.nytimes.com/1990/12/07/world/standoff-in-the-gulf-iraqi -leader-s-message-to-national-assembly.html?scp=14&sq=iraq%20hostages&st =nyt&pagewanted=1.

Iraq Liberation Act of 1998, Pub. L. No. 105–338, 112 Stat. 3178–3181 (1998).

Isaacs, Stephen. "Authority Is Cited for Use of Force." *Washington Post*, May 14, 1975, A1.

Jakobsen, Peter Viggo. *Western Use of Coercive Diplomacy after the Cold War: A Challenge for Theory and Practice*. London: Macmillan, 1998. http://dx.doi .org/10.1057/9780230373570.

Jehl, Douglas. "Clinton Addresses Nation on Threat to Invade Haiti; Tells Dicta- tors to Get Out." *New York Times*, September 16, 1994. http://www.nytimes .com/1994/09/16/world/showdown-haiti-white-house-clinton-addresses -nation-threat-invade-haiti-tells.html?scp=1&sq=clinton%20address%20 haiti%20september%201994&st=cse.

Jervis, Robert. *The Logic of Images in International Relations*. Morningside ed. New York: Columbia University Press, 1989.

———. *Why Intelligence Fails: Lessons from the Iranian Revolution and the Iraq War*. Ithaca, NY: Cornell University Press, 2010.

———. "Why Nuclear Superiority Doesn't Matter." *Political Science Quarterly* 94, no. 4 (Winter 1979–80): 617–33. http://dx.doi.org/10.2307/2149629.

"Joint Statement, Baghdad, 20 January 2003." UNMOVIC: Selected Security Council Briefings. January 20, 2003. http://www.unmovic.org/.

Kagan, Frederick W. "The U.S. Military's Manpower Crisis." *Foreign Affairs* 85, no. 4 (2006): 97–110. http://dx.doi.org/10.2307/20032044.

Kahl, Colin H. "In the Crossfire or the Crosshairs? Norms, Civilian Casualties, and U.S. Conduct in Iraq." *International Security* 32, no. 1 (2007): 7–46. http://dx.doi.org/10.1162/isec.2007.32.1.7.

Kalyvas, Stathis N. *The Logic of Violence in Civil War*. Cambridge, UK: Cambridge University Press, 2006. http://dx.doi.org/10.1017/CBO9780511818462.

Kant, Immanuel. "Perpetual Peace." In *Kant: Political Writings*, edited by Hans Reiss and translated by H. B. Nisbet, 93–131. Cambridge, UK: Cambridge University Press, 1991.

Karol, David, and Edward Miguel. "The Electoral Cost of War: Iraq Casualties and the 2004 U.S. Presidential Election." *Journal of Politics* 69, no. 3 (2007): 633–48. http://dx.doi.org/10.1111/j.1468-2508.2007.00564.x.

Keaney, Thomas A., and Eliot A. Cohen. *Gulf War Air Power Survey Summary Report*. Washington, D. C.: Government Printing Office, 1993.

Kennedy, Robert F. *Thirteen Days: A Memoir of the Cuban Missile Crisis*. New York: W. W. Norton, 1999.

Kifner, John. "Confrontation in the Gulf: Arab Vote to Send Troops to Help

Saudis; Boycott of Iraqi Oil Is Reported Near 100%; Baghdad Isolated."
    New York Times, August 11, 1990. http://www.nytimes.com/1990/08/11
    /world/confrontation-gulf-arab-vote-send-troops-help-saudis-boycott-iraqi
    -oil-reported.html?scp=2&sq=&pagewanted=1.

Kirkpatrick, David D. "Libyans Offer Credible Case of Death by Airstrike."
    New York Times, March 30, 2011. http://www.nytimes.com/2011/03/31
    /world/africa/31casualty.html.

————, and Kareem Fahim. "Qaddafi Warns of Assault on Benghazi as U.N.
    Vote Nears." *New York Times*, March 17, 2011. http://www.nytimes.com
    /2011/03/18/world/africa/18libya.html.

————, Steven Erlanger, and Elisabeth Bumiller. "Allies Open Air Assault
    on Qaddafi's Forces in Libya." *New York Times*, March 19, 2011. http://
    www.nytimes.com/2011/03/20/world/africa/20libya.html?pagewanted+all.

————. "Qaddafi Pledges 'Long War' as Allies Pursue Air Assault on Libya." *New
    York Times*, March 20, 2011. http://www.nytimes.com/2011/03/21/world
    /africa/21libya.html.

Knowlton, Brian. "Acts of Defiance 'Totally Unacceptable,' Perry Tells Baghdad;
    U.S. Warns Iraq over Its Threats to Kuwait." *New York Times*, September 13,
    1996. http://www.nytimes.com/1996/09/13/news/13iht-iraq.t_13.html?scp=1
    27&sq=iraq&st=nyt.

Korb, Lawrence. "Fixing the Mix: How to Update the Army's Reserves." *Foreign
    Affairs* 83, no. 2 (2004): 2–7. http://dx.doi.org/10.2307/20033897.

Koring, Paul. "Libyan Military Widely Regarded as Murderous Thugs." *Globe
    and Mail*, February 21, 2011. http://www.theglobeandmail.com/news
    /world/africa-mideast/libyan-military-widely-regarded-as-murderous-thugs
    /article1915393/.

Krass, Caroline D. "Authority to Use Military Force in Libya: Memorandum
    Opinion for the Attorney General." Opinions of the Office of Legal Counsel
    in Volume 35. April 1, 2011. http://www.justice.gov/sites/default/files/olc
    /opinions/2011/04/31/authority-military-use-in-libya.pdf.

Kuperman, Alan J. "A Model Humanitarian Intervention?: Reassessing NATO's
    Libya Campaign." *International Security* 38, no. 1 (2013): 105–36. http://
    dx.doi.org/10.1162/ISEC_a_00126.

————. "Obama's Libya Debacle: How a Well-Meaning Intervention Ended in
    Failure." *Foreign Affairs* 94, no. 2 (2015): 66–77.

Lacquemont, Richard A. "The Casualty-Aversion Myth." *Naval War College
    Review* 57, no. 1 (2004): 39–57.

Larson, David L., ed. *The "Cuban Crisis" of 1962: Selected Documents and Chro-
    nology*. Boston: Houghton Mifflin, 1963.

Larson, Eric V. *Casualties and Consensus: The Historical Role of Casualties in
    Domestic Support for U.S. Military Operations*. Santa Monica, CA: RAND,
    1996.

————, and Bogdan Savych. *American Public Support for U.S. Military Opera-
    tions from Mogadishu to Baghdad*. Santa Monica, CA: RAND, 2005.

Layne, Christopher. "The Waning of U.S. Hegemony—Myth or Reality?: A Review Essay." *International Security* 34, no. 1 (2009): 147–72. http://dx.doi .org/10.1162/isec.2009.34.1.147.

Lerner, Mitchell B. *The* Pueblo *Incident: A Spy Ship and the Failure of American Foreign Policy*. Lawrence: University Press of Kansas, 2002.

"Libya Declares Ceasefire but Fighting Goes On." Al Jazeera. March 18, 2011. http://www.aljazeera.com/news/africa/2011/03/2011318124421218583.html.

"Libya Pays to End Terrorism Cases." *New York Times*, November 1, 2008. http:// www.nytimes.com/2008/11/01/world/africa/01libya.html?ref=0.

"Libya—Revolution and Aftermath (2011)." *New York Times*, November 22, 2011. http://topics.nytimes.com/top/news/international/countriesandterrito ries/libya/index.html?scp=1-spot&sq=libya&st=cse.

Little, Douglas. "A Puppet in Search of a Puppeteer? The United States, King Hussein, and Jordan, 1953–1970." *International History Review* 17, no. 3 (1995): 512–44. http://dx.doi.org/10.1080/07075332.1995.9640719.

Litwak, Robert S. *Regime Change: U. S. Strategy through the Prism of 9/11*. Washington, DC: Woodrow Wilson Center Press, 2007.

Long, Scott J. *Regression Models for Categorical and Limited Dependent Variables*. Thousand Oaks, CA: Sage Publications, 1997.

Lyall, Jason. "Does Indiscriminate Violence Incite Insurgent Attacks? Evidence from Chechnya." *Journal of Conflict Resolution* 53, no. 3 (2009): 331–62. http://dx.doi.org/10.1177/0022002708330881.

Mack, Andrew. "Why Big Nations Lose Small Wars: The Politics of Asymmetric Conflict." *World Politics* 27, no. 2 (1975): 175–200. http://dx.doi.org /10.2307/2009880.

Maoz, Zeev. "Resolve, Capabilities, and the Outcomes of Interstate Disputes, 1816–1976." *Journal of Conflict Resolution* 27, no. 2 (1983): 195–229. http:// dx.doi.org/10.1177/0022002783027002001.

Marsh, John O., Jr. "Active and Reserve Forces." *Annals of the American Academy of Political and Social Science* 517, no. 1 (September 1991): 94–105. http:// dx.doi.org/10.1177/0002716291517001007.

Mayer, Jane. "The Predator War: What Are the Risks of the CIA's Covert Drone Program?" *New Yorker*, October 26, 2009, 36–45.

Mazzetti, Mark, and Eric Schmitt. "C.I.A. Steps Up Drone Attacks on Taliban in Pakistan." *New York Times*, September 27, 2010. http://www.nytimes .com/2010/09/28/world/asia/28drones.html.

———, Eric Schmitt, and Robert F. Worth. "Two-Year Manhunt Led to Killing of Awlaki in Yemen." *New York Times*, September 30, 2011. http://www.ny times.com/2011/10/01/world/middleeast/anwar-al-awlaki-is-killed-in-yemen .html.

McNamara, Robert. "Reflections on War in the Twenty-First Century." *Interdisciplinary Science Reviews* 23, no. 2 (1998): 125–34. http://dx.doi.org/10.1179 /isr.1998.23.2.125.

Mercer, Jonathan. *Reputation and International Politics*. Ithaca, NY: Cornell University Press, 1996.

Merom, Gil. *How Democracies Lose Small Wars: State, Society, and the Failures of France in Algeria, Israel in Lebanon, and the United States in Vietnam*. Cambridge, UK: Cambridge University Press, 2003. http://dx.doi.org/10.1017/CBO9780511808227.

"Militia Holding Libyan Port Offers to Talk with Government." Al Jazeera. March 15, 2014. http://america.aljazeera.com/articles/2014/3/15/libyan-port-rebelstotalkwithgovernment.html.

Miller, Greg. "CIA Seeks to Expand Drone Fleet, Officials Say." *Washington Post*, October 18, 2012. http://articles.washingtonpost.com/2012-10-18/world/35502344_1_qaeda-drone-fleet-cia-drones.

Mitchell, Alison. "U.S. Launches Further Strike against Iraq after Clinton Vows to Extract 'Price.'" *New York Times*, September 4, 1996. https://www.nytimes.com/1996/09/04/world/us-launches-further-strike-against-iraq-after-clinton-vows-he-will-extract-price.html?scp=29&sq=iraq&st=nyt&pagewanted=1.

Monteiro, Nuno P. *Theory of Unipolar Politics*. Cambridge, UK: Cambridge University Press, 2014. http://dx.doi.org/10.1017/CBO9781107449350.

Morrow, James D. "Capabilities, Uncertainty, and Resolve: A Limited Information Model of Crisis Bargaining." *American Journal of Political Science* 33, no. 4 (1989): 941–72. http://dx.doi.org/10.2307/2111116.

"Muammar Gaddafi Urges Followers to Turn Libya 'into a Hell.'" *Guardian*, September 1, 2011. http://www.theguardian.com/world/2011/sep/01/muammar-gaddafi-libya-into-hell.

Mueller, John E. "The Search for the 'Breaking Point' in Vietnam: The Statistics of a Deadly Quarrel." *International Studies Quarterly* 24, no. 4 (1980): 497–519. http://dx.doi.org/10.2307/2600287.

———. *War, Presidents and Public Opinion*. New York: John Wiley & Sons, 1973.

Myers, Steven Lee. "U.S. Attacks Military Targets in Iraq." *New York Times*, September 3, 1996. http://www.nytimes.com/1996/09/03/world/us-attacks-military-targets-in-iraq.html?scp=17&sq=iraq&st=nyt&pagewanted=1.

———, and Judy Dempsey. "NATO Showing Strain over Approach to Libya." *New York Times*, April 14, 2011. http://www.nytimes.com/2011/04/15/world/africa/15nato.html?pagewanted=all.

National Intelligence Council. *National Intelligence Estimate: Iraq's Continuing Programs for Weapons of Mass Destruction*. October 2002. http://nsarchive.gwu.edu/NSAEBB/NSAEBB129/nie.pdf.

National Security Council. "The National Security Strategy of the United States of America." September 2002. http://georgewbush-whitehouse.archives.gov/nsc/nss/2002/index.html.

"NATO Takes Command in Libya Air Operations." North Atlantic Treaty Organization. March 31, 2011. http://www.nato.int/cps/en/natolive/news_71867.htm.

Nichols, Michelle. "Libya Arms Fueling Conflicts in Syria, Mali and Beyond: U.N. Experts." Reuters. April 9, 2013. http://www.reuters.com/article/2013 /04/09/us-libya-arms-un-idUSBRE93814Y20130409.

Obama, Barack. "Remarks by the President on the Situation in Libya." Office of the Press Secretary. March 18, 2011. http://www.whitehouse.gov/the-press-office /2011/03/18/remarks-president-situation-libya.

"Obama on Muammar Gaddafi Death: President Obama Addresses Death of Libyan Leader." *Huffington Post*, October 20, 2011. http://www.huffingtonpost .com/2011/10/20/obama-muammar-gaddafi-dead_n_1022106.html.

Odom, Thomas P. *Dragon Operations: Hostage Rescues in the Congo, 1964–1965*. Leavenworth Papers No. 14. US Army Command and General Staff College, Fort Leavenworth, KS, Combat Studies Institute. July 1988. http://usacac .army.mil/cac2/cgsc/carl/download/csipubs/odomLP14.pdf.

Office of Management and Budget. *Historical Tables: Budget of the U.S. Government, Fiscal Year 2011*. Washington, DC: Government Printing Office, 2010.

———. *Historical Tables: Fiscal Year 2014 Budget of the U.S. Government*. Washington, DC: Government Printing Office, 2013. http://www.whitehouse.gov /sites/default/files/omb/budget/fy2014/assets/hist.pdf.

———. "Table 3.1—Outlays by Superfunction and Function: 1940–2015." *Office of Management and Budget: Historical Tables*, 2010. http://www.white house.gov/omb/budget/Historicals/.

Office of the Under Secretary of Defense for Personnel and Readiness. *Population Representation in the Military Services: Fiscal Year 2008 Report Summary*. 2010. http://prhome.defense.gov/portals/52/Documents/POPREP/poprep2008 /summary/poprepsummary2008.pdf .

Oh, John K. "South Korea 1976: The Continuing Uncertainties." *Asian Survey* 17, no. 1 (1977): 71–80. http://dx.doi.org/10.1525/as.1977.17.1.01p02605.

O'Hanlon, Michael. *Technological Change and the Future of Warfare*. Washington, DC: Brookings Institution Press, 2000.

Organski, A. F. K., and Jacek Kugler. *The War Ledger*. Chicago: University of Chicago Press, 1980.

Pape, Robert A. *Bombing to Win: Air Power and Coercion in War*. Ithaca, NY: Cornell University Press, 1996.

———. "The Limits of Precision-Guided Air Power." *Security Studies* 7, no. 2 (1997): 93–114. http://dx.doi.org/10.1080/09636419708429343.

Parker, James. "Should Our Volunteers Be Raised by Conscription?" *North American Review* 166, no. 498 (1898): 570–84.

Pastor, Robert A. "The Delicate Balance between Coercion and Diplomacy: The Case of Haiti, 1994." In Art and Cronin, *The United States and Coercive Diplomacy*, 119–55.

Paust, Jordan J. "The Seizure and Recovery of the *Mayaguez*." *Yale Law Journal* 85, no. 6 (1976): 774–806. http://dx.doi.org/10.2307/795719.

Poggioli, Sylvia. "Gadhafi's Military Muscle Concentrated in Elite Units." National

Public Radio. March 10, 2011. http://www.npr.org/2011/03/10/134404618/
gadhafis-military-muscle-concentrated-in-elite-units.

Preble, Christopher A. *The Power Problem: How American Military Dominance
Makes Us Less Safe, Less Prosperous, and Less Free*. Ithaca, NY: Cornell University Press, 2009.

Press, Daryl G. *Calculating Credibility: How Leaders Assess Military Threats*. Ithaca,
NY: Cornell University Press, 2005.

———. "The Myth of Air Power in the Persian Gulf War and the Future of Warfare." *International Security* 26, no. 2 (2001): 5–44. http://dx.doi.org/10.1162
/016228801753191123.

Rachman, Gideon. "Think Again: American Decline." *Foreign Policy* 184 (Janu-
ary/February 2011): 59–63.

"Remarks and a Question-and-Answer Session with Reporters in Aspen, Colorado, following a Meeting with Prime Minister Margaret Thatcher of the
United Kingdom." George Bush Presidential Library and Museum: Public
Papers. August 2, 1990. http://bush41library.tamu.edu/research/public-papers
/2124.

"Remarks and an Exchange with Reporters on the Iraqi Invasion of Kuwait."
George Bush Presidential Library and Museum: Public Papers. August 5,
1990. http://bush41library.tamu.edu/research/public-papers/2138.

"Remarks at the Aspen Institute Symposium in Aspen, Colorado." George Bush
Presidential Library and Museum: Public Papers. August 2, 1990. http://bush
41library.tamu.edu/archives/public-papers/2128.

"Report of the Secretary-General on the Activities of the Special Commission
Established by the Secretary-General pursuant to Paragraph 9 (b) (i) of Reso-
lution 687 (1991)." United Nations. October 6, 1997. http://www.un.org
/Depts/unscom/sres97-774.htm.

Rich, Spencer. "Members Briefed." *Washington Post*, May 15, 1975, A1.

Ricks, Thomas E. *Fiasco: The American Military Adventure in Iraq*. New York:
Penguin, 2006.

Risen, James. "U.S. Seeks Means to Bring Suspect from Afghanistan." *New York
Times*, August 19, 1998. http://www.nytimes.com/1998/08/20/world/us
-seeks-means-to-bring-suspect-from-afghanistan.html?scp=33&sq=afghanistan
&st=nyt.

Rosen, Steven. "War Power and the Willingness to Suffer." In *Peace, War, and
Numbers*, edited by Bruce M. Russett, 167–83. Beverly Hills, CA: Sage Publications, 1972.

Rosenthal, Andrew. "President Calls Panama Slaying a Great Outrage." *New
York Times*, December 18, 1989. http://www.nytimes.com/1989/12/19
/world/president-calls-panama-slaying-a-great-outrage.html?scp=19&sq
=panama&st=nyt &pagewanted=1.

Rostker, Bernard. *I Want You!: The Evolution of the All-Volunteer Force*. Santa
Monica, CA: RAND, 2006.

Rusk, Dean. *As I Saw It*. As told to Richard Rusk. Edited by Daniel S. Papp. New York: W. W. Norton, 1990.

Sanger, David E., and Thom Shanker. "Gates Warns of Risks of a No-Flight Zone." *New York Times*, March 2, 2011. http://www.nytimes.com/2011/03/03/world /africa/03military.html?pagewanted=all.

Schelling, Thomas. *Arms and Influence*. New Haven, CT: Yale University Press, 1966.

Schiavenza, Matt. "China Economy Surpasses US in Purchasing Power, but Americans Don't Need to Worry." *International Business Times*, October 8, 2014. http://www.ibtimes.com/china-economy-surpasses-us-purchasing -power-americans-dont-need-worry-1701804.

Schlesinger, Arthur M., Jr. *A Thousand Days: John F. Kennedy in the White House*. Boston: Houghton Mifflin, 1965.

Schmitt, Eric. "Forces Not Ready for January War, U.S. General Says." *New York Times*, December 19, 1990. http://www.nytimes.com/1990/12/20/world /standoff-in-the-gulf-forces-not-ready-for-january-war-us-general-says.html ?scp=45&sq=iraq+baker&st=nyt.

Sechser, Todd S. "Goliath's Curse: Coercive Threats and Asymmetric Power." *International Organization* 64, no. 4 (2010): 627–60. http://dx.doi.org/10 .1017/S0020818310000214.

———. "Militarized Compellent Threats, 1918–2001." *Conflict Management and Peace Science* 28, no. 4 (2011): 377–401. http://dx.doi.org/10.1177/073 8894211413066.

Shenon, Philip. "U.S. Is Preparing Bigger Air Strikes on Targets in Iraq." *New York Times*, September 12, 1996. http://www.nytimes.com/1996/09/12 /world/us-is-preparing-bigger-air-strikes-on-targets-in-iraq.html?scp=117&sq =iraq&st=nyt.

———. "U.S. Pressing Kabul to Oust Saudi Linked to Bombings." *New York Times*, August 18, 1998. http://www.nytimes.com/1998/08/19/world/us -pressing-kabul-to-oust-saudi-linked-to-bombings.html?scp=27&sq=afghani stan&st=nyt.

"Showdown in Haiti; In the Words of the President: The Reasons Why the U.S. May Invade Haiti." *New York Times*, September 16, 1994. http://www .nytimes.com/1994/09/16/world/showdown-haiti-words-president-reasons -why-us-may-invade-haiti.html?pagewanted=all&src=pm.

Simons, William E. "The Vietnam Intervention, 1964–65." In George, Hall and Simons, *The Limits of Coercive Diplomacy: Laos, Cuba, Vietnam*, 144–210.

Singer, P. W. *Corporate Warriors: The Rise of the Privatized Military Industry*. Updated ed. Ithaca, NY: Cornell University Press, 2008.

———. "Outsourcing War." *Foreign Affairs* 84, no. 2 (2005): 119–32. http:// dx.doi.org/10.2307/20034280.

———. "The Regulation of New Warfare." Brookings. February 2010. http:// www.brookings.edu/research/opinions/2010/02/27-defense-regulations-singer.

———. *Wired for War: The Robotics Revolution and Conflict in the Twenty-first Century*. New York: Penguin, 2009.

Sly, Liz, and Greg Jaffe. "Allied Strikes Pummel Libya's Air Force but Do Little to Stop Attacks on Civilians." *Washington Post*, March 22, 2011.

———, Debbi Wilgoren, and Craig Whitlock. "U.S. Jet Crashes in Libya, but Pilots Safe; Gates Sees Airstrikes Slowing Soon." *Washington Post*, March 22, 2011. http://www.washingtonpost.com/world/us-jet-crashes-in-libya-pilots -safe-gates-says-air-strikes-should-slow-soon-/2011/03/22/ABNC0lCB_story .html?hpid=z1.

Smith, R. B. "The International Setting of the Cambodia Crisis, 1969–1970." *International History Review* 18, no. 2 (1996): 303–35. http://dx.doi.org/10.1 080/07075332.1996.9640745.

Snyder, Glenn H. "'Prisoner's Dilemma' and 'Chicken' Models in International Politics." *International Studies Quarterly* 15, no. 1 (1971): 66–103. http:// dx.doi.org/10.2307/3013593.

Snyder, Jack, and Erica D. Borghard. "The Cost of Empty Threats: A Penny, Not a Pound." *American Political Science Review* 105, no. 3 (2011): 437–56. http:// dx.doi.org/10.1017/S000305541100027X.

Spence, Michael. "Job Market Signaling." *Quarterly Journal of Economics* 87, no. 3 (1973): 355–74. http://dx.doi.org/10.2307/1882010.

Stanger, Allison. *One Nation under Contract: The Outsourcing of American Power and the Future of Foreign Policy.* New Haven, CT: Yale University Press, 2009.

"Statement by Press Secretary Fitzwater on President Bush's Letter to President Saddam Hussein of Iraq." George Bush Presidential Library and Museum: Public Papers. January 12, 1991. http://bush41library.tamu.edu/archives /public-papers/2617.

Stigler, Andrew L. "A Clear Victory for Air Power: NATO's Empty Threat to Invade Kosovo." *International Security* 27, no. 3 (Winter 2002–3): 124–57. http://dx.doi.org/10.1162/01622880260553651.

Stiglitz, Joseph E., and Linda J. Bilmes. *The Three Trillion Dollar War: The True Cost of the Iraq Conflict.* New York: W. W. Norton, 2008.

Sullivan, Patricia L. "War Aims and War Outcomes: Why Powerful States Lose Limited Wars." *Journal of Conflict Resolution* 51, no. 3 (2007): 496–524. http://dx.doi.org/10.1177/0022002707300187.

———, and Michael T. Koch. "Military Intervention by Powerful States, 1945– 2003." *Journal of Peace Research* 46, no. 5 (2009): 707–18. http://dx.doi .org/10.1177/0022343309336796.

Taubman, Philip. "Officials Doubt Soviet Freighter Contains MIG's." *New York Times*, November 10, 1984. http://www.nytimes.com/1984/11/10/world /officials-doubt-soviet-freighter-contains-mig-s.html?scp=6&sq=nicaragua +soviet+ship& st=nyt.

———. "U.S. Warns Soviet It Won't Tolerate MIG's in Nicaragua." *New York Times*, November 8, 1984. http://www.nytimes.com/1984/11/08/world/us -warns-soviet-it-won-t-tolerate-mig-s-in-nicaragua.html?scp=1&sq=nicaragua +soviet+ship& st=nyt.

"Text of Bush's Speech at West Point." *New York Times*, June 1, 2002.

http://www.nytimes.com/2002/06/01/international/02PTEX-WEB.
html?pagewanted=all.

Thomas, David L., II. "The U.S. Army: A Business? Return on Investment?"
Military.com. December 3, 2004. http://www.military.com/NewContent
/1,13190,120304_ArmyBusiness-P1,00.html.

Tilly, Charles. "Reflections on the History of European State-Making." In *The
Formation of National States in Western Europe*, edited by Charles Tilly, 3–83.
Princeton, NJ: Princeton University Press, 1975.

Trachtenberg, Marc. "Audience Costs: An Historical Analysis." *Security Studies*
21, no. 1 (2012): 3–42. http://dx.doi.org/10.1080/09636412.2012.650590.

"Transcript of U.S. Statement about Measures against Iraq." *New York Times*,
August 12, 1990. http://www.nytimes.com/1990/08/13/world/confrontation
-in-the-gulf-transcript-of-us-statement-about-measures-against-iraq.html?scp
=4&sq=iraq&st=nyt.

Truman, Harry S. "295—The President's News Conference: November 30,
1950." *The American Presidency Project*, edited by John Woolley and Gerhard
Peters. http://www.presidency.ucsb.edu/ws/index.php?pid=13673.

Twomey, Christopher P. *The Military Lens: Doctrinal Difference and Deterrence
Failure in Sino-American Relations*. Ithaca, NY: Cornell University Press, 2010.

"UK, US and Spain Won't Seek Vote on Draft Resolution, May Take 'Own Steps'
to Disarm Iraq." UN News Centre. March 17, 2003. http://www.un.org/apps
/news/story.asp?NewsID=6472#.VdyJWc4Q50c.

United Nations Security Council (UNSC). "Resolution 660 (1990)." August 2,
1990. http://daccess-dds-ny.un.org/doc/RESOLUTION/GEN/NR0/575/10
/IMG/NR057510.pdf?OpenElement.

———. "Resolution 661 (1990)." August 6, 1990. http://daccess-dds-ny.un.org
/doc/RESOLUTION/GEN/NR0/575/11/IMG/NR057511.pdf?OpenElement.

———. "Resolution 662 (1990)." August 9, 1990. http://daccess-dds-ny.un.org
/doc/RESOLUTION/GEN/NR0/575/12/IMG/NR057512.pdf?OpenElement.

———. "Resolution 678 (1990)." November 29, 1990. http://daccess-dds-ny.un
.org/doc/RESOLUTION/GEN/NR0/575/28/IMG/NR057528.pdf?Open
Element.

———. "Resolution 686 (1991)." March 2, 1991. http://daccess-dds-ny.un.org
/doc/RESOLUTION/GEN/NR0/596/22/IMG/NR059622.pdf?OpenElement.

———. "Resolution 687 (1991)." April 3, 1991. http://daccess-dds-ny.un.org/doc
/RESOLUTION/GEN/NR0/596/23/IMG/NR059623.pdf?OpenElement.

———. "Resolution 1284 (1999)." December 17, 1999. http://daccess-dds-ny
.un.org/doc/UNDOC/GEN/N99/396/09/PDF/N9939609.pdf?OpenElement.

———. "Resolution 1441 (2002)." November 8, 2002. http://daccess-dds-ny
.un.org/doc/UNDOC/GEN/N02/682/26/PDF/N0268226.pdf?OpenElement.

———. "Resolution 1973 (2011)." March 17, 2011. http://daccess-dds-ny.un.org
/doc/UNDOC/GEN/N11/268/39/PDF/N1126839.pdf?OpenElement.

———. "Spain, United Kingdom of Great Britain and Northern Ireland and

United States of America: Draft Resolution." March 7, 2003. http://www
.un.org/News/dh/iraq/res-iraq-07mar03-en-rev.pdf.

United States Bureau of Labor Statistics. "CPI Inflation Calculator." Accessed
March 9, 2015. http://www.bls.gov/data/inflation_calculator.htm.

United States Department of Defense (USDOD). *Conduct of the Persian Gulf
War: Final Report to Congress, April 1992*. Washington, DC: Government
Printing Office, 1992.

———. *Quadrennial Defense Review 2014*. March 2014. http://www.defense
.gov/pubs/2014_Quadrennial_Defense_Review.pdfQ3.

———. *Sustaining U.S. Global Leadership: Priorities for 21st Century Defense*.
January 2012. http://www.defense.gov/news/Defense_Strategic_Guidance
.pdf

United States Department of the Army. *The U.S. Army / Marine Corps Counterinsurgency Field Manual*. Chicago: University of Chicago Press, 2007.

United States Department of the Navy. "Korean War: Chronology of U.S. Pacific
Fleet Operations, June–December 1950." Naval History and Heritage Center.
April 10, 2005. http://www.history.navy.mil/research/library/online-reading
-room/title-list-alphabetically/k/korean-war-chronology/june-dec-1950.html.

United States Department of State. *Official Texts on Iraq, 1998*. 1998. http://1997
-2001.state.gov/www/regions/nea/iraq_remarks98.html.

"United States Department of State Memorandum of Conversation: Secretary
James A. Baker III and Foreign Minister Tariq Azziz." The James A. Baker III
Institute for Public Policy, Rice University. January 9, 1991.

"US Imposes Sanctions on Libya." *Washington Post*, February 25, 2011. http://
www.washingtonpost.com/wp-dyn/content/article/2011/02/25/AR20110225
06702.html.

"US Issues Travel Ban for Senior Gadhafi Officials." *Washington Post*, February
26, 2011. http://www.washingtonpost.com/wp-dyn/content/article/2011/02
/26/AR2011022603058.html.

"US Secretary of State Colin Powell's Statement on Iraq's Weapons Declaration."
Guardian, December 20, 2002. http://www.theguardian.com/world/2002
/dec/20/iraq.usa1.

"U.S. Threat Cited in '62 Cuba Crisis." *New York Times*, April 26, 1963.

Waltz, Kenneth N. *Theory of International Politics*. Boston: McGraw-Hill, 1979.

Warden, John A., III. "Success in Modern War: A Response to Robert Pape's
Bombing to Win." *Security Studies* 7, no. 2 (Winter 1997–98): 172–90.
http://dx.doi.org/10.1080/09636419708429345.

"'We Have the Forces,' Clinton Warns Hussein." *New York Times*, November 15,
1997. http://www.nytimes.com/1997/11/15/world/we-have-the-forces
-clinton-warns-hussein.html?scp=42&sq=iraq&st=nyt.

Weisman, Steven R. "A Test of Wills between Iran and the West." *New York
Times*, January 11, 2006. http://www.nytimes.com/2006/01/12/international
/middleeast/12diplo.html.

"White House Statement of the President, May 15, 1962." The Pentagon Papers. 2011. http://www.archives.gov/research/pentagon-papers/.

Wilkenfeld, Jonathan, and Michael Brecher. "Codebook for ICB2—International Crisis Behavior Project, Actor-Level Dataset—July 2010, Version 10.0." The International Crisis Behavior Project. http://www.cidcm.umd.edu/icb/data/.

Williams, Gary. "Prelude to an Intervention: Grenada 1983." *Journal of Latin American Studies* 29, no. 1 (1997): 131–69. http://dx.doi.org/10.1017/S00 22216X9600466X.

Woods, Kevin M., David D. Palkki, and Mark E. Stout, eds. *The Saddam Tapes: The Inner Workings of a Tyrant's Regime, 1978–2001*. Cambridge, UK: Cambridge University Press, 2011. http://dx.doi.org/10.1017/CBO9781139 061506.

———, with Michael R. Pease, Mark E. Stout, Williamson Murray, and James G. Lacey. *Iraqi Perspectives Project: A View of Operation Iraqi Freedom from Saddam's Senior Leadership*. Norfolk, VA: United States Joint Forces Command Joint Center for Operational Analysis, 2006.

Woodward, Bob. *Plan of Attack: The Definitive Account of the Decision to Invade Iraq*. New York: Simon & Schuster, 2004.

World Bank. "GDP (current US$)." http://data.worldbank.org/indicator/NY .GDP.MKTP.CD.

———. "GDP per capita (current US$)." http://data.worldbank.org/indicator /NY.GDP.PCAP.CD/countries.

———. "Military expenditure (% of GDP)." http://data.worldbank.org/indicator /MS.MIL.XPND.GD.ZS.

Zelikow, Philip D. "Force without War, 1975–1982." *Journal of Strategic Studies* 7, no. 1 (1984): 29–54. http://dx.doi.org/10.1080/01402398408437175.

Zimmermann, Tim. "Coercive Diplomacy and Libya." In George and Simons, *The Limits of Coercive Diplomacy*, 2nd ed., 201–28.

Index

Page numbers in italics refer to tables.